AF394677

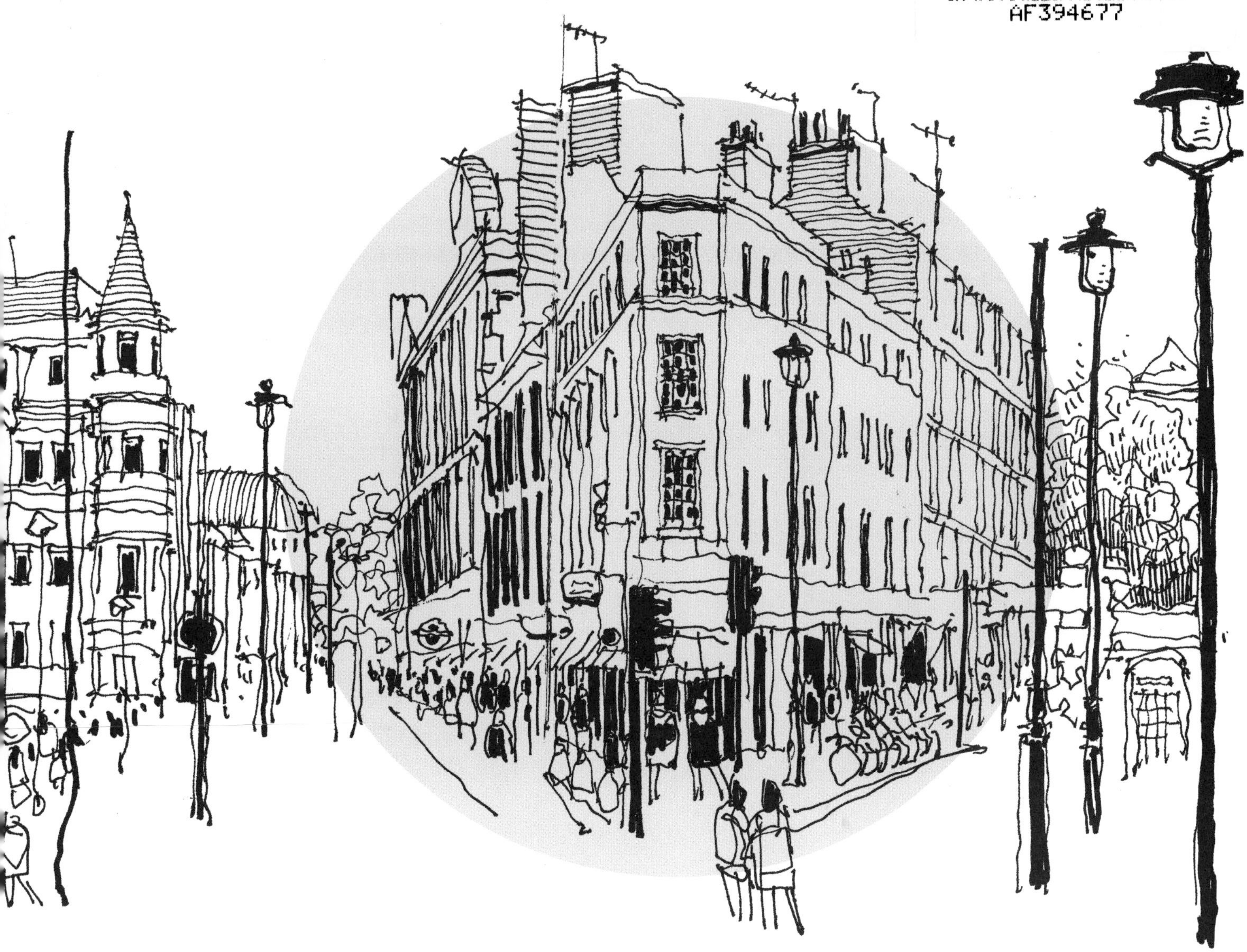

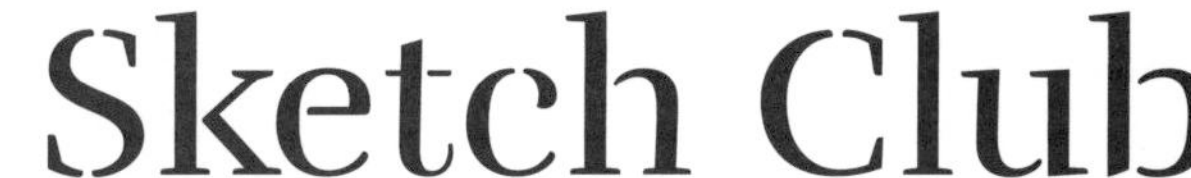

Sketch Club

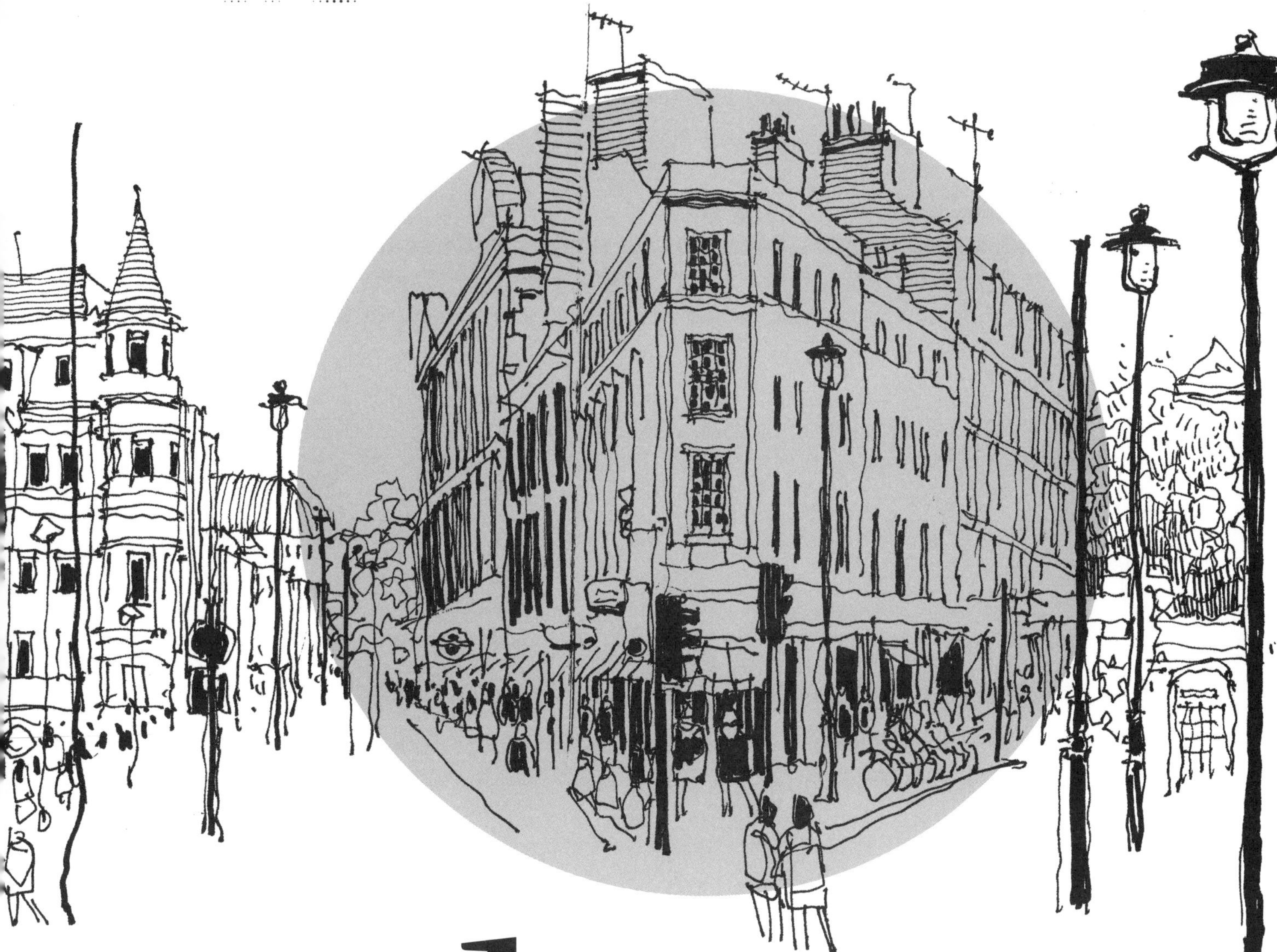

Phil Dean

Urban Drawing

ilex

An Hachette UK Company
www.hachette.co.uk

First published in the United Kingdom in 2020 by
ILEX, an imprint of Octopus Publishing Group Ltd
Octopus Publishing Group
Carmelite House
50 Victoria Embankment
London, EC4Y 0DZ
www.octopusbooks.co.uk

Design and layout copyright © Octopus Publishing
Group 2020
Text and illustrations copyright © Phil Dean 2020

Publisher: Alison Starling
Commissioning Editor: Ellie Corbett
Managing Editor: Rachel Silverlight
Junior Editor: Stephanie Hetherington
Editorial Assistant: Ellen Sandford O'Neill
Art Director: Ben Gardiner
Assistant Production Manager: Lucy Carter
Design: JC Lanaway

Ilex is proud to partner with Tate; supporting the
gallery in its mission to promote public understanding
and enjoyment of British, modern and contemporary art.

ISBN 978-1-78157-775-2

A CIP catalogue record for this book
is available from the British Library

Printed and bound in China

1 0 9 8 7 6 5

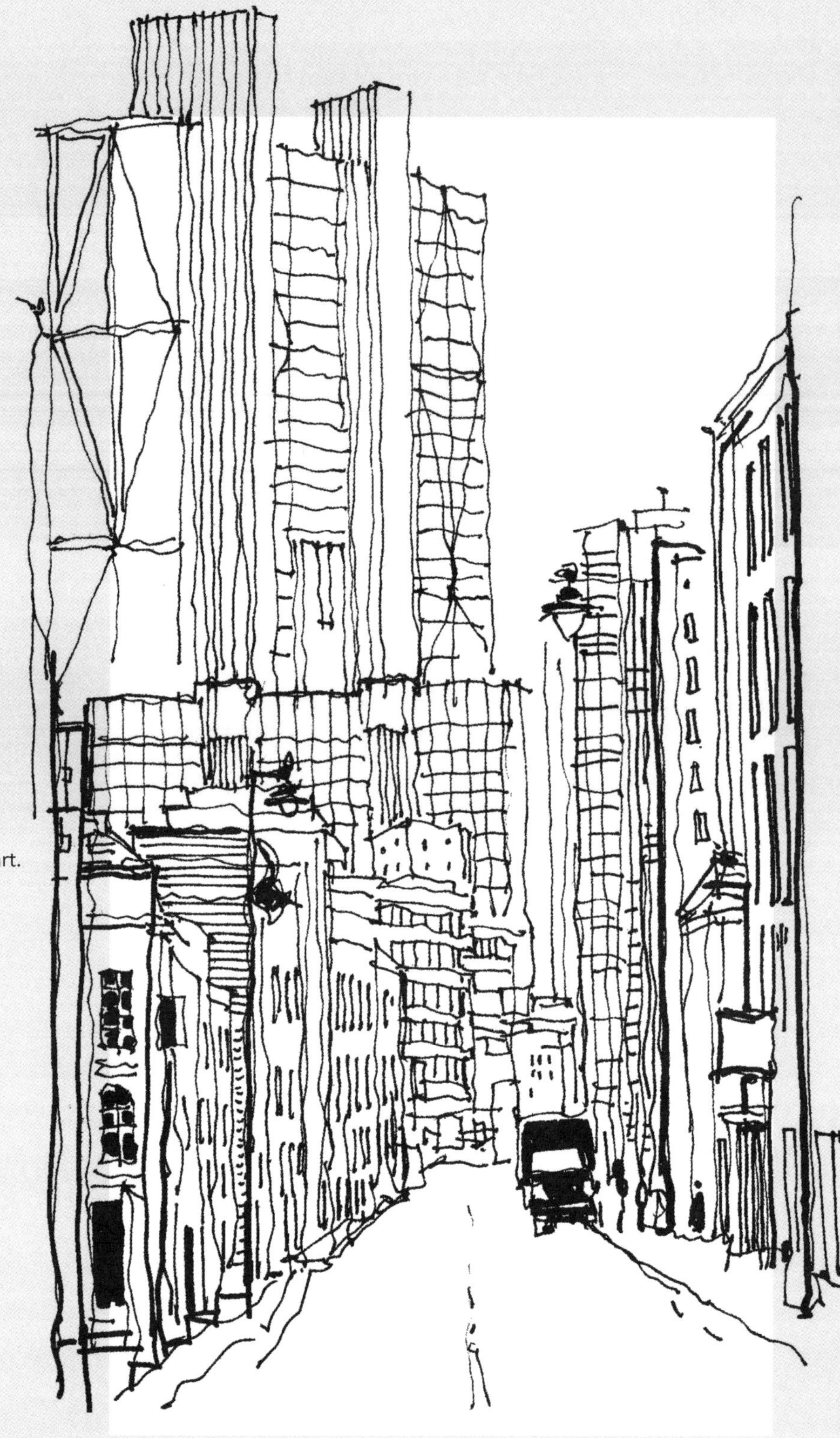

Contents

6   **INTRODUCTION**

8   Equipment

10   Sketchbook

12   Materials

16   Getting Started

18   Etiquette

20   **CHAPTER 1: LOOSENING UP**

22   Getting Sketch Ready

24   Looking for Sketching Potential

32   **CHAPTER 2: BUILDING A SCENE**

34   Measuring

40   Composition

48   Perspective

54   Small-Scale Sketching

58   Sweeping Scale

62   **CHAPTER 3: TONE AND CONTRAST**

64   Tone

76   **CHAPTER 4: TAKING IT FURTHER**

78   People

84   Creativity

90   Details

94   Colour

100   **CHAPTER 5: FINISHING TOUCHES**

102   Tips and Tricks

108   When to Stop

110   Sharing Your Work

112   Acknowledgements

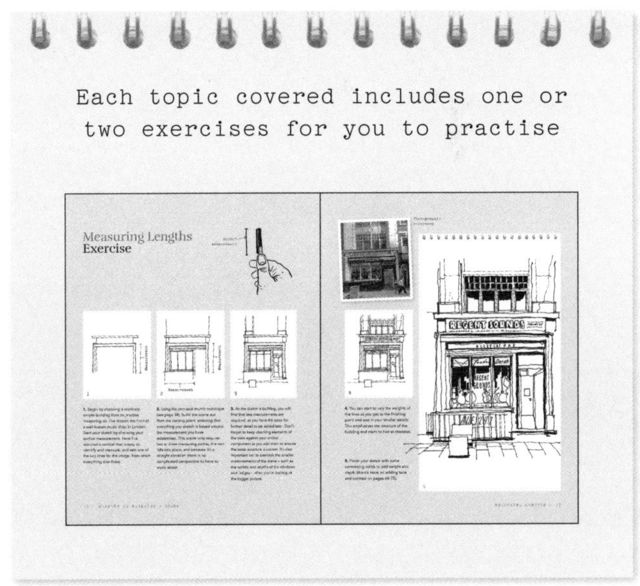

Introduction

Sketching in a city environment is an exciting experience. The streets throb with energy and pulse with life. From the soaring skyscrapers of New York to Rome's ancient architecture, wherever you turn, the city offers unique sketching opportunities.

Drawing in urban spaces also gives you a completely new way in which to engage with a city – to sketch a place is to truly see it. This could mean experiencing a new city through the lens of a sketcher or seeing a familiar area with fresh eyes.

Urban sketching is very different to studio-based drawing such as figure drawing or still life. You are out in a public environment, part of the landscape and embedded in the city. In the studio, the artist has control over the environment and the subject matter, but live sketching on the streets is a different matter. You have to embrace the combinations of static buildings and ever-moving people and vehicles.

I got hooked on urban sketching when I moved to London in 2013 – the diverse architecture of the city inspired me to pick up my pencil. My first few sketches

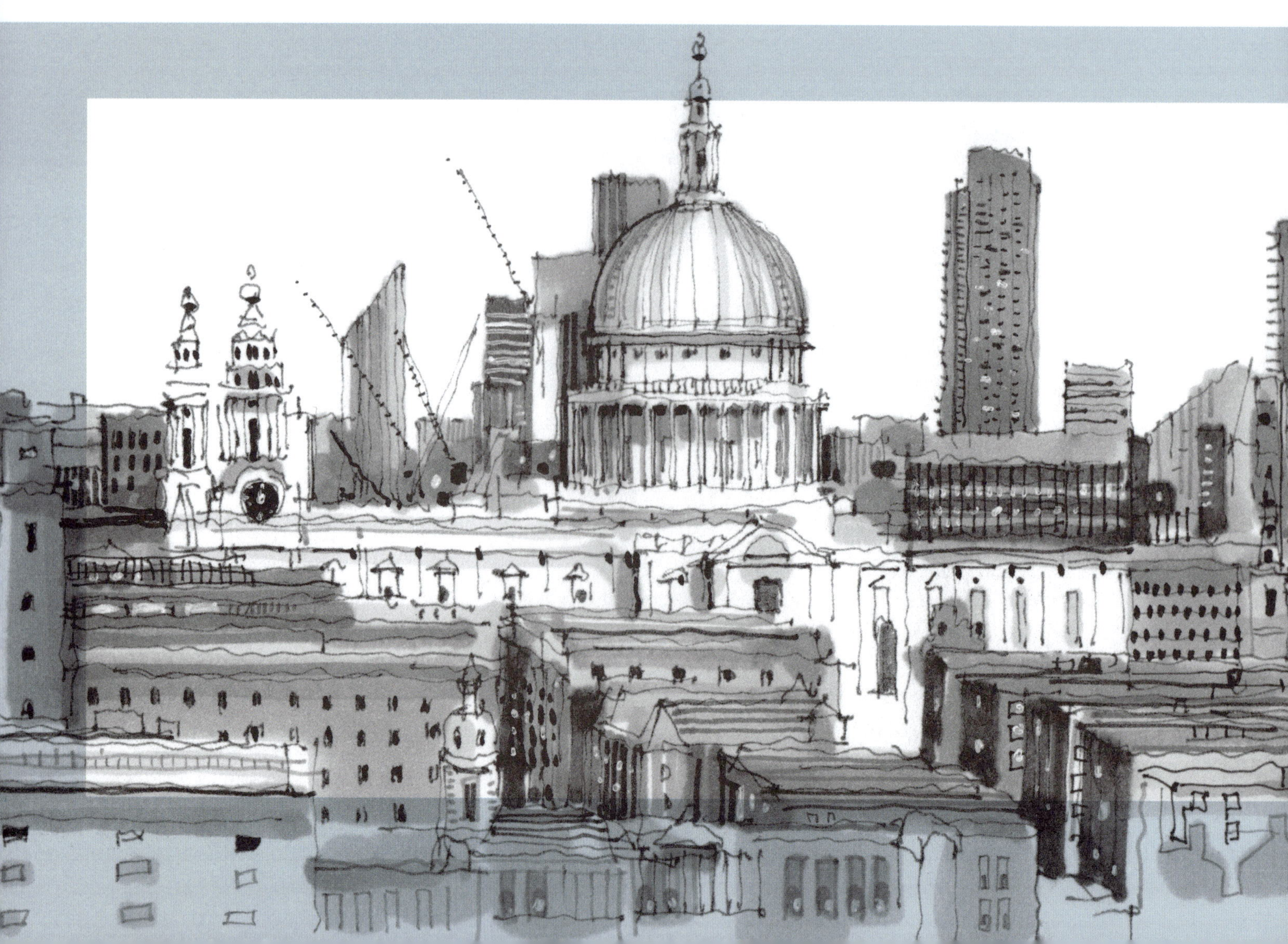

were a bit clunky but I was determined to draw without worrying about the outcome. Over time, I got into a groove and found that my eye improved with each sketch. I began producing more and more faithful representations of the city scenes that I observed, be they calm, hectic, noisy, quiet, relaxed or full on – I just drew what I saw.

I searched hungrily for more examples of urban sketching online, and seeing how passionate and prolific other sketchers were pushed me on to sketch even more. Seeing the work of artists such as Simone Ridyard, who has depicted Manchester's brutalist architecture in delicate watercolour, and the stunning complexity of the European cityscapes of Gérard Michel inspired me further, while the boldness and immediacy of James Hobbs's London sketches helped me to explore a more direct style in my own work.

The aim of this book is to inspire you to sketch in the urban environment. It contains many of the hard-won tips and tricks that I've learned over a lifetime of sketching. What I have come to appreciate over the years is that the more you are exposed to the different styles, works and approaches of other artists, the better you become at your own craft. Sketching is a very personal thing, and you will discover that you naturally have your own style.

This book starts out at the beginning of the sketching journey – how to get the right equipment and materials, and how to get yourself sketch-ready – and concludes with ways of adding the finishing touches that complete your artworks. In between, we will explore ways to loosen up on location and learn the basics of perspective, composition and measurement. We also investigate how adding tone and colour can be transformative. Each section is accompanied by an exercise so you can put what you are reading into practice and see your skills develop as you move through the book.

Let's get sketching!

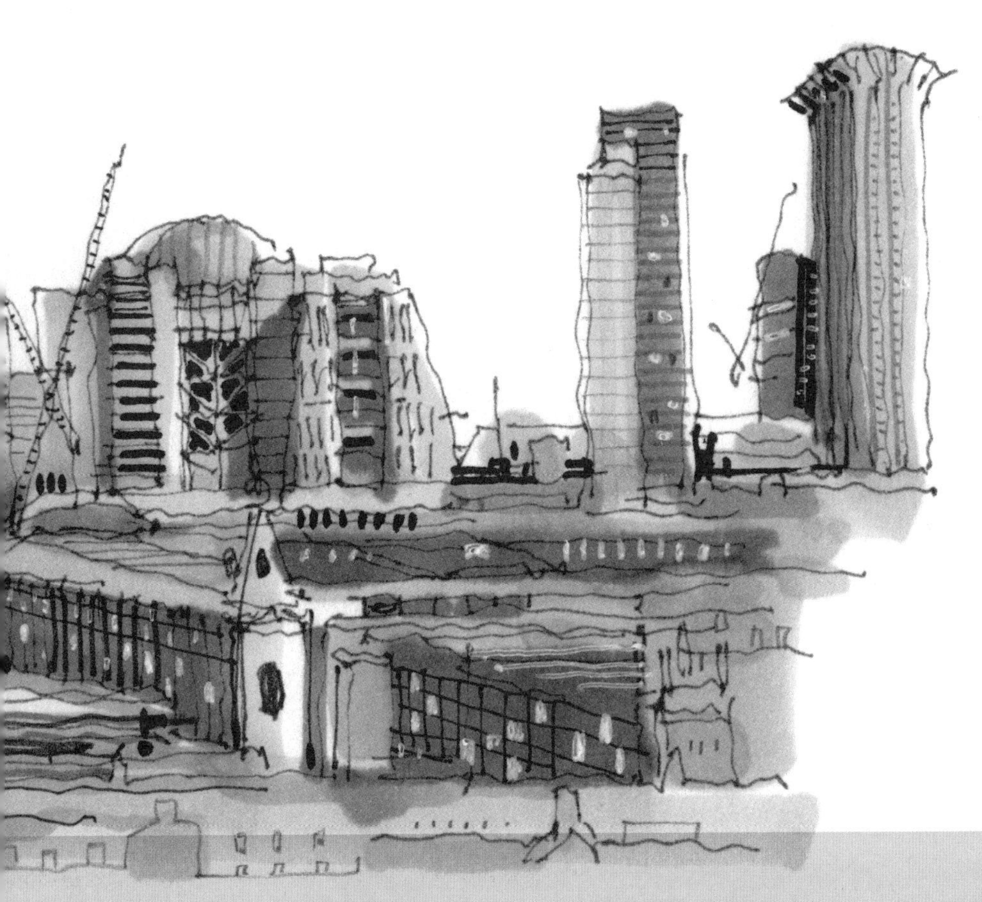

There are no hard-and-fast rules in this book — just simple advice to help you create better art.

London skyline

Equipment

The beauty of urban sketching is that it doesn't require a huge investment in materials and equipment to get started. That said, it helps to ensure you have the right equipment to be able to sketch live and spontaneously. Working with the right equipment will help you produce artwork that really stands out. This chapter sets out what equipment you will need to get started.

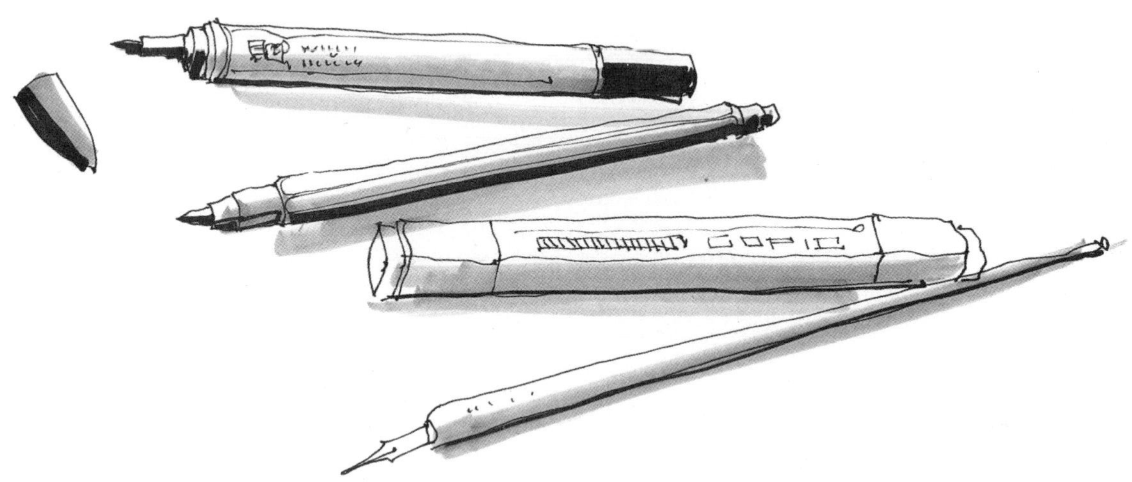

If, like me, you are seduced by the latest sketchbooks or pens, then embrace this. But sketching doesn't have to be expensive; you can simply use what is available. Some of my best sketches have been on napkins or scrap paper with a cheap fibre-tip pen. Some of the finest examples of urban sketches I've seen have been created with the most basic equipment. The humble ballpoint pen is a subtle and effective sketching implement. Ultimately, it's about what you feel comfortable with, and once you get into a rhythm with your sketching, you can then experiment with new media.

The huge choice of artists' materials available can seem overwhelming, even for the experienced sketcher. My advice is to keep things simple and stick to a small kit of tried-and-tested sketch materials. Over time, you can supplement these with new products to keep things fresh. All you really need to get started is something to draw with and something to draw on.

When sketching in an urban environment, I find sketchbooks more practical than drawing on loose sheets of paper. You can whip a sketchbook out anywhere to grab a few minutes of sketch time. I like the convenience of a book as it keeps all my drawings in one place. On the other hand, some artists prefer to use loose paper sheets attached to a board, which give you more options when it comes to drawing size, and means you can frame your finished pieces easily.

Although all your material needs can be met online, I recommend visiting your local art supplies shop – most large towns and cities have them – to try out the pens before you buy them. I like to support my local art retailers and they often give good advice.

In addition to the basics of some paper and a pen, these are other pieces of equipment that you may find useful as you start sketching:

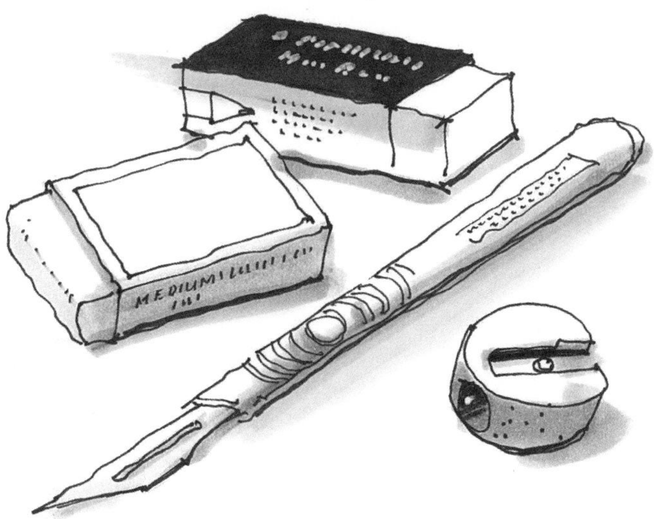

- **Large drawing board and paper clips** – Very useful for large-scale drawings (see page 58) and can be portable. Make sure the wood is soft enough to take drawing pins or, with harder wood, use low tack masking tape to hold the paper in place.

- **Easel** – Some artists like using an easel for large-scale sketching, but they are often too cumbersome to be useful to the average urban sketcher.

- **Sharpeners** – This is essential when using pencil and charcoal to give crisp lines. Old-school sketchers use a craft knife or scalpel (widely available in art supplies shops), but remember to pack these in your hold luggage if you're travelling by plane, otherwise they will be confiscated!

- **Erasers** – It is useful to have both a hard eraser for rubbing out pale lines and a kneadable one for blending and shading. Experiment with both: erasers are not just for getting rid of mistakes.

- **Masking tape** – Use low tack tape to hold loose paper in place. Masking tape or magic tape will not damage the paper when you remove it carefully.

- **Fixative spray** – This 'fixes' charcoal (and very soft pencil) drawings on the paper and stops them from smudging. Spray your finished sketches before you pack them away.

- **Cutting mat** – An A3 cutting mat is very useful for cropping finished sketches and for when you want to cut out a sketch and paste it physically onto another.

- **Spray mount** – This is a light glue spray in aerosol form that will help you overlay multiple sketches to create interesting collages. Remember to use it in a well-ventilated space.

- **Scanner** – Most desktop printers have a scanning function that is useful for scanning your work to edit or share digitally. If you don't have such a printer, I suggest purchasing a small stand-alone scanner; good-quality scanners are relatively inexpensive if bought online.

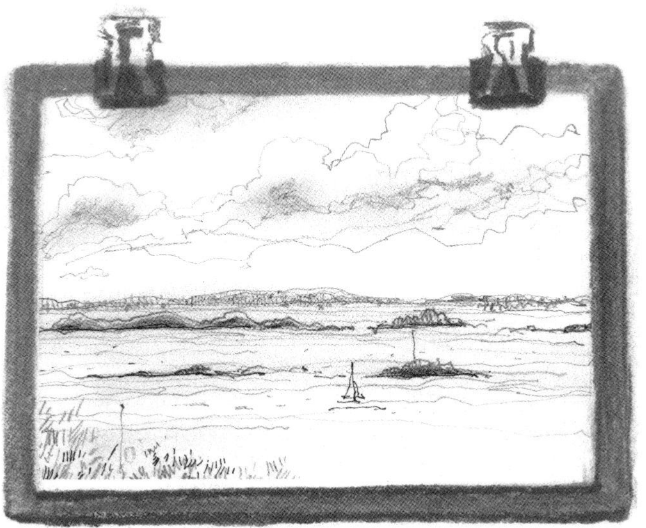

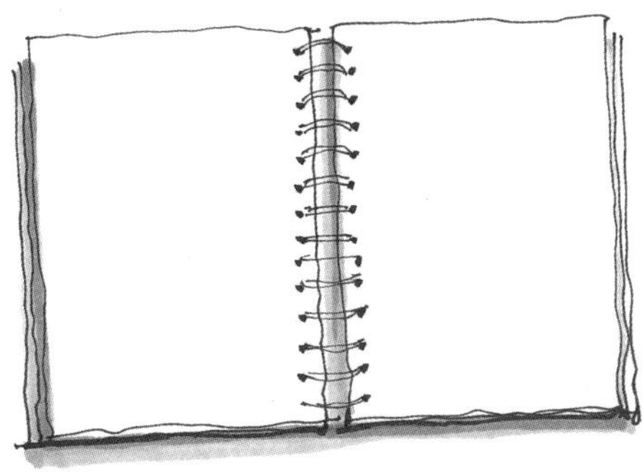

Sketchbook

A sketchbook for urban drawing has to be robust enough to cope with being thrown into a bag, jammed in a case, dropped on the ground and having liquid spilled over it. The binding needs to be strong and should allow the book to lie flat to enable sketches to stray across both sides of the spread.

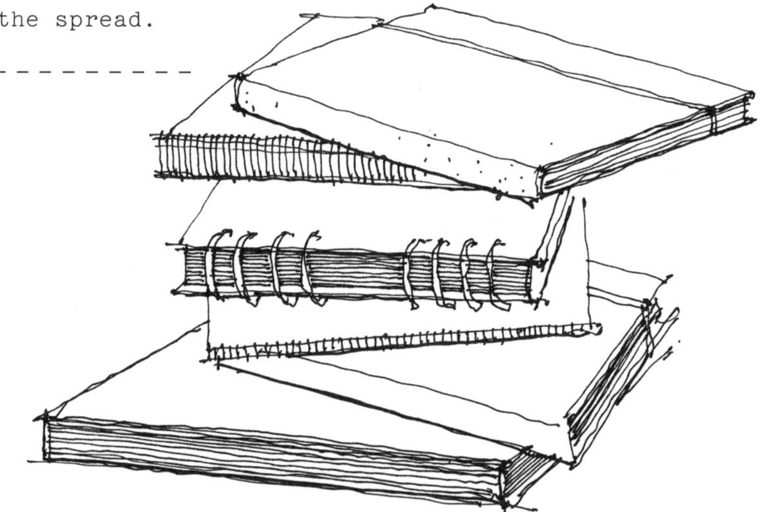

It's important to think about what size of sketchbook will work best for your purpose. I find a smaller A5 sketchbook is the ideal size for sketching on the go. It's agile, practical and unobtrusive, and the double-page spread is large enough to capture the bigger scenes, while also being perfect for more intimate sketches.

Many brands of sketchbook are available and my favourite is the Moleskine sketchbook range. There are cheaper alternatives, but some poorer-quality books shed pages too easily or are bound too tightly to lie flat. My advice would be to buy two or three different books and try out each one using different media – ink, marker, pencil, charcoal – to see which you prefer.

Landscape or portrait?
Although a portrait A5 sketchbook is my go-to size and format, other styles can spark inspiration just by virtue of their different size or shape. It's a good idea to have a few alternative book types in your bag, in case a different style of book is better suited to the scene you're sketching.

Wide landscape sketchbooks are great for cityscapes and sweeping vistas, square books provide an Instagram-friendly canvas and portrait-format sketchbooks can be great for fitting in taller buildings.

Paper
Smooth paper that takes a line easily is ideal for both pen and pencil. The paper should be fine grain, which does not allow ink to soak in too much, keeping the integrity of the linework intact. As a general rule, the smoother the paper, the faster the line. If you intend to add watercolour to your sketches, you will need specialist watercolour paper that is designed to absorb watercolour paint. Most pads will accommodate most media, but as a general rule, the thicker the paper, the more likely it is to take all manner of paint and ink.

Coloured paper is an interesting option that can add a different dimension to your sketches. The smooth, tinted paper and pale background colours are perfect for urban sketching as you can add white highlights to give an instant depth to your linework. Textured paper can also add another dimension to pencil and charcoal sketches.

Sketchbook 'rules'

It's good to establish some sketchbook 'rules' before you get started because, rather paradoxically, these can help you get to know what works best for you. Some artists use their book as a pristine collection of artworks and others use it to jot and sketch everything they see. I'm in the latter camp and I prefer to see my sketchbook as a visual journal. It can be liberating to give yourself permission to make mistakes and move on to the next page. It's also satisfying to look back on the abandoned sketches among the more successful drawings – it's all part of your sketching journey.

The main rule for the urban sketcher, however, is simply to carry your book and pens with you at all times. I can never stress this enough as it's the only way to ensure you draw constantly, which will continuously improve your work. You never know when you might see something that is crying out to be sketched, or find yourself with a spare 15 minutes while you grab a cup of coffee. Get your book out of your bag and get sketching!

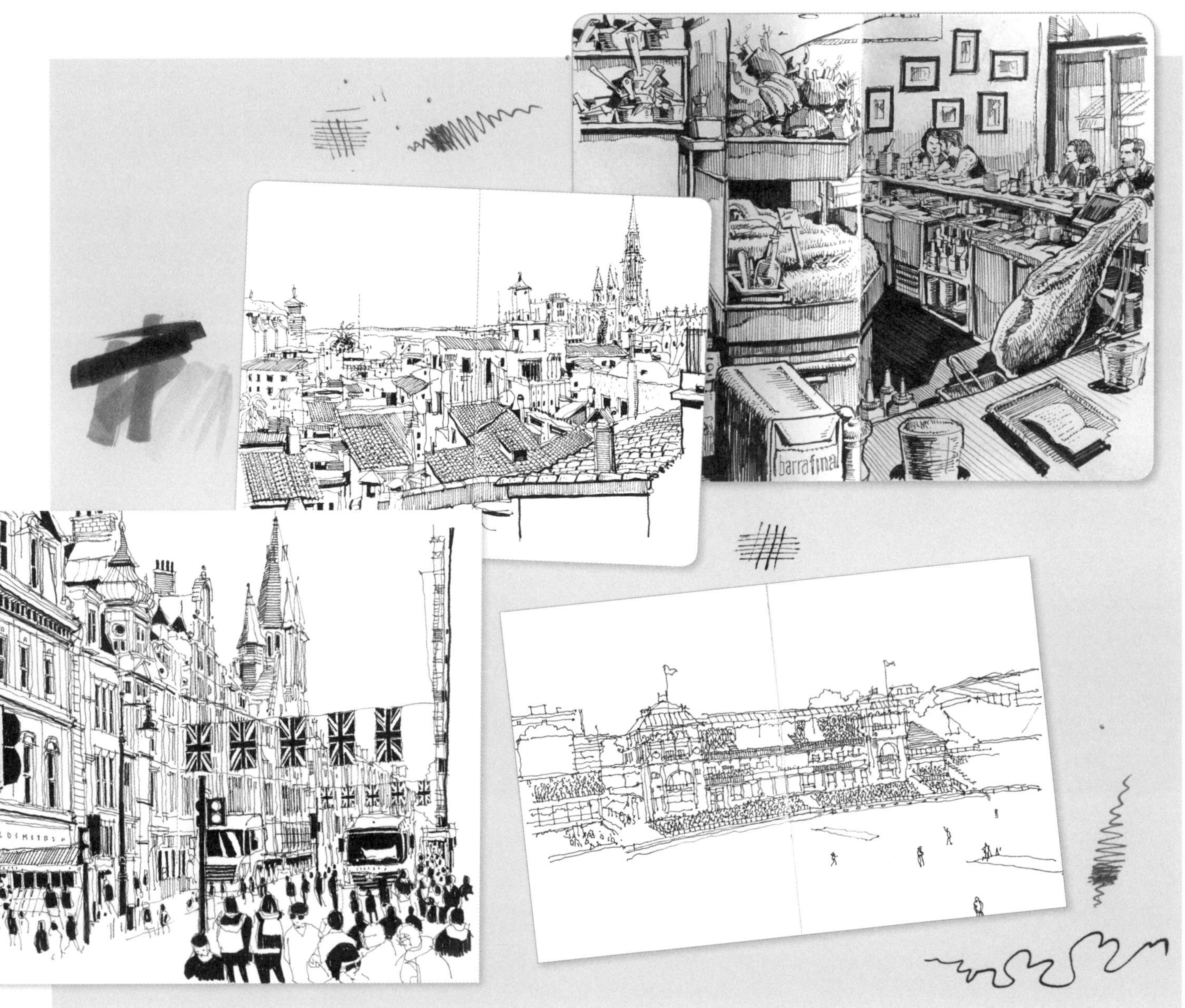

Materials

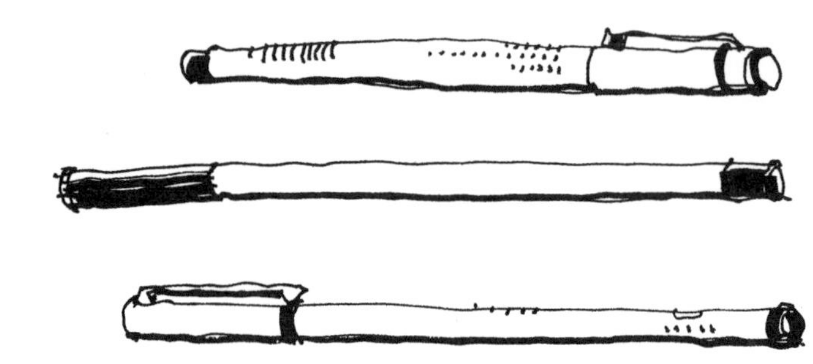

A pen is my preferred medium for urban sketching. It can take time to build up the confidence to draw in ink, but there is a freedom and immediacy to it that is quite exhilarating and addictive. However, experiment with other mediums as well to find your own preference. Here are a few examples to get you started.

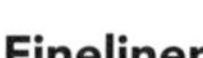

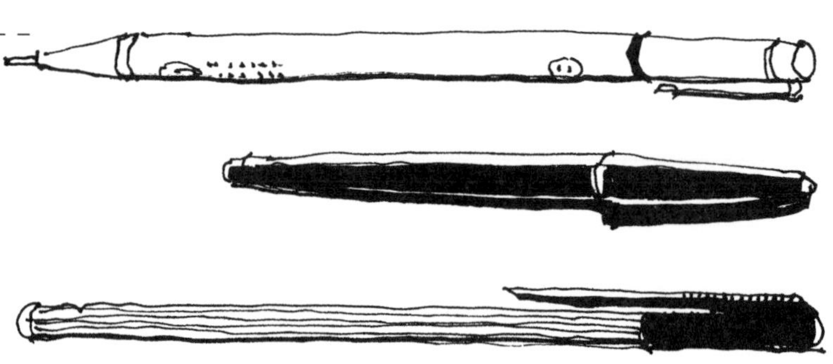

Fineliner

This is a pen with a fibre tip enclosed in metal or plastic. It comes in various line weights, from super-thin to chunky. The fineliner is the ultimate line-drawing pen, delivering fluid and precise lines. I suggest starting with a 0.3mm nib as it's a good all-rounder for line drawing. It is worth noting that some fineliners are not waterproof, so the ink will run if you add watercolour or colour with marker pens afterwards. Also, if you are sketching in wet weather, I advise using a waterproof pen to avoid splodges.

Ballpoint pen

Ballpoint is a surprisingly forgiving pen for sketching, with almost pencil-like qualities such as the ability to adjust line strength and stroke. On the whole, with ballpoints, the finer the nib, the better. It's always worth keeping a ballpoint in your bag for fast sketches of people.

Fountain pen

The old-fashioned fountain pen has seen a renaissance with sketchers in recent times (albeit in a modern, easy-to-use guise) and the lovely lines it delivers make it a favourite for many urban sketchers. The advantage of sketching with a fountain pen is the range of lines and thicknesses that you can achieve by adjusting how much pressure you put on the nib. Waterproof ink can also be used with a fountain pen, so adding watercolour will not cause the ink to run.

Brush pen

The brush pen can be a hard pen to master but it delivers bold and fluid results. It is particularly suited for scenes with people – capturing movement and vibrancy in economic strokes. These pens come in a wide range of colours and are definitely worth experimenting with.

Charcoal

To this day, I can't use charcoal without it taking me back to the arduous life drawing sessions at art school. But charcoal can be great to sketch with, giving fast, bold and immediate lines, and you can easily correct any mistakes with a kneadable eraser and some white chalk. The urban landscape is quite challenging for this medium and I would only really recommend using it when there is a lot of organic content in your scene; trees, rivers and people, for example. Geometric shapes are quite difficult to capture accurately in charcoal, but it can be really effective when drawing a more expressive or abstract sketch. If you do use charcoal, don't forget your fixative spray to ensure your finished piece doesn't smudge.

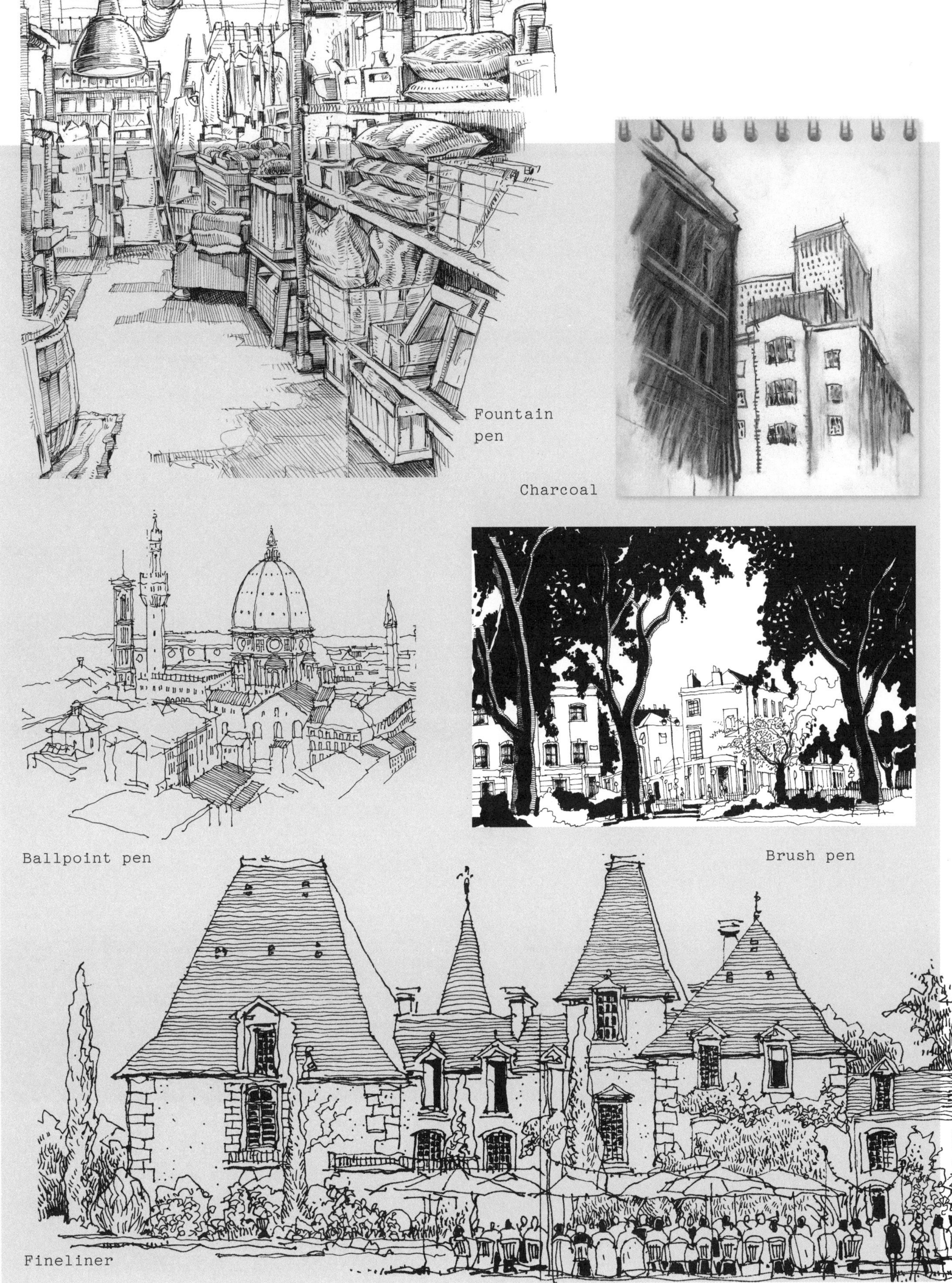
Fountain
pen

Charcoal

Ballpoint pen

Brush pen

Fineliner

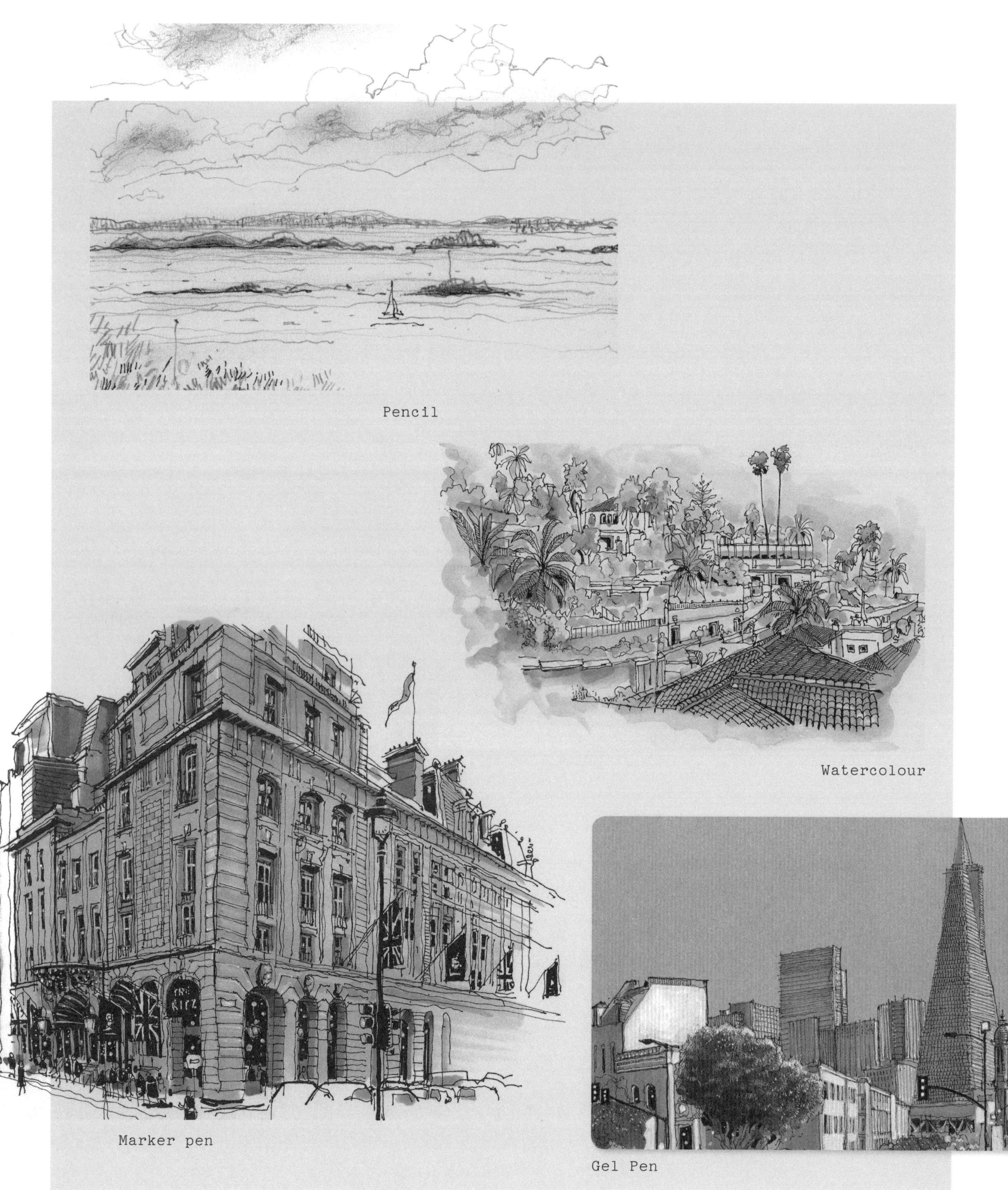

Pencil
Watercolour
Marker pen
Gel Pen

Pencil

Pencil is a wonderful medium to capture cityscapes with. Most of us are familiar with drawing with pencil from our school days, so it's an unintimidating media to work with. It is also extremely flexible and very forgiving for the beginner sketcher lacking in confidence. I always have some pencils in my bag in case the subject matter lends itself more to that medium. To save time when out and about, I use mechanical pencils that don't need sharpening. Softer pencils (HB–9B) deliver heavy shadows and more line weight, while harder pencils (H–9H) are great for adding detail.

Coloured pencils are amazing to sketch with on their own and white pencils are great for adding highlights to sketches on dark paper.

Marker pen

Marker pen is my favourite method of adding colour to my sketches – probably due to the fact that when I was a graphic designer, using computers wasn't yet the norm so I predominantly used marker pens in my work. Marker pens are an easy way to add tone and colour to your sketches, and you'll see lots of examples in this book of how to achieve this. They are also good for laying flat and graduated tones, while brush markers are good for softer 'watercolour' effects. It's worth experimenting with a small set of greys or basic colours to add a splash of colour or tonal depth to your line sketches.

The downside to these pens is that they are not particularly cheap and they have the annoying habit of drying out (although refills can be bought for some brands).

Gel pen or paint pen

Gel pens or paint pens are great for adding extra colour on top of your sketches. They are particularly good for adding highlight detail. These pens are a cheap way to boost your sketching arsenal.

Watercolour

Watercolour can seem a little daunting at first but don't be put off. It can be an extremely useful medium for adding some colour to your sketches once you get them home. While only the most enthusiastic (and experienced) urban sketchers tend to use watercolour on location, it can deliver great results in situ, since the artist can see the colours and represent them faithfully. Though it can take some time to master watercolour techniques, it's definitely worth the effort. I recommend you buy a cheap beginners' set (available in all art supplies shops) and have some fun experimenting – it's hard to go too wrong as long as you remember that less is more.

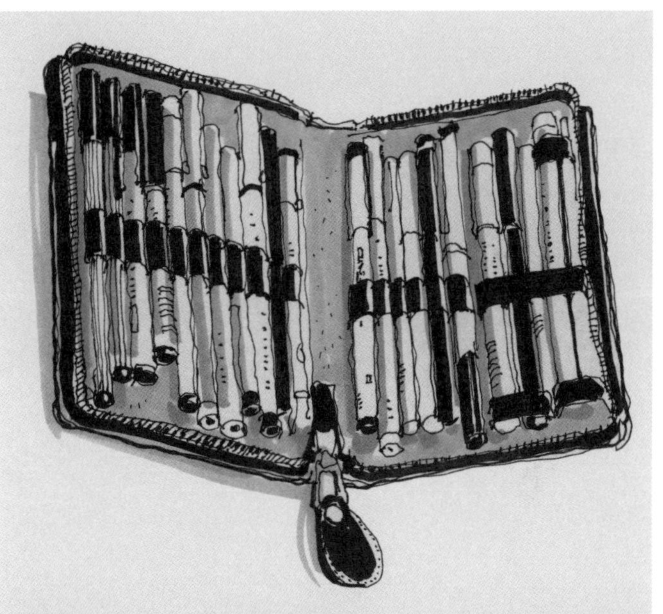

PEN AND PENCIL CASE

It's important to keep your sketching kit in good order so that you can locate what you need when you need it. A case with elasticated loops can be more user-friendly than a traditional pencil case as it allows you to carry the basic sketching gear in an ordered and easy-to-access format. I carry mine everywhere with me, along with my sketchbook.

Getting Started

Now that you have your sketchbook and materials, you're ready to get out into the urban environment. Here are a few tips to get you started.

Travel light

Some artists prefer to have lots of kit, easels and large-format sketchbooks, but I find the less encumbered I am by the kit, the easier it is to focus on the drawing. If you always travel with a small selection of pens and an A5 sketchbook, you will be able to set up camp anywhere and get drawing quickly wherever you are.

Pick a subject that interests you

There is absolutely no point in sketching something that doesn't excite you. The fact is, you're more likely to get a great result with something that interests you. Start with whatever catches your eye.

Get comfortable

I like standing to draw as it gives me space and the impetus to work quickly, but for beginners, less-confident artists and people who work at a slower pace, a seated position may be more comfortable and allow for more accuracy. Find a location where you can easily sit on a wall or chair to give yourself more time to capture the scene. Bars and restaurants can be great spots for sketching, and you can enjoy some refreshments at the same time.

Remember that a drawing is not a photograph

Don't fall into the trap of trying to faithfully capture the scene you are drawing as if it were a photograph. A sketch is an expression of what you're looking at, not an exact reproduction. Keeping this in mind will loosen the shackles of realism and help you be more satisfied with the finished result. Don't get too hung up on the mistakes – learn to celebrate them!

Set yourself a time limit

It can be useful to give yourself a time limit on your live drawings. This helps to focus the mind and instil your drawings with energy, and it forces you to move on to another view. Quick sketches often capture much more than an overworked piece.

Work in a medium that you feel comfortable with

I love drawing with pen – straight in, with no pencil. But I'm very aware this requires a lot of confidence and my advice to beginners is always to start with a medium you feel comfortable with. This might well be pencil or charcoal, both of which are quite forgiving.

Stop and come back to it later

Don't be afraid to call time on a sketch even though it's not 'finished'. Remember, you are the one to decide what's finished and what's not. A great tip is to take a quick photo of the view you're sketching on your phone and then use the image as a reference for adding more detail, tone or colour later on. This is especially helpful if the weather turns and you still want to add more to the sketch.

Keep at it

Practise makes perfect, and a sketch a day is a great way to train your eye. Draw mundane things such as bus journeys, sandwich shops, mugs on desks and drab buildings. You'll quickly become adept at looking for interesting views, and soon your sketchbook will become a record of your travels.

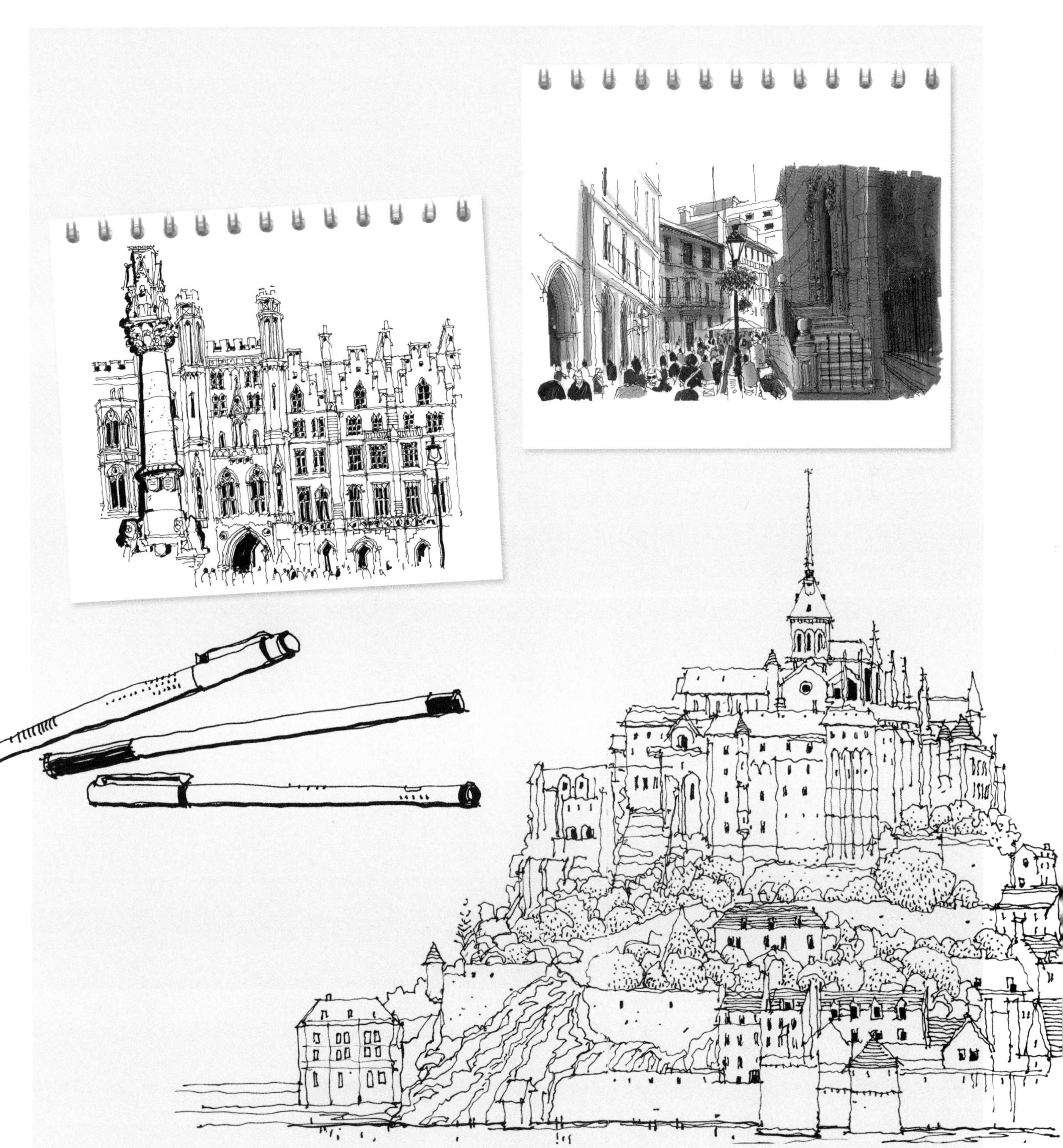

Etiquette

There aren't any rules for sketching in public, but I like to think there is an unwritten 'sketcher's code of conduct'. Firstly, it's worth remembering that sketching in public these days is actually quite unusual. Nobody ever bats an eyelid when people are taking snaps with their devices, but when someone is taking the time to sketch, it can be a different story. Here are a few pointers that you might find useful when you're sketching outside.

- -

Permission

It's legal to sketch on the streets in most countries, but if you're sketching somewhere new, do check that the local laws permit it. Authorities in some countries can be very suspicious of studious-looking individuals loitering with sketchbooks. If there are security guards in the vicinity, ask them if you are allowed to sketch there. I always ask for permission if I want to sketch in a location such as a museum, church, gallery or any kind of private property, and of course it's absolutely necessary if you ever want to get access to a roof for a rooftop sketch. In most cases, people are happy for you to do so, but it's always worth checking first. It's a little-known fact that many galleries and museums have fold-away stools hanging on walls that can be used by artists when a seat is needed for a long drawing.

Keep out of the way

A key thing I have learned is that if you are sketching in a busy city centre or bustling location, you need to find a spot that is out of the way. It helps to be invisible to the subject you are sketching, so find a quiet corner where you can observe and sketch without being jostled.

Don't be shy

When people see you sketching on the street, you will inevitably be asked: 'Can I have a look?'. We all have our own limits of what we feel comfortable with, but always be polite and try not to be self-conscious about your work, no matter what stage you are at on your sketch journey. If you receive a compliment on your artwork, then accept it graciously in the spirit it is given – this will help your sketching confidence no end.

Sketching people

Sketching people at fairly close quarters is another area where the sketcher has to be respectful and sensitive to what is going on around them. If your subject notices you, don't try to hide the fact you are sketching them. Simply show them your book and pen and ask if they are happy for you to continue. In my experience, 99 percent of the time people don't mind being the subject of your sketch, but if not, simply close your book and move on. Don't worry if your drawing is not a brilliant likeness and don't be afraid to show your work to your subject. People often love the attention. That said, it never fails to astonish me how many people are so absorbed with their electronic devices that you could sketch them all day long and they would be completely oblivious!

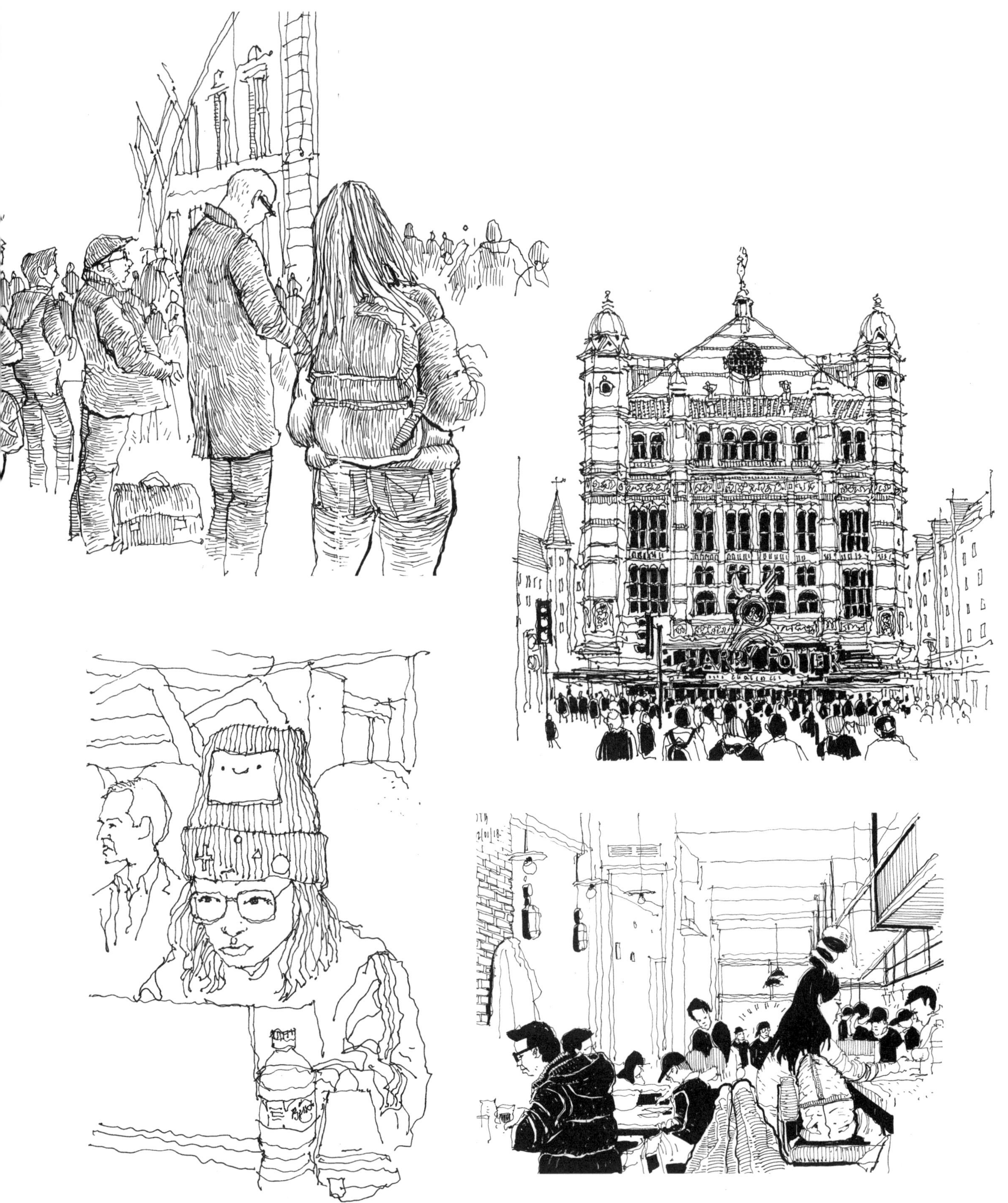

HARRY POTTER

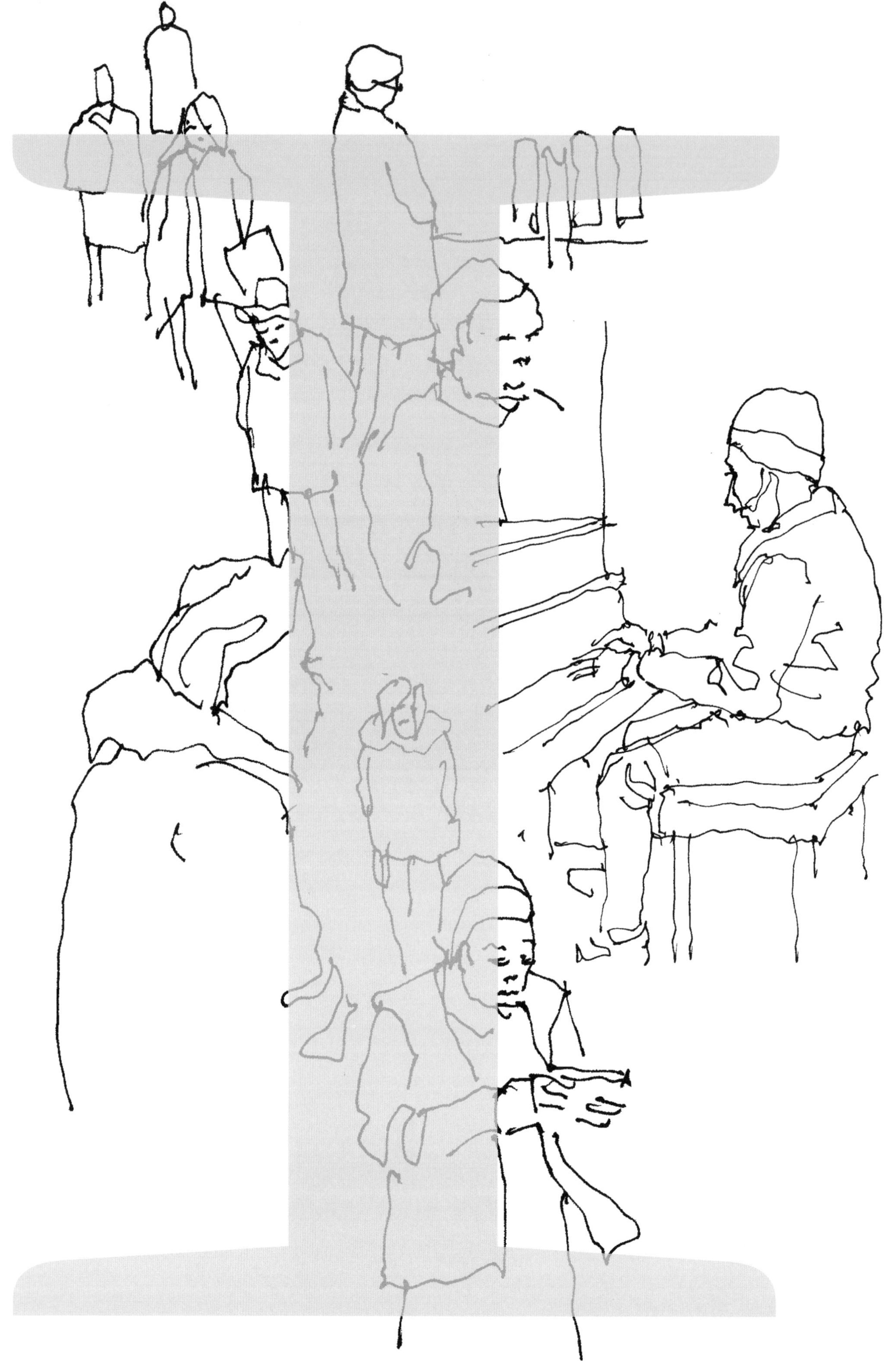

Loosening Up

Sketching is like a muscle: the more you exercise it, the stronger it will become. It follows, therefore, that it's essential to warm up — just as you would before any exercise — to make the most of your activity. Loosening up before sketching is hugely helpful to get you into the zone, shake off any stiffness and relieve any nervousness about the initial mark-making.

People sometimes feel a lot of pressure over getting started as tackling a blank page can often seem challenging, even daunting. This is where loosening-up exercises can help. When I run workshops, I find that people produce much more accomplished work when they are relaxed, and a short quick-sketch session is always time well spent. We all have pressures in our daily lives and doing a few quick practise sketches often takes the pressure off so you can then go on to create something really great.

Getting Sketch Ready

Urban sketching is about the connection between the artist and their observations in an urban environment. If you live in a town or city and are used to exploring the area, you may already have a good sense of the place. However, if you spend a lot of time in your car, or you need to travel into an urban environment to sketch, take time to walk the streets and get a real feel for them. Look carefully at the architecture and see what views are interesting and attractive to you. Look for intriguing buildings or streets and take note of the locations that draw your attention.

Photographers will often undertake a 'recce' (short for reconnaissance) before starting a photographic commission, and this is also useful when setting out on an urban sketching mission. Walk around and assess your options – 30 minutes scoping out an area will be time well invested to find a place that excites and inspires you. You can use a map app on your phone to log locations to come back to another time.

When you walk the streets looking for a scene to capture, remember to look up as well as around you at eye level. Regular city dwellers do not always observe in the way that an artist does; it is our job to take notice of everything with an almost obsessive curiosity so that we can translate the city effectively onto paper. You will soon become familiar with the styles of architecture that you sketch, the periods they are from and the materials from which they are constructed.

David Gentleman is a great example of an artist taking the time to immerse himself in a city to really understand what makes it tick. In his book, *London, You're Beautiful: An Artist's Year*, Gentleman teaches us to look again at London as he draws his way through the city over the space of a year.

When you do eventually get settled down to sketch, remember not to stop looking around you!

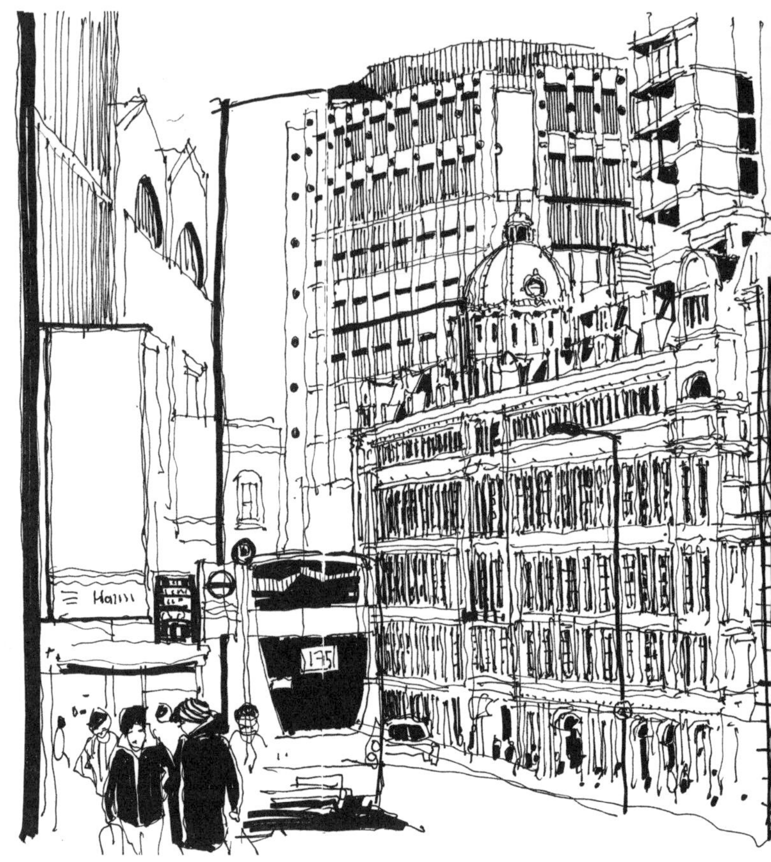

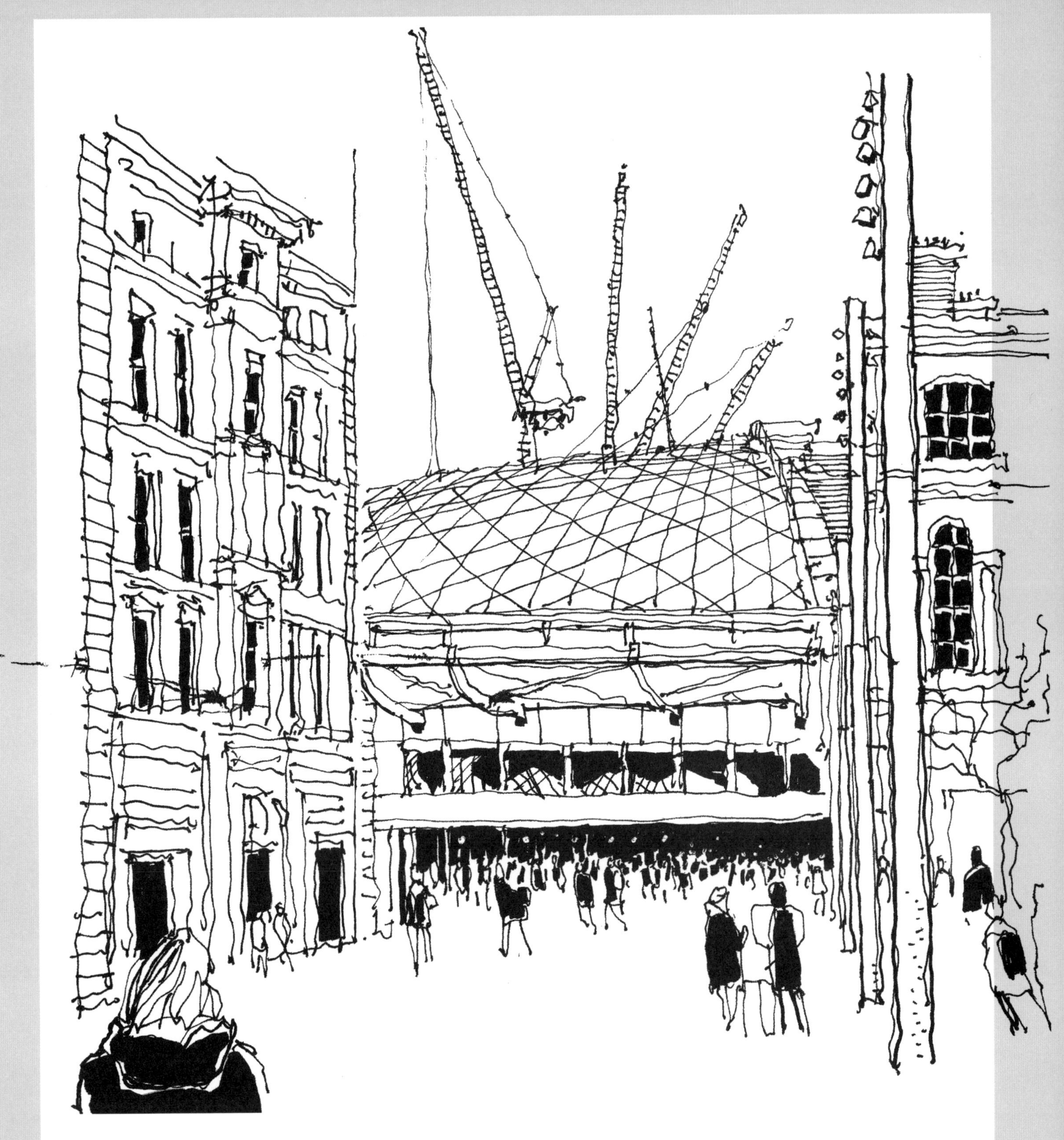

Looking for Sketching Potential

When you're heading out sketching, sometimes the pressure of
what to actually draw can be a barrier to getting started. I've
picked out a few of my go-to subjects to give you some ideas,
but remember the key to successful sketching is in finding
something that you personally find interesting.

- -

Vistas

I love a good rooftop and find there is no better place to start drawing than up high, with a view of a city. You can zoom in on details or, if desired, explore the entire vista. Urban sketchers relish the opportunity to draw above ground level and the elevated position offers the artist unparalleled freedom and a new perspective.

Mundanity

Often a scene that you wouldn't ordinarily look at twice will be amazing in sketch form – locals sat outside a small café in the sun drinking coffee, students doing their washing in a laundromat, a dog sitting under a table, for instance. All of these scenes might look quite uninteresting as a photograph, but drawing can bring a level of artistic gravitas to everyday views. Sketching opportunities are everywhere, especially where you don't expect them!

Travelling

Travel and sketching go hand in hand. Buses, trains, planes, and cars are all great sketching locations. Everything you pass on the way from A to B offers new opportunities for the urban sketcher, and then when you arrive, there will be a plethora of new people, architecture, streets and nature to explore. Whether you are heading off to the other side of the world or on your daily commute, always remember to pack your drawing kit!

Architectural mayhem

Old, new, classical, brutalist…the more varied the architectural styles are in a sketch, the better. A scene where the architecture tells the story of the city will always be interesting and challenging. In London, for example, you could look for a location where the beautiful old architecture of Sir Christopher Wren combines with the modernist towers of Norman Foster.

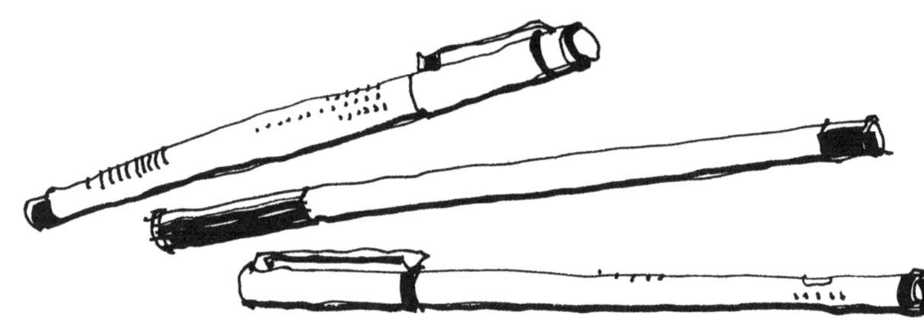

The exercises that follow are designed to get you in the mood for sketching. They are quick sessions that will help you settle in to the task at hand by being free and relaxed. If your style is naturally slower, they will challenge you to try drawing at a quicker pace, building your confidence in what you can achieve in a short time. If you are naturally fast, then these will help you be more accurate and challenge you to use new materials.

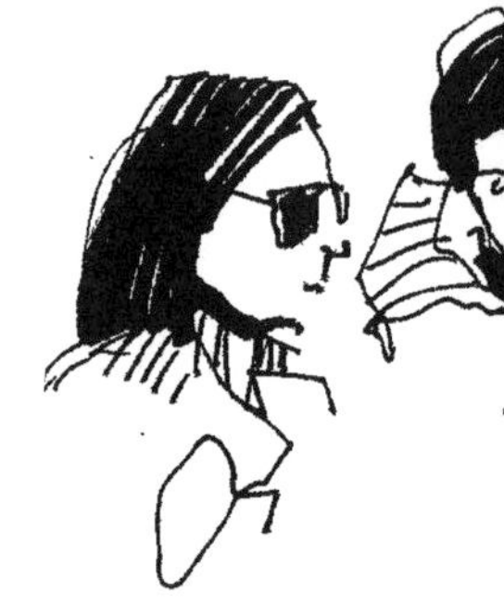

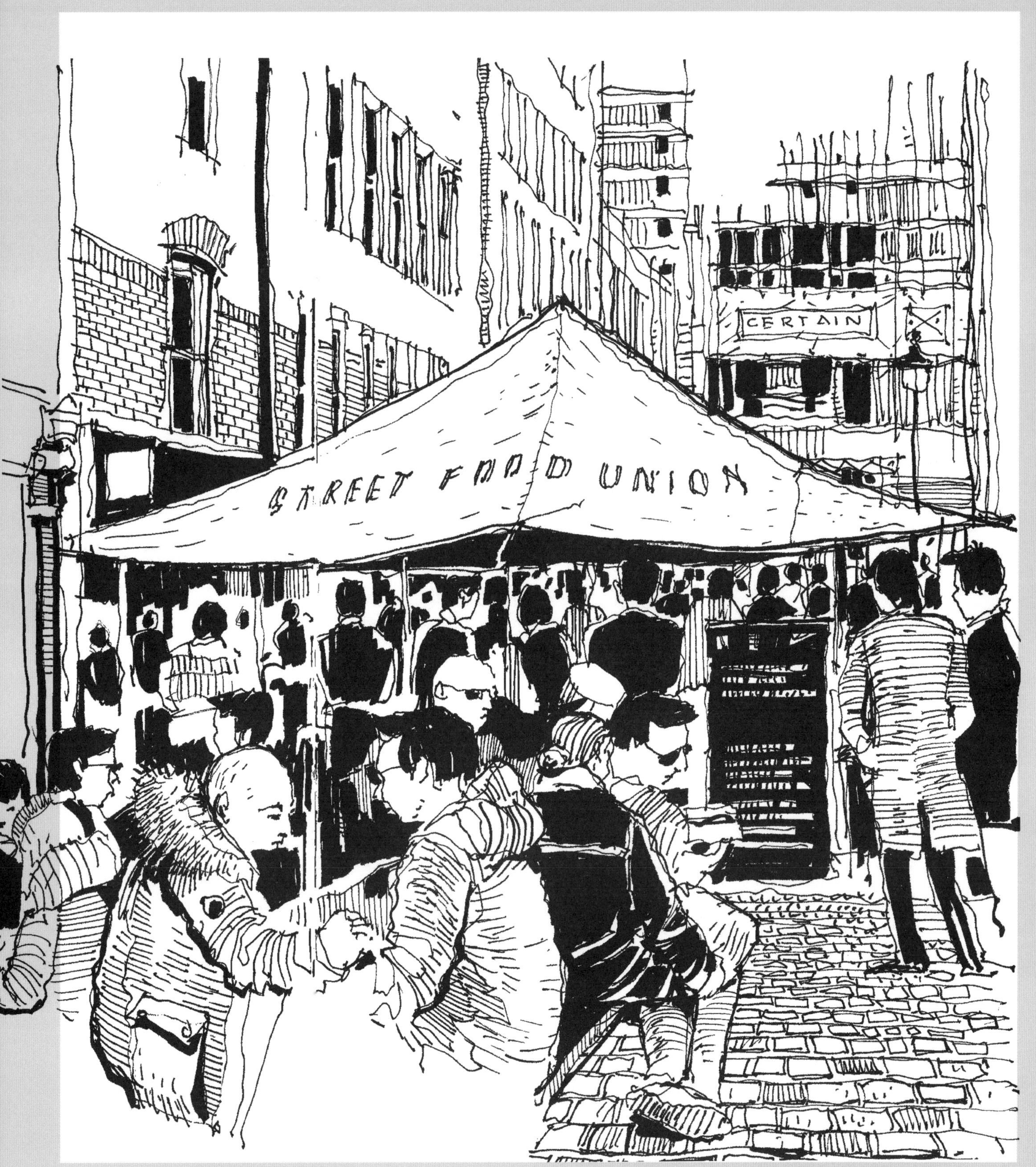

STREET FOOD UNION
CERTAIN

Five-Minute Thumbnail Sketches Exercises

If you haven't sketched for a while, doing a few quick sketches is a good way to loosen up and build your confidence. These exercises are all about working quickly and challenging yourself to use different media. The objective is to capture the essence of the subject swiftly, and not worry about the accuracy of the sketch. Try to use the opposite of what you would normally use to sketch the subject matter – for instance, if the scene is delicate and complex, use a fat pen or large chunk of charcoal. Start by selecting three or four different types of media: pen, pencil, charcoal and brush pen, for example. Work in a sketchbook no larger than A4 to keep your sketching focused and fast. Find a location with multiple angles and views. Try to vary the scene in each of your sketches – for example, a close-up of a plant or tree in the foreground in one sketch, and a particular feature of a building in another. Allow yourself five minutes to capture each view.

Exercise 1

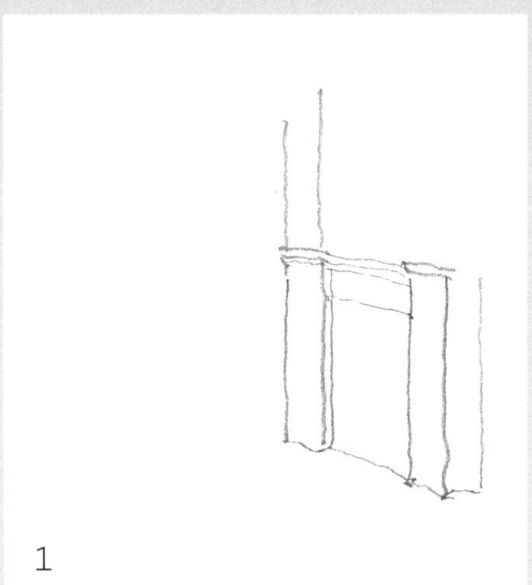

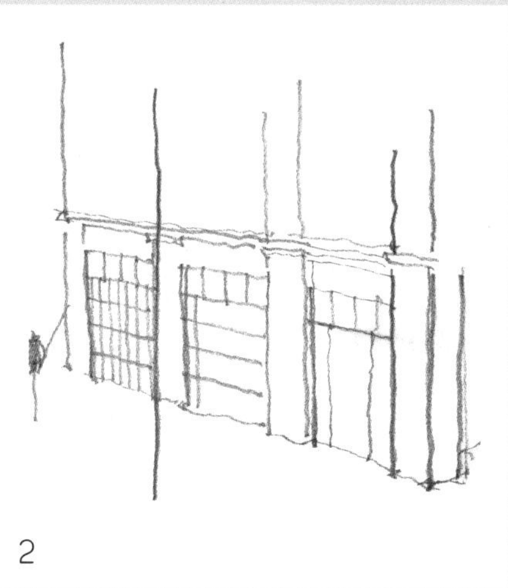

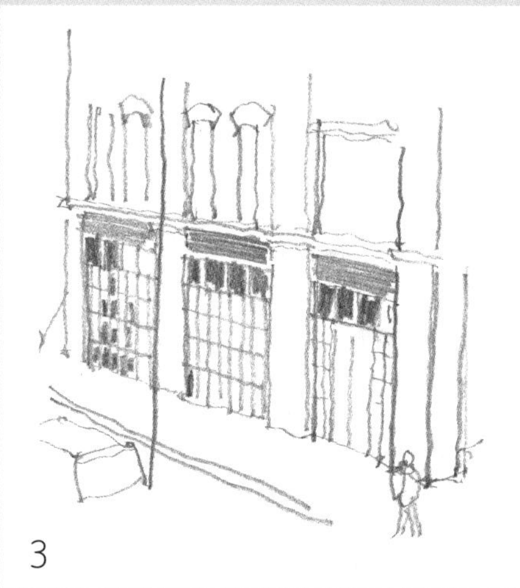

1. Choose your first medium, set a timer and start making marks immediately, beginning with the key structural shapes.

2. Focus your attention on small areas of the larger scene and fill these in quickly. See if you can use lines created by buildings or lampposts to frame your wider scene.

3. Keep your eyes on your subject for the majority of the time you are sketching. The more you look, the better your sketches will be. Once you've got the basic shapes down, add detail to build up your sketch.

- -

FOR THIS SKETCH
I used a Koh-I-Noor clutch pencil
with a 4B 4mm lead — not what I
would normally use for a tightly
rendered building, but the result
is a soft and soulful interpretation.

FOR THIS SKETCH
I used a Tombow black brush marker pen —
again, it is not my first pen of choice
for architectural subject matter. It's hard
to control the finer detail, but it does
deliver bold and impactful lines.

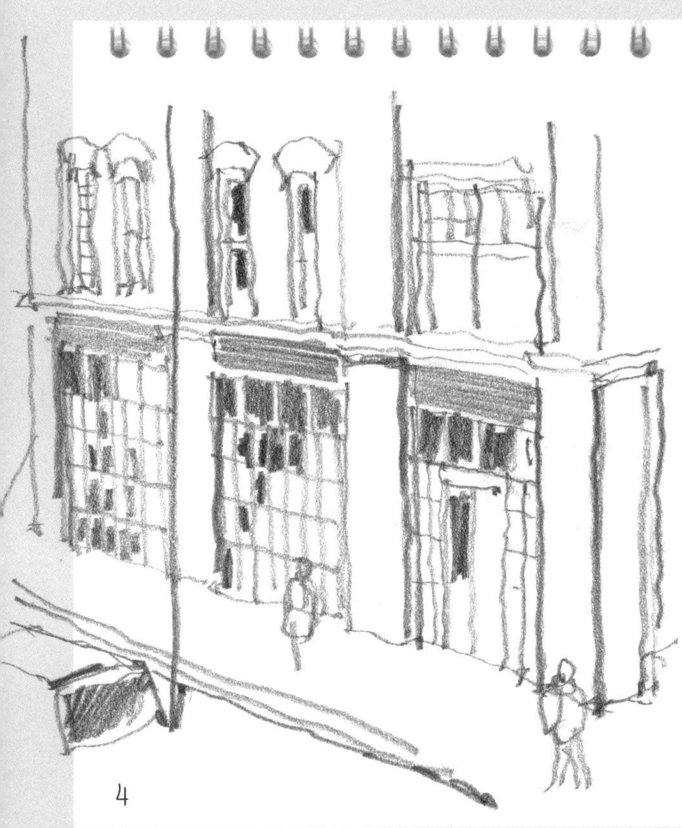

4

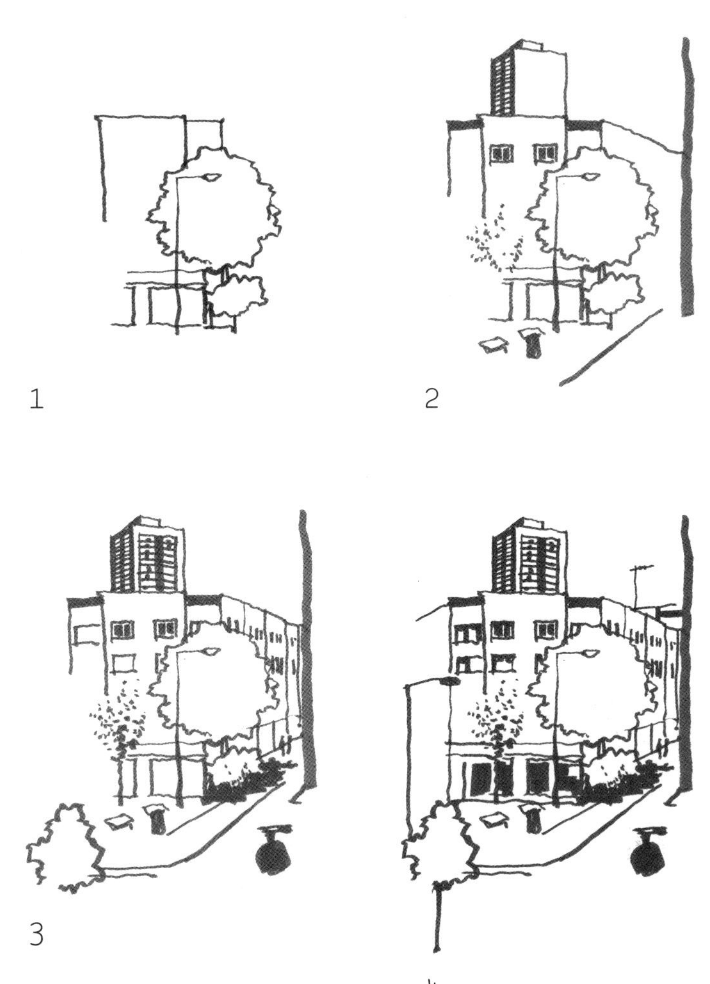

1

2

3

4

4. Just before your time runs out, add any final details.
You could add some tone and shadows, or a person.
Try to include as many details as possible in the time
you have, but don't labour your marks – keep your
movements quick and relaxed. When the timer
sounds, turn the page, reset it and go again with a
different subject and medium. Repeat this exercise
three or four times and you will be surprised by how
quickly you can fill your sketchbook, and how each
medium gets you to work differently.

Contour Line Drawing Exercise

Contour line drawing (sometimes called 'blind drawing') is sketching without looking at the paper. It can feel quite strange to draw without knowing where your marks are going, but it can also be very liberating. The object of the exercise is to concentrate purely on looking and seeing. The key to successful urban sketching is spending at least 50 percent of your time looking, so that you're drawing what you *really* see rather than what you *expect* to see. The results are often wild and loose, but they can also capture nuance and character in a way that you wouldn't think possible.

• Select materials you are comfortable with. Contour line drawing is a perfect exercise for experimenting with ink, as it takes away the nervousness about making the initial mark. Brush pens are also great for this exercise, as you can vary the weights of the lines; the same is true for thick, chisel-pointed pencils.

This exercise is best conducted sitting down. Find a quiet corner to sit, preferably surrounded by plenty of people. Railway stations, libraries, bars, restaurants and coffee shops are all ideal, as people will tend to be less mobile and easier to sketch. Try to pick somewhere that has an interesting backdrop that you can bring into your sketch.

• Start by sketching quick outlines of a person and remember to keep your eyes on your subject all the time. Imagine your pen going around the edge of their silhouette. Feel free to add detail like clothes or hats. Build up your scene with multiple drawings across the spread of your sketchbook. Try using a couple of colours too – red and black look very effective when combined. Don't forget to add details in the background to give context to the drawings.

• After 15 minutes of sketching, and when you have filled your sketchbook spread with multiple drawings, move to another location and repeat the exercise. Mix up the weights of your selected medium – use bold and chunky lines alongside fine and delicate ones. If you need to take a glance at your paper occasionally to get your bearings, feel free to do so; it's helpful in complex scenes to get your position on the page.

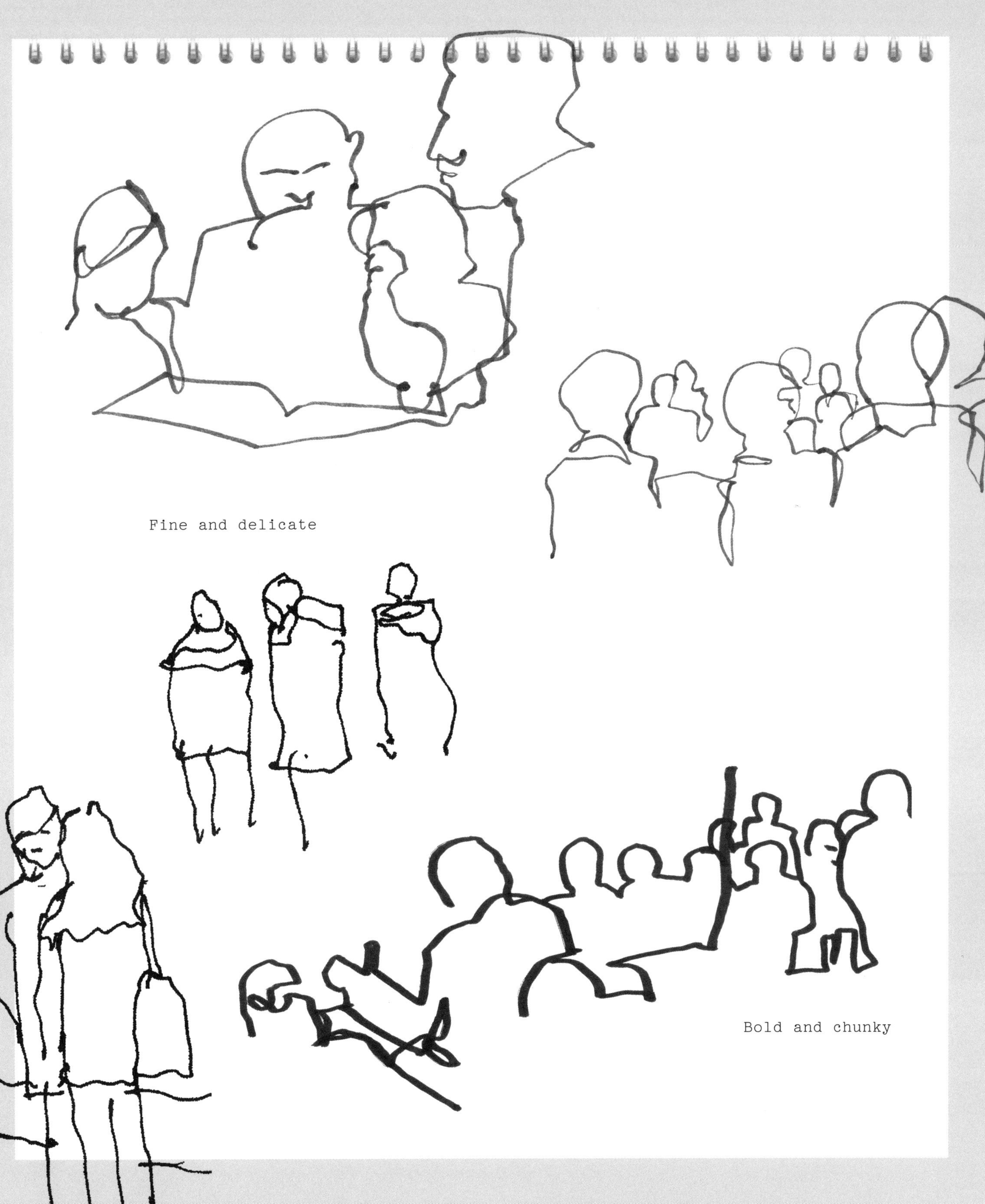

Fine and delicate
Bold and chunky

Sketching People in a Busy Location Exercise

This exercise will help you learn to work unselfconsciously and quickly in a busy location. Sketching people quickly is also great practise for when you want to capture human activity as part of your sketch. Find a quiet spot in a bustling environment where you can observe people and sketch unnoticed. Allow yourself no more than three minutes per view and work in either pen or pencil – whichever you feel most comfortable with for sketching at speed.

1. Find a secluded corner and identify someone who is in a fairly static position to give you a chance to capture their pose. In my sketch, this man was momentarily standing still, occupied with his mobile device, so he was in the perfect position for me to sketch him. Start drawing the facial features, beginning with the eyes and building the head from there. Then work down the shoulder to the hand and the device, the central point of this sketch. Look at the shapes and angles being made by the limbs and let your pen follow the outline. Keep your lines free and fearless!

2. Now change your view and identify another candidate who's not moving too much and try to sketch them from a different angle. Don't worry about accuracy – it's the immediacy of the lines that we are interested in. Again, start with the eyes and work down the face; eyes looking down are easier to sketch, as just a simple line will denote the form. Get the shape of the head right – you'll notice here it is almost egg-shaped due to the angle. This man's baggy sweatshirt is key to the believability of the drawing, so I took care to capture the folds. If you have time, then add in more fabric folds to help depict a realistic form.

3. Next, select people who are moving. This sketch will have a different energy: note the unfinished nature of my drawings. Even though these are quick captures, there is movement and action. The smaller sketches are purposely basic – sketch simple figures using an egg-shaped head and rectangular torso and experiment with the shapes to reflect different body sizes. If someone is looking down, reflect that in your lines, if they are looking at you, notice the angle of the head. You must keep looking at your subjects all the time, taking only quick glances at your paper every few seconds. Bring the sketches together as you draw in a single montage on the page and be playful with the composition. Vary the size of the people you draw too – show some smaller people that are farther away and some closer and larger.

IF YOU HAVE MORE TIME and you enjoyed the freedom of fast lines, start again with four further views. When you have conducted this exercise a few times, you will notice that you have increased your drawing speed, buying yourself valuable time when you are live sketching.

4. If you see someone doing something different or unexpected, take the opportunity to sketch them. This pianist in a train station was a gift for me to draw – although his hands were moving, his pose remained static. I started on his hat and worked down through his face and head, onto his arms and back to get the posture. Because he was playing the piano, it was important to get a sense of his hands, as they are inevitably where the eye lands. Hands are hard to draw quickly so don't waste time trying to make each finger look realistic. Small lines for each digit will work – try to get a sense of the shapes as the fingers move and flex.

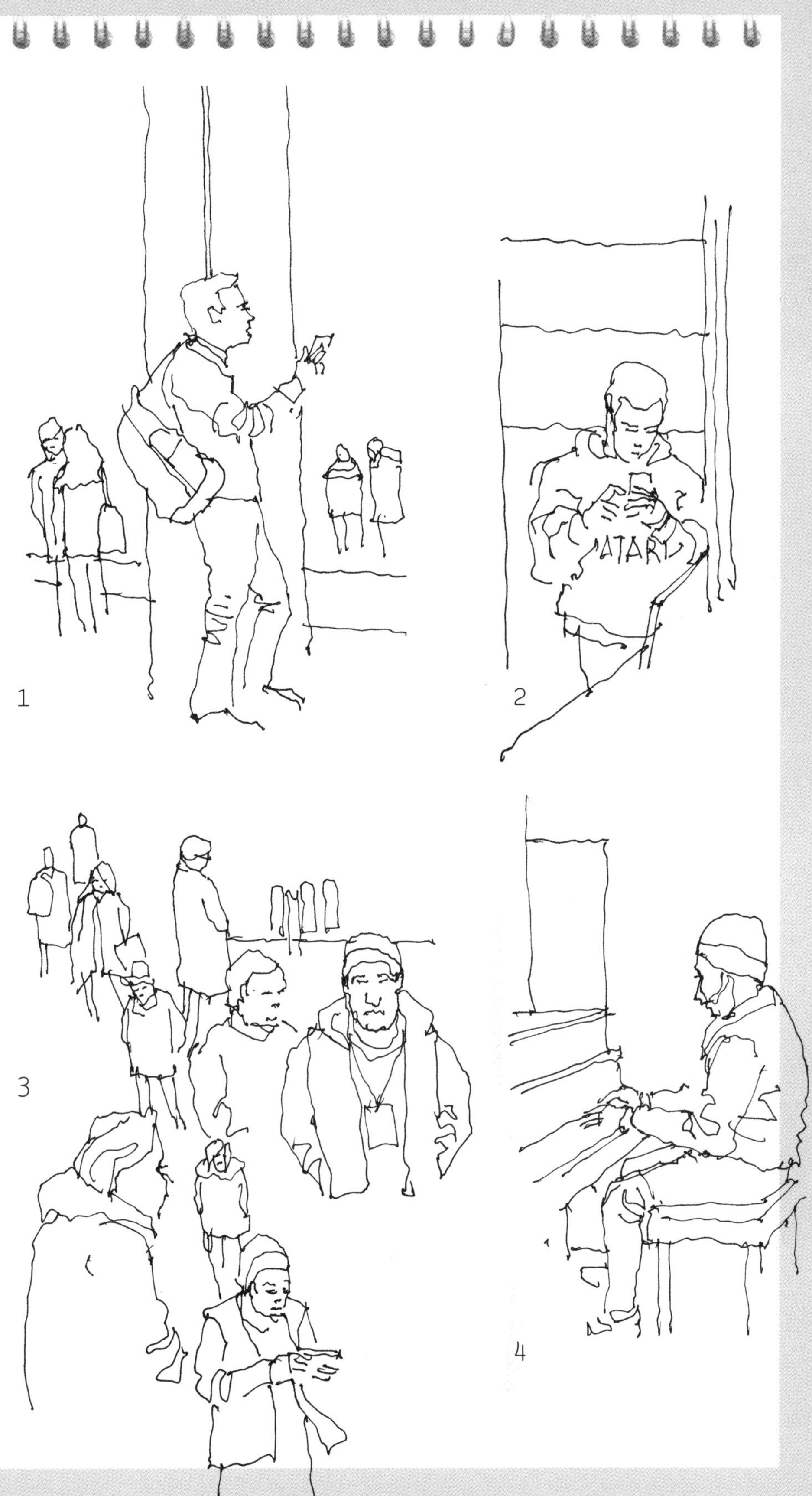

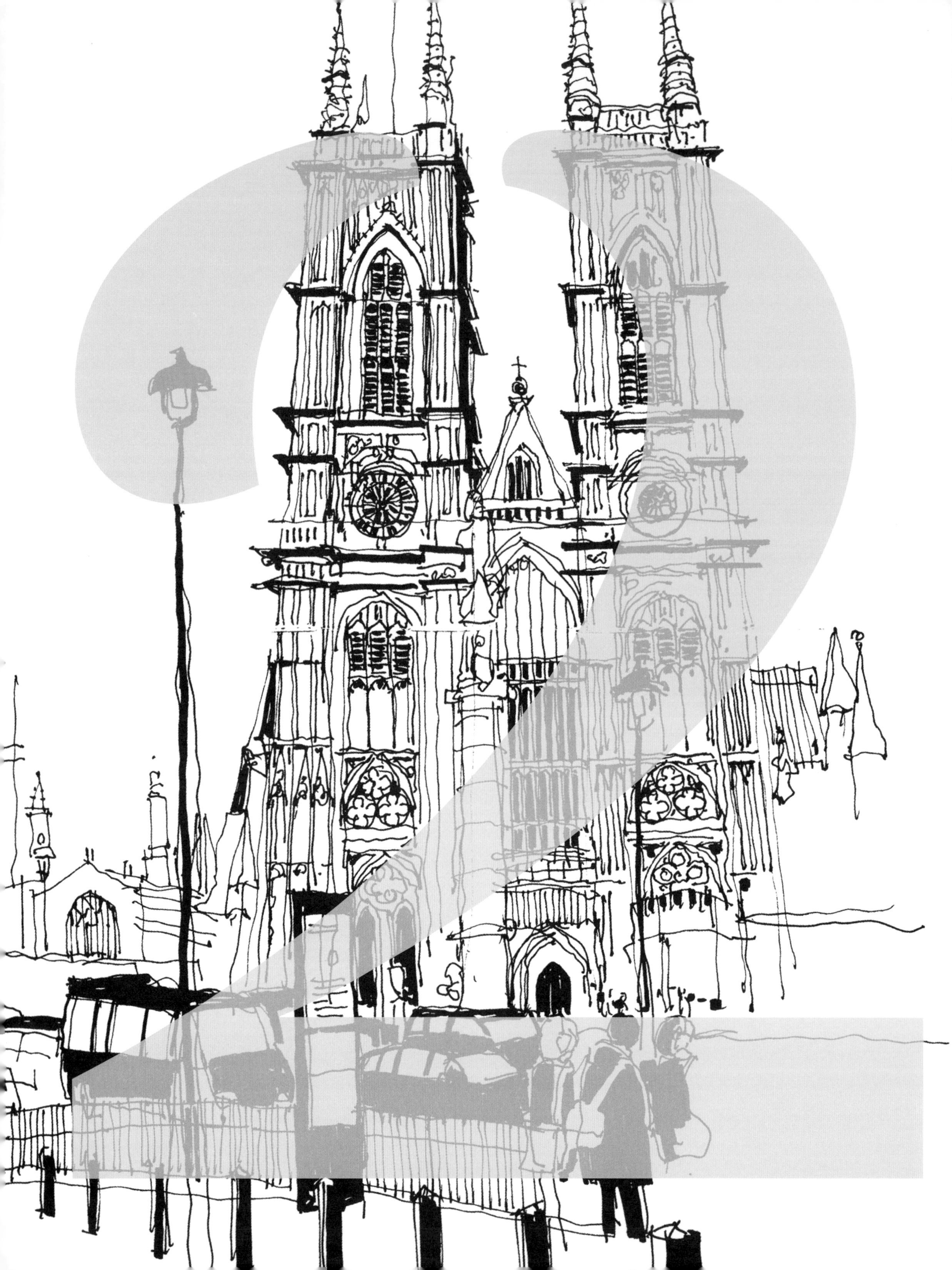

Building a Scene

Now that you are warmed up and ready for sketching, we will begin to explore how to build a scene in more detail, and we'll look at some techniques that will make your work stand out on the page.

Although drawing is a creative process, relying on the artistic interpretation of a scene, it can be enhanced by some technical knowledge. Simple exercises in measurement and perspective will help you master the challenging angles and many shapes of cities, allowing you to accurately translate the proportions of your scene onto the page.

We will also look at composition — how to arrange your scene on the page to maximize its impact — including how negative space around the subject matter can enhance your sketches, what to leave out of a drawing, and how to make sure it looks balanced.

The size and format of the sketch is a key component of the finished image, and in this chapter we also consider how the choice between a large canvas and small sketchbooks can affect the finished artwork and bring personality and attitude to your work.

Measuring

A lot of seemingly complex talk about measurement techniques can make sketching a daunting experience for the beginner or intermediate artist. The truth is, proportions are important in every sketch, but once you understand the basic approach to getting them right, you'll be able to tackle the most complex scenes with confidence.

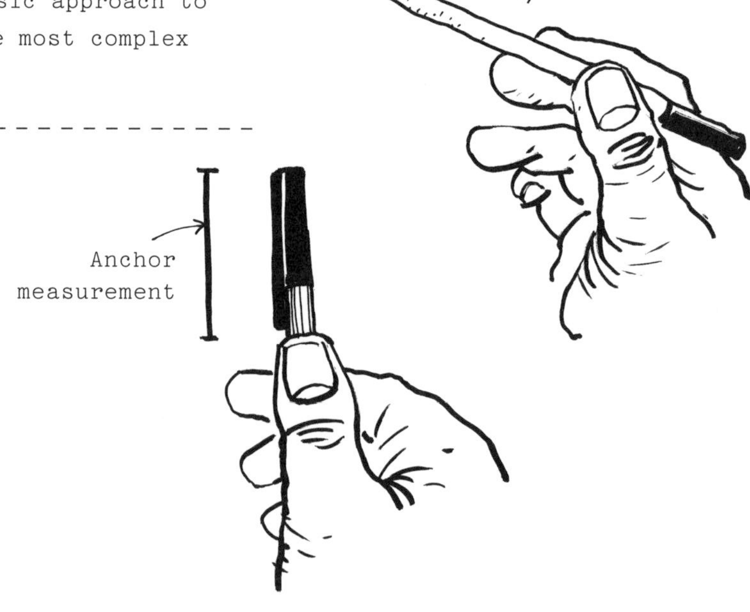

Often you will find that it's the looser sketches that are the most charming, and which best capture the personality of a scene. It is the sound construct of an artwork, rather than its perfect accuracy, that puts the eye at ease and allows the viewer to appreciate the overall effect. The purpose of using techniques like those outlined below is not to stifle free-flowing sketching, but to help you ensure the framework of the sketch is robust, allowing for creative interpretation that is built on solid foundations.

Fortunately, you have all the basic measuring tools you will need for urban sketching in the pen or pencil you have in your hand. It is a good idea to start each sketch with an 'anchor measurement' that sets the scale of your piece. I recommend that you select a point at the heart of the scene and use this as the benchmark for all subsequent components, loosely measuring adjacent items to ensure the scale is broadly in line.

Begin by choosing two key points in the scene you are sketching. I often choose the distance between the top of a building and another high point in the scene. Hold your pen or pencil out straight in front of you at arm's length, and align the end of your pen with your first key point. Align your thumb on the pen with the other key point (see the illustration). This measurement is your anchor measurement against which you can measure everything else in the scene. For instance, the height of your building might be six times this anchor measurement. A person in your scene could be half an anchor measurement tall. Remember to use it as a scaled measurement rather than trying to directly translate this length on your page.

While complex perspectives and angles are covered in detail in the next chapter, there is also a very simple way of measuring angles quickly, using a similar technique to the one above. Align the length of your pen or pencil with a key angle in your scene and then, holding your hand as steady as possible to maintain the angle, bring your pen down to lay against your page and trace the line of the angle (see the illustration). This is your starting angle, and it can be a very good way to understand the basic perspective of a scene without getting bogged down with the technicalities. Generally, all that is needed to get a sketch off to a good start is a relatively accurate angle line, but you can repeat this technique whenever you get stuck.

The examples opposite and the exercises over the following pages demonstrate how these simple principles can help you to work out the relationships between different elements in your drawings.

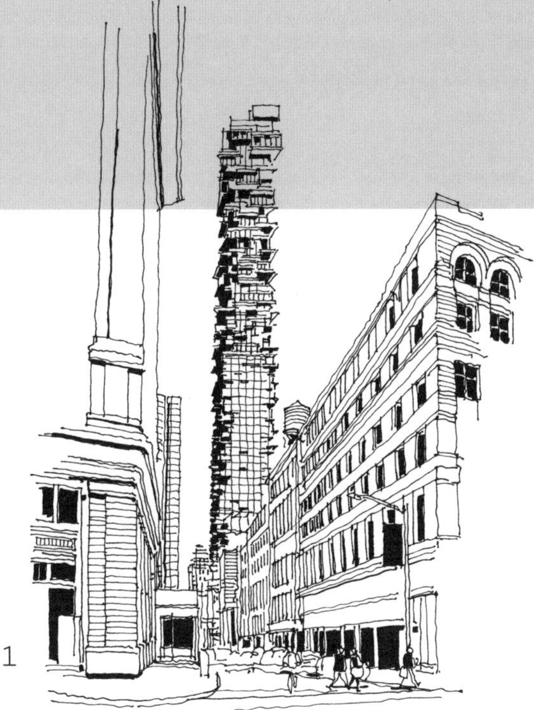

1

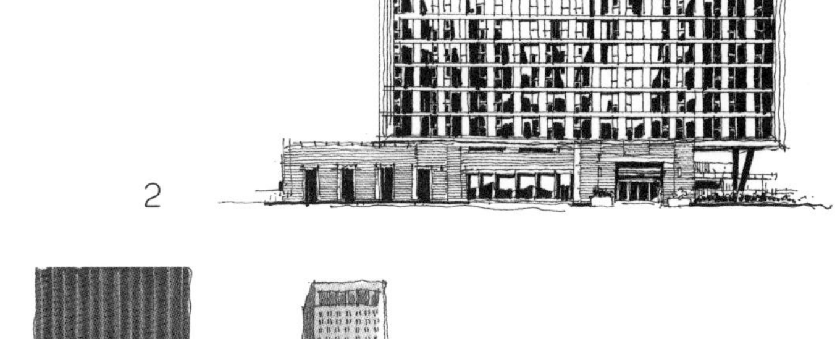

2

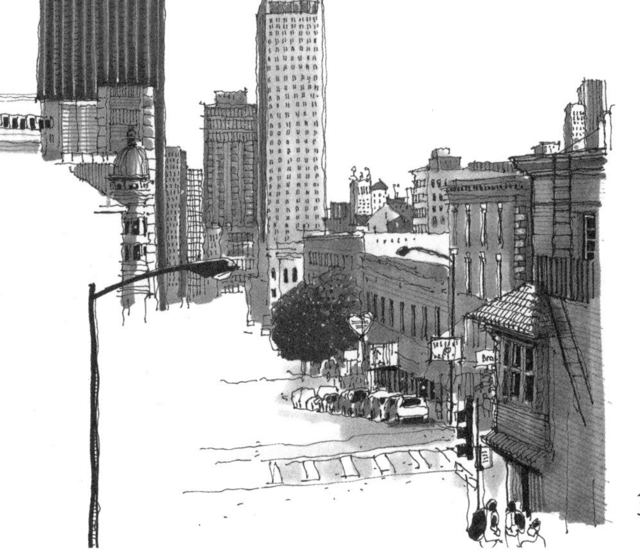

3

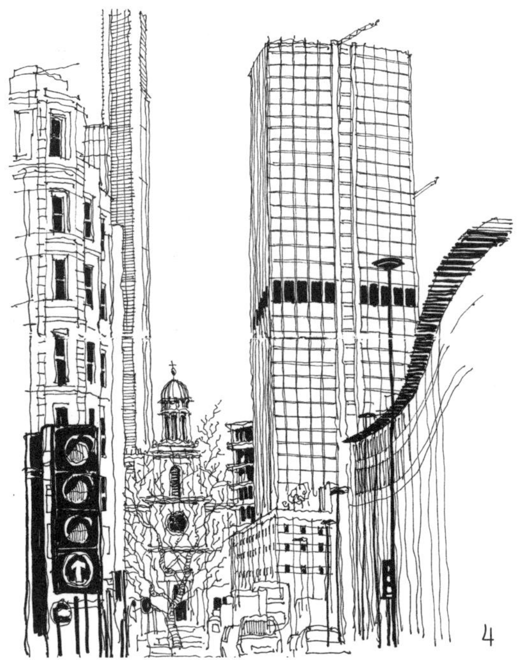

4

1. New York, USA

I aligned my thumb and the end of my pen with half the height of the main vertical tower. Then I measured all other lengths from this. I aligned my pen with the top of the building on the right to see the extreme angle of perspective.

2. Chicago, USA

In this flat elevation with no perspective to speak of, I measured three storeys to anchor myself vertically and then I built out from there. I used the same measure horizontally to get the overall proportion correct and used a pencil to construct the shape of the buildings before finishing it with pen.

3. San Francisco, USA

Here, using the central tower as the anchor made it easy to bring all the surrounding towers into proportion. There are some tricky perspective lines in this sketch due to San Francisco's hilly urban landscape, so I was constantly checking the angles using the anchor measurement technique.

4. London, UK

I used the church peeking between the buildings as the anchor measurement to set the scale for the taller buildings around it. Very tricky, steeply curved angles on the right were solved by aligning the pen to the broad angle and not worrying about the curve.

Measuring Lengths
Exercise

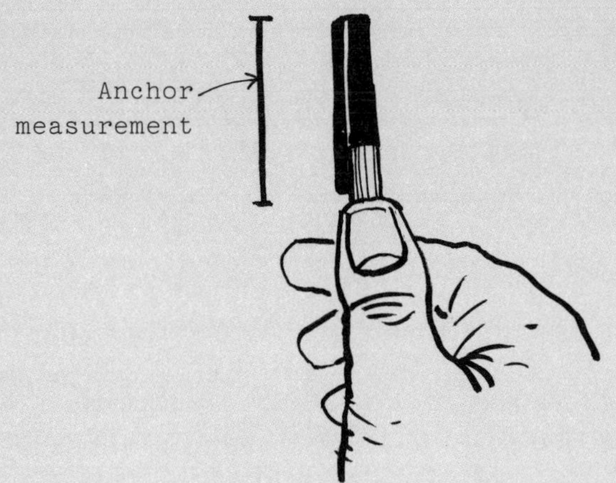

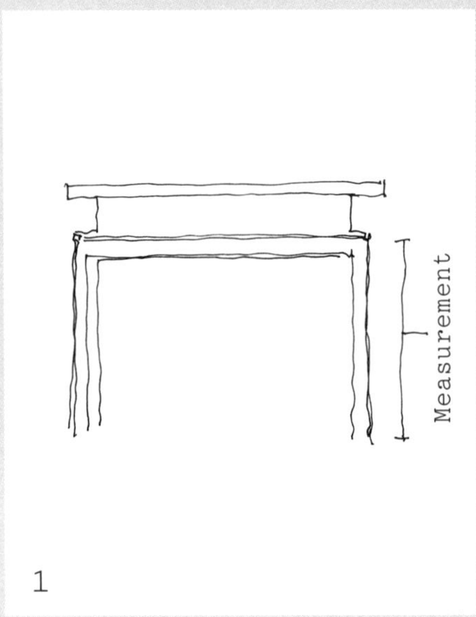

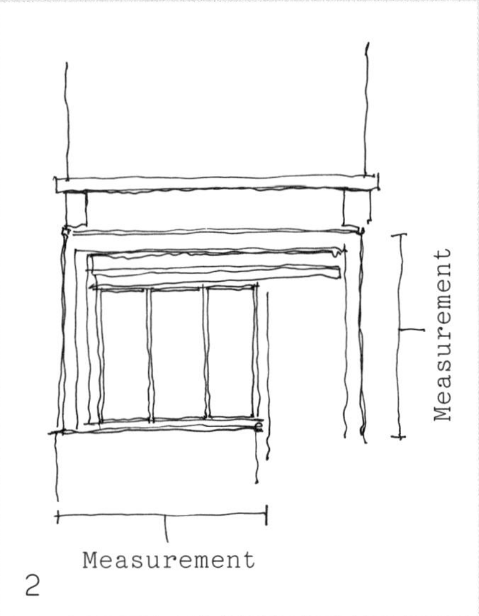

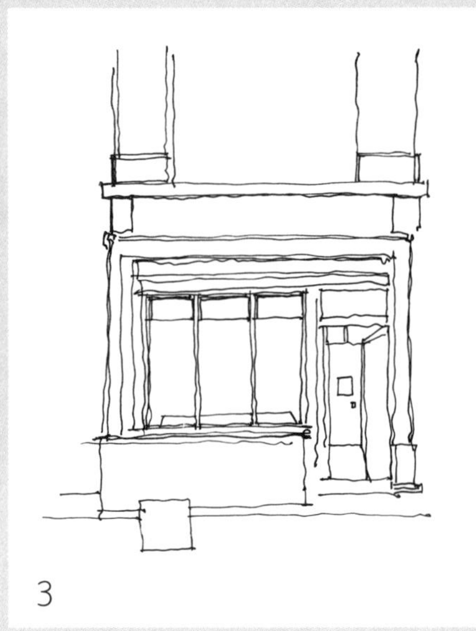

1. To practise measuring, choose a relatively simple building front as your subject matter. I've chosen the front of a well-known music shop in London. Start your sketch by choosing your anchor measurement. Here, I selected a vertical that was easy to identify and measure – it's also one of the key lines for the image, from which everything else flows.

2. Build the scene up and out from the starting point, ensuring that everything you sketch is based around the anchor measurement you have established, adding further anchors as required. This simple scene required only two or three anchor measurements to construct the basic structure of the building, and because it's a straight elevation, there was no complicated perspective to worry about.

3. As the sketch develops, you will find that fewer measurements are required, as it's easy to add details once you've got the basic shapes and proportions. Don't stop checking elements of the view against your anchor components as you add them, though. It is also important not to overlook the smaller measurements of the scene – such as the widths and depths of the windows and ledges – when you're looking at the bigger picture.

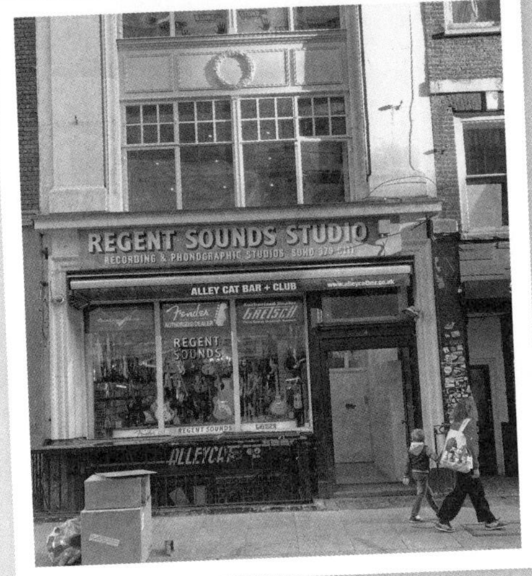

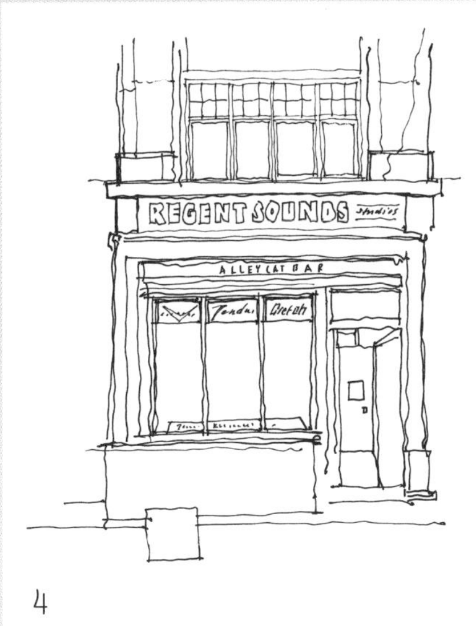

4

4. Once the basic structure is done, you can start to vary the weights of the lines (see pages 70–1) , which helps to emphasize the structure of the building and starts to hint at shadows. Begin adding a few details.

5. Finish your sketch with some contrasting solid blocks of tone to add weight and depth (see pages 68–9).

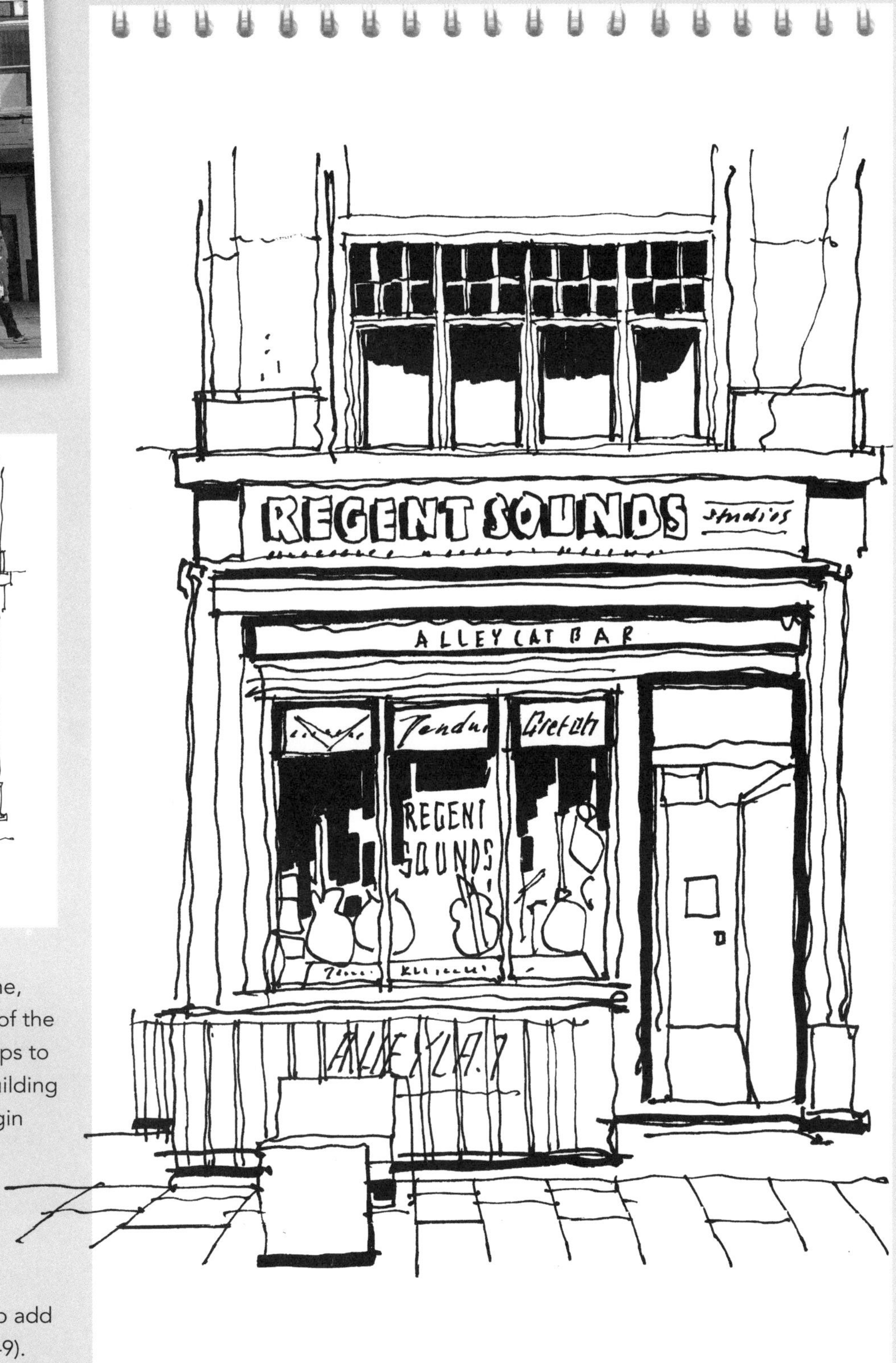

5

Measuring Angles
Exercise

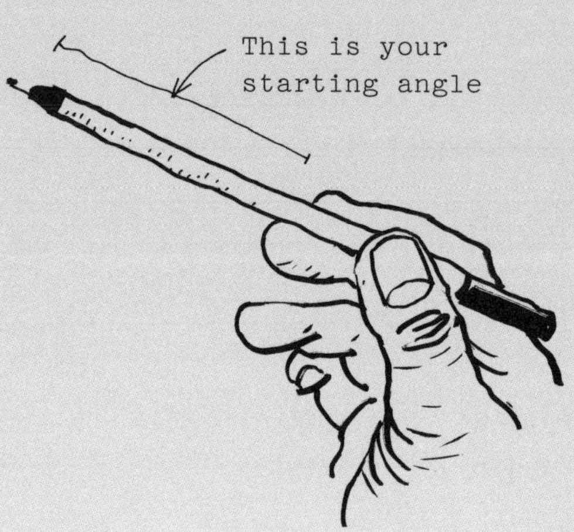

1. Find a complex scene with multiple lines of perspective to give yourself plenty of tricky angles to practise measuring. Begin your sketch in the middle of the scene and select a main angle to anchor it – I chose the bold gantry to the left of the composition. Align your pen or pencil with your chosen element and carefully transfer that line to the paper, following the angle as faithfully as you can. You will be surprised at how acute most angles are compared to your perception of the view.

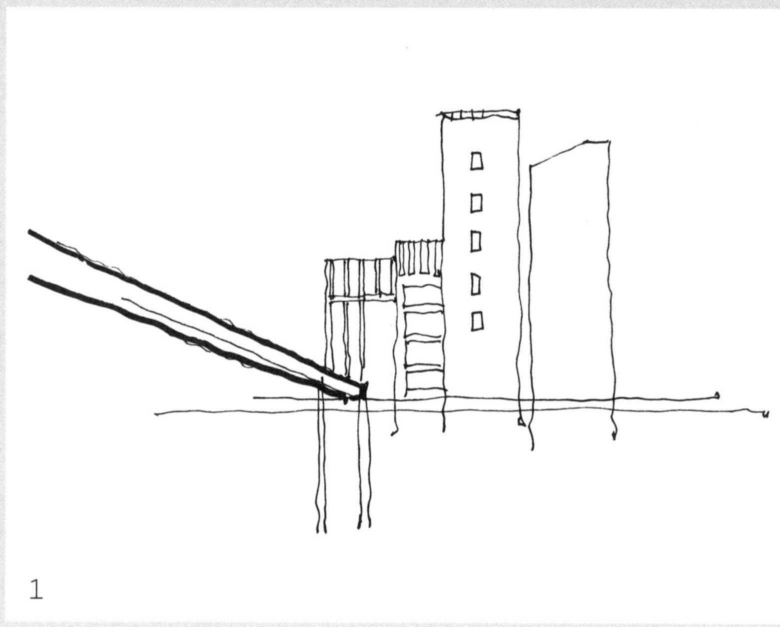

1

2. Apply the same technique when you approach the main lines of each structure you tackle, whether they are vertical or angled. This technique is particularly useful for guiding oblique angles, and always delivers a more accurate rendition of the scene than the human eye can comprehend alone. To accentuate the sense of scale and perspective suggested by angles in the foreground, keep most background angles perpendicular (at right angles) to the horizon. Remember that your pen can help with this part too.

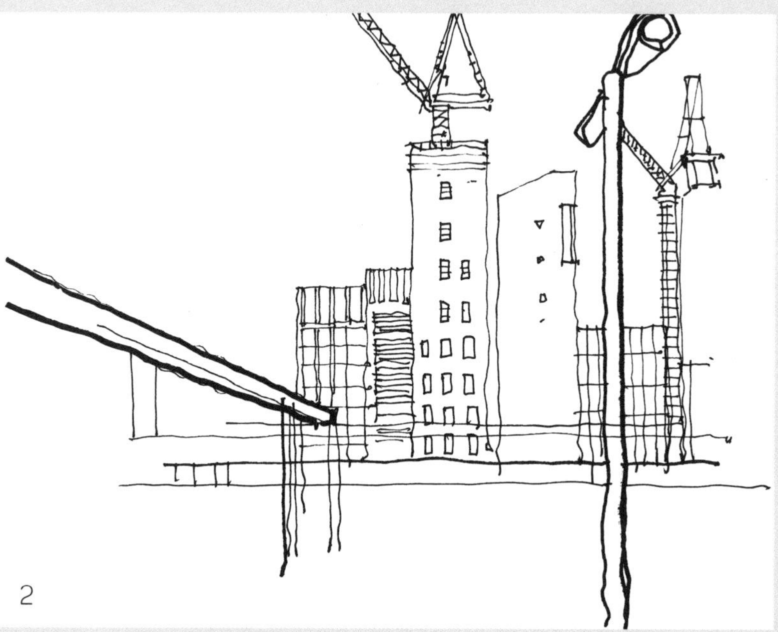

2

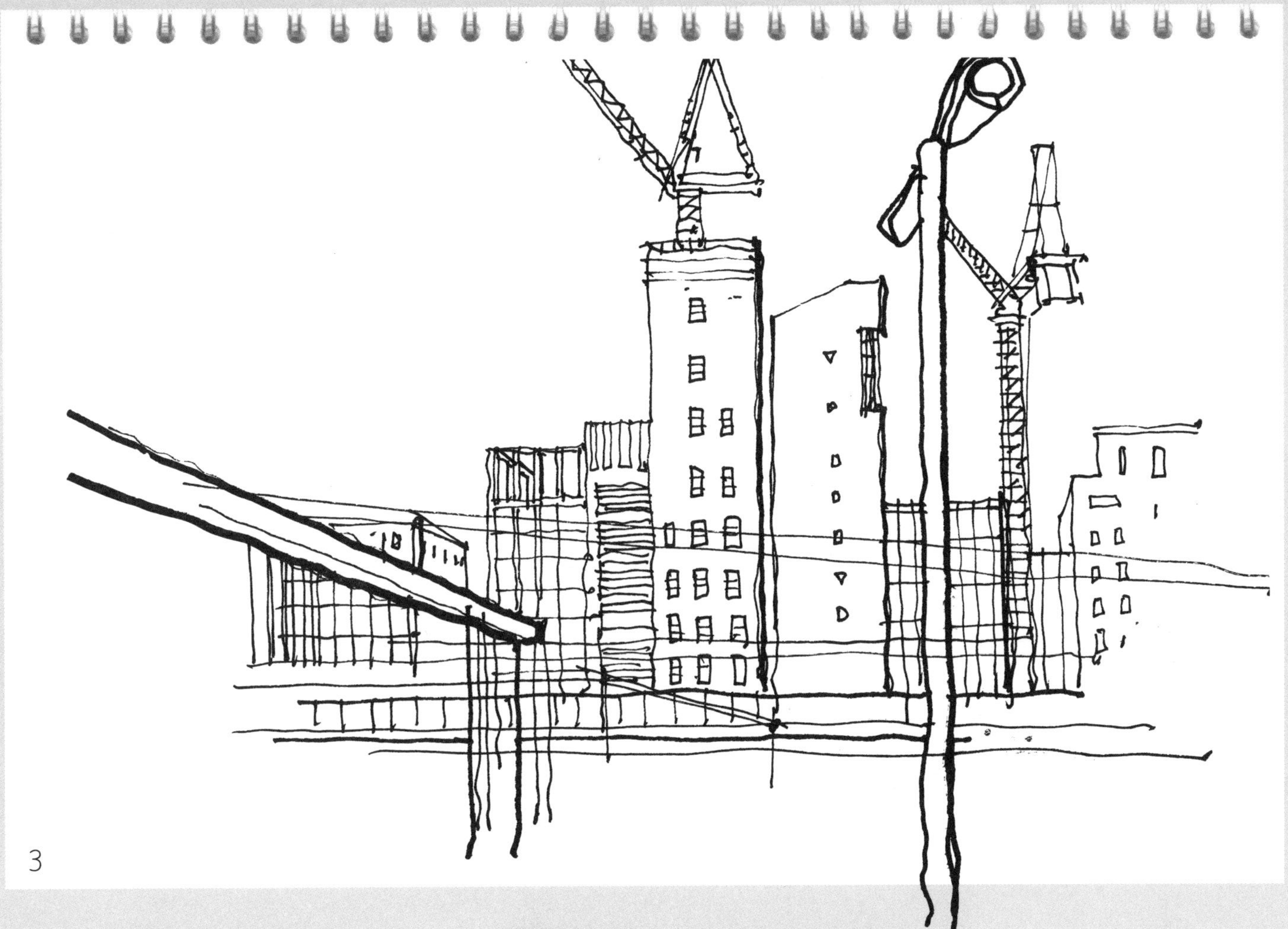

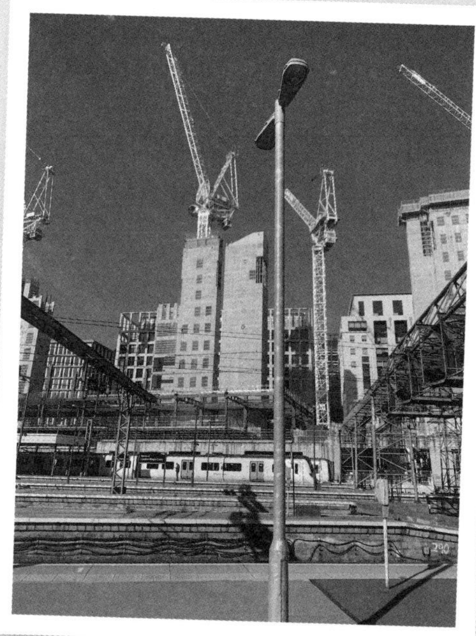

3

3. Once you've established the basic composition, add details until you are happy with your sketch. Even though this technique isn't a comprehensive measure of perspective (we'll see more on perspective on pages 48–53), if you keep checking the angles with the pen as you proceed, you will find that your sketch will still be realistic. It's very satisfying to sketch using this simple technique. In fact, once you get the hang of it, it's quite addictive and will likely become your go-to angle trick!

Photographic
reference

Composition

Composition is about the way we choose to arrange a scene on the page to maximize the visual impact of the drawing. There are certain techniques we can use to give our drawings different moods and atmospheres, to draw our viewers into the scene, to add a sense of depth or dynamism, and to attract attention to the most important elements.

When you start a sketch, think about your subject matter and how it will be arranged on the page. A useful tip is to first loosely sketch out the view you want to capture before you commit to a more permanent medium. At the same time, remember that in life we don't always see things in entirety – buildings overlap one another, or extend out of our field of vision. In a similar way, we can position elements to be cut off by the frame of our page edge to make our sketches appear more natural and even to give them a sense of intrigue.

One of the best lessons in composition is learning not to fill every bit of white space on the page – a little empty space, also known as 'negative space', complements the busier areas of a drawing and leads the eye towards the subject. When a page is too full, it can be hard for the eye to know where to look. Equally, a sketch floating in too much white space will look lost. Think of your drawing area as your canvas – whether it's a thumbnail space you've marked out, a half-page or an entire double-page spread in a sketchbook – and consider the final sketch in its entirety in this space. The aim is to find the perfect balance between image and space.

The 'rule of thirds' is a handy principle, used in all visual art forms from cinema to painting, that can help you work out a balanced composition. To follow this 'rule', imagine your page divided into three (horizontally, vertically or both) and place key elements along the lines of thirds; for example, major structural anchors, or the line of the horizon. The idea is to create something more interesting than a symmetrical composition in the middle of the page, which feels safe and ordinary, and gives the eye no impetus to wander around

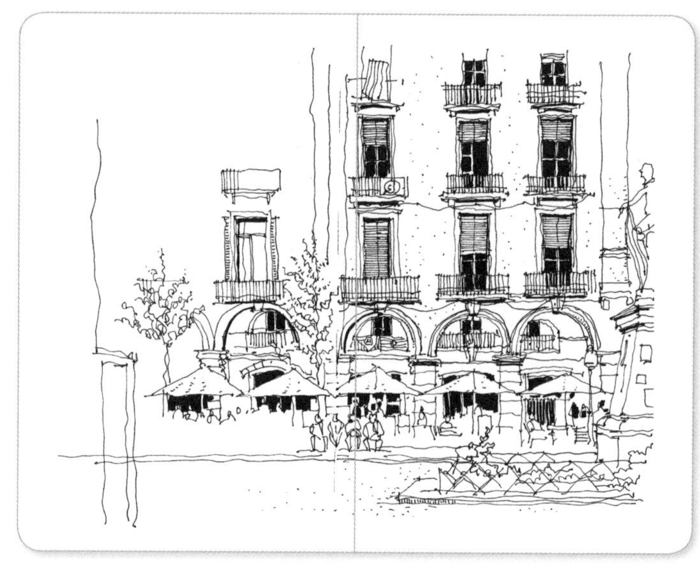

Balance

the rest of the scene. Once you start thinking in thirds, you will notice how subtle and effective this principle can be.

British artist David Hockney provides a masterclass in composition with his early line drawings of California. His spare, crisp and confident lines are elegantly arranged on the page, often using the rule of thirds and enjoying plenty of white space around them. Another British artist, Lucinda Rogers, also provides plenty of inspiration in her drawings of New York and London. Her sketches are crammed full of exquisite details that exude bustling street life, they are scrupulously composed on the page. The negative space she employs is just as important as the drawing it surrounds.

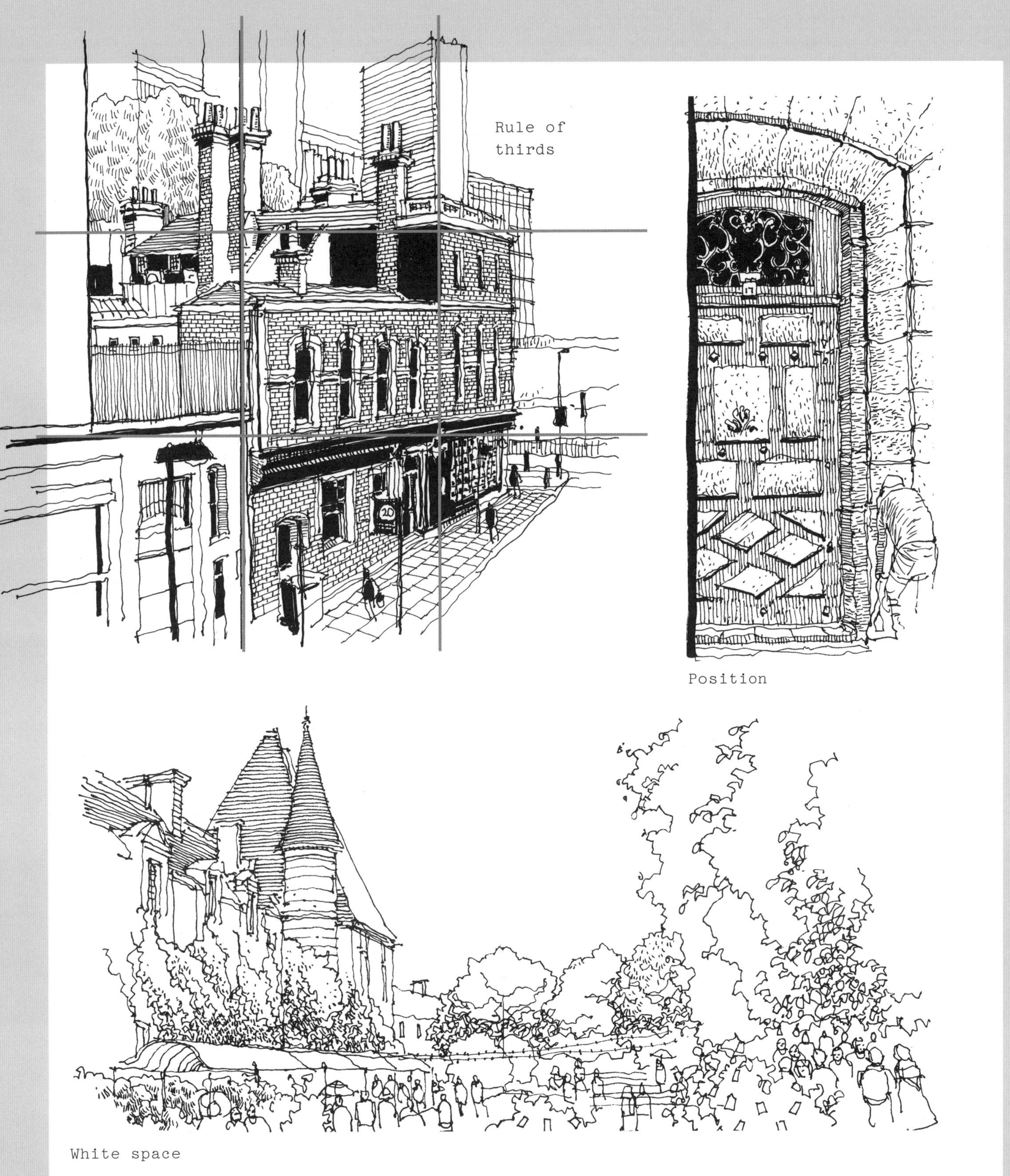
Rule of
thirds
Position
White space

Composition Exercise

To get to grips with the principles of composition, try starting a sketch tightly in the corner of a page and working out from this point along lines of thirds. As you work, leave parts of the drawing unfinished to see how this affects the way the scene feels. At first you will likely be tempted to fill in all the gaps in your sketch, but remember not to be afraid of white space. Completely jam-packed compositions work for some scenes and styles, but as a general principle, giving your drawing space to breathe is much better than filling every inch of your page.

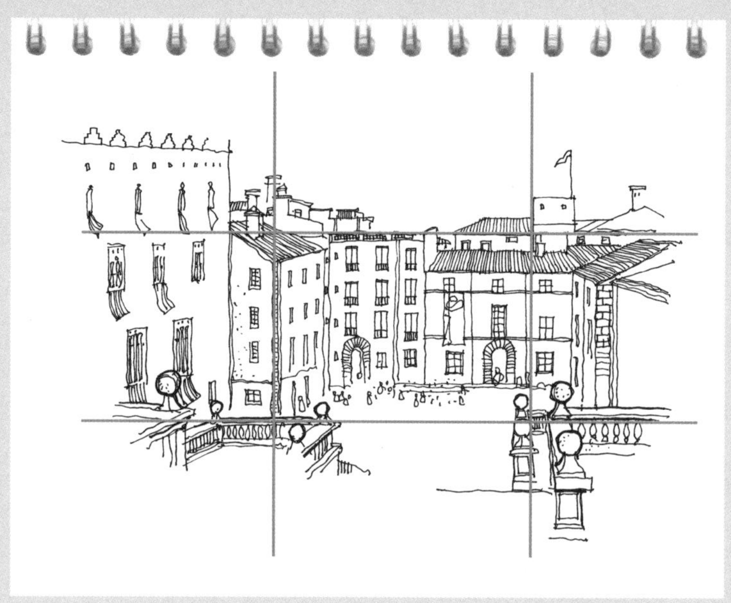

Rule of thirds

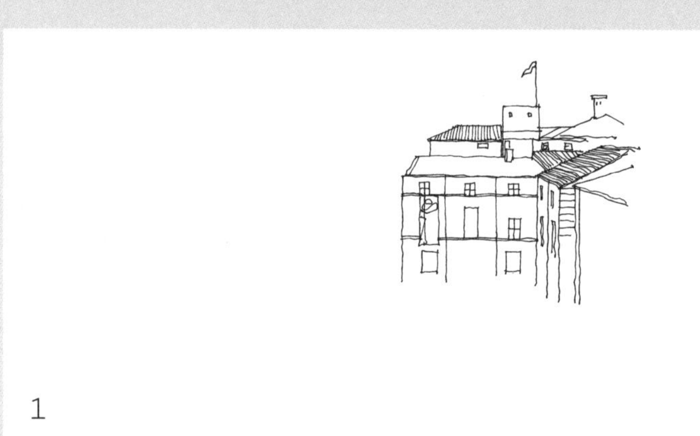

1

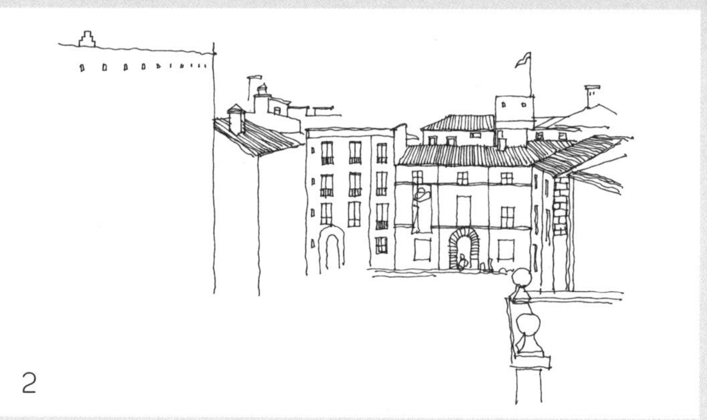

2

1. Start your sketch from a focal point in the scene – a building that catches your eye or a road that draws you into the scene. With practise, you will become attuned to the kinds of elements that will reliably act as a creative catalyst (and where to place them) for your sketch to unfold.

2. Focus on different sides of the sketch – top, bottom, left and right – thinking about where to leave some empty or less detailed spaces. Try not to draw an outline and work inwards to fill it in, but draw outwards from a point of interest. There is a magic to this stage of the sketch that is intoxicating; try to go with the flow and get caught up in the visual journey your pen is following.

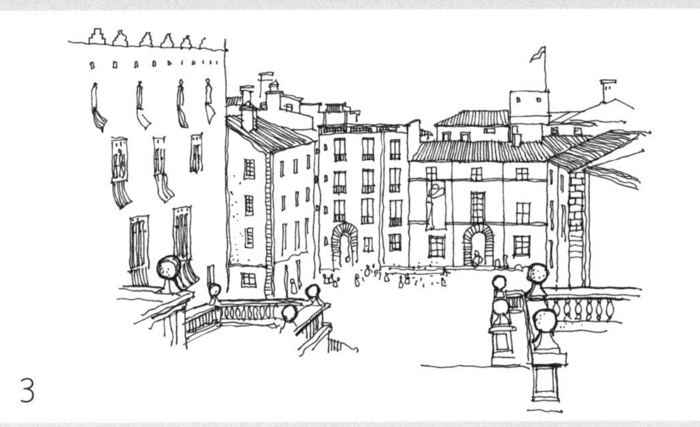

3. Stay focused on the balance of the sketch as it emerges and keep in mind the compositional principle of thirds. Don't fill every possible space, but focus on areas of detail like brickwork or roof tiles (which you only need to suggest) that will add texture and realism to the overall picture.

4. Add more details, concentrating on adding these final touches to the focal point(s) where you want the eye to linger. Allow less important elements to fade out, with less detail, into the white space and the edges of the page beyond. Give yourself permission to leave detail out if it helps the overall balance of the artwork; stand back from your sketch to help you see it more objectively and in its entirety. Add some blocks of solid black and heavy-weight lines to help the overall balance and create a harmonious composition.

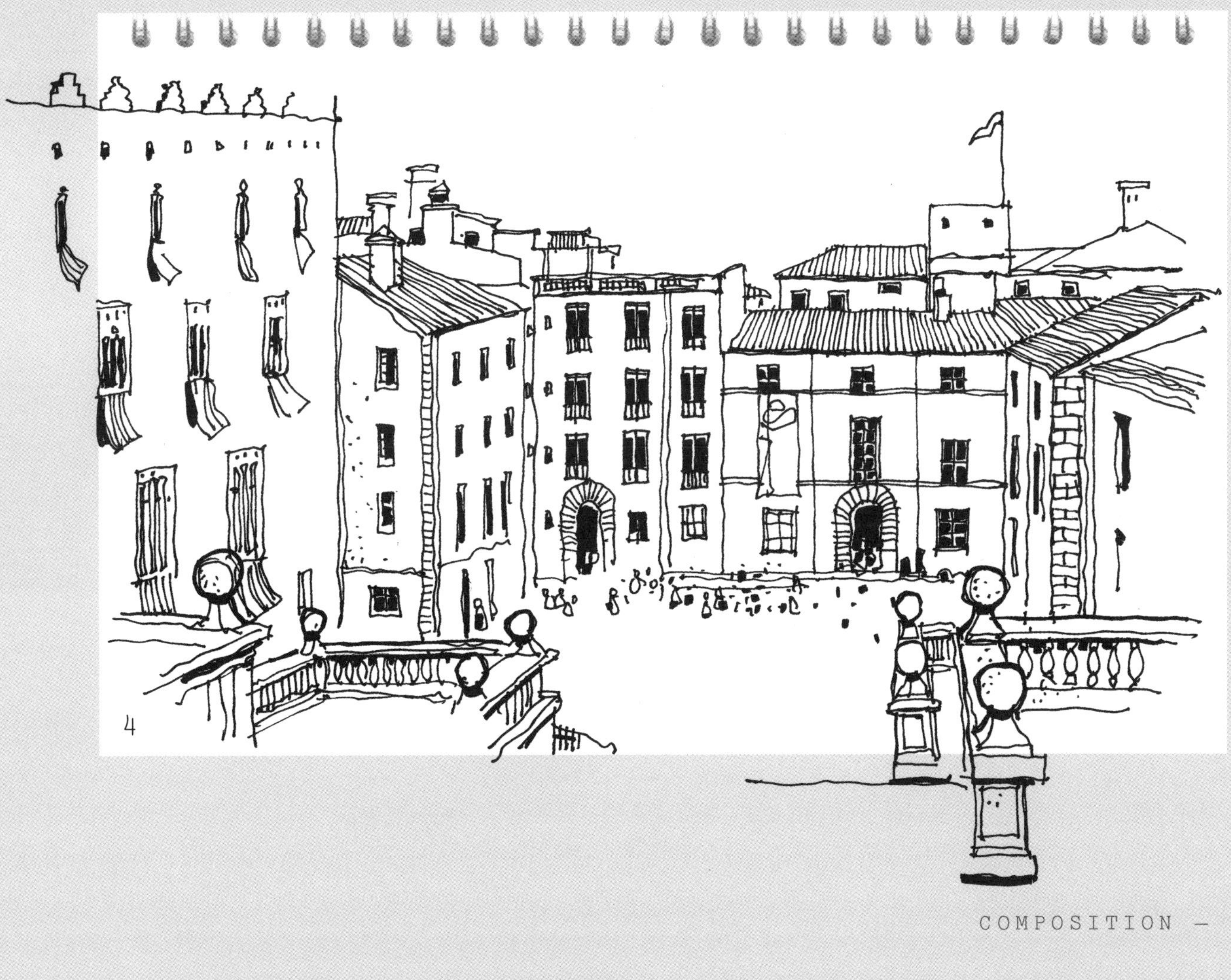

White Space Exercise

White space can be the most magnetic element in a drawing – you don't have to fill the whole page in order to produce a great sketch. This exercise highlights the importance of negative space, so that you can learn how it relates to and amplifies the entire piece. Pick a busy scene where there is lots going on: a hectic market scene, a packed airport departure lounge, a bustling train station. The aim is to restrict the sketch to fill no more than a third of the frame of your drawing area, so you will need to separate what's important from the noise.

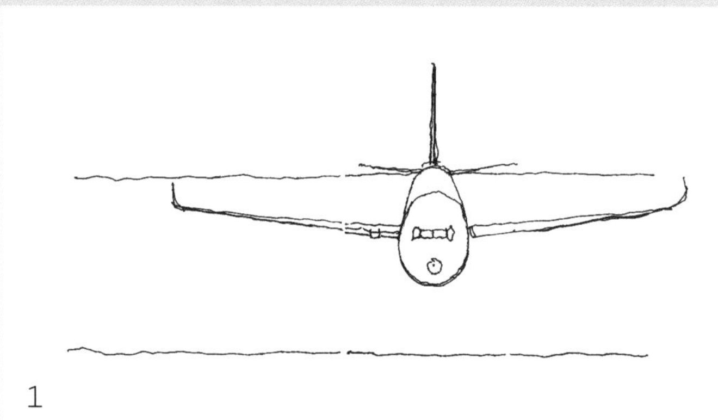

1

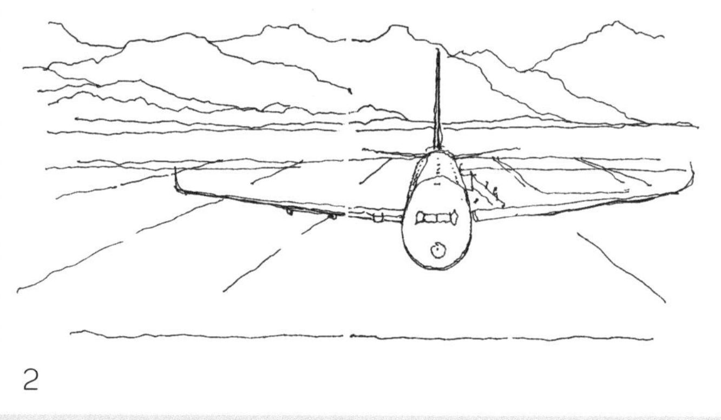

2

1. Find a strong horizontal or vertical edge to anchor the sketch, and slowly and carefully start to build out from there. My sketch began with the horizon line and the wings and body of the plane, as these were the most dominant parts of the scene.

2. As you progress, try to use restraint and think carefully about the whole canvas, checking that it looks balanced as it develops. Consider the view before you and think about which details add to the scene and which are superfluous. What is the simplest way you can convey an element and it still be recognizable?

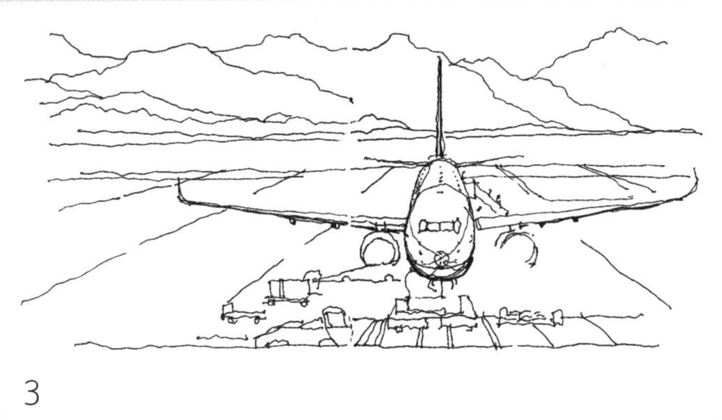

3. Having elements in both the foreground and the background will help to give your sketch a sense of depth, and it can help to give more detail to what appears in the foreground. Find and follow any perspective lines as faithfully as you can, measuring the angles with your pen all the time. Work as fast as you dare – I had to bear in mind that airports (usually) have a very fast turnaround!

4. It's hard to know when to stop, but it's almost always before you think it is. Be confident in your empty spaces, just adding a few final details that give the scene life, such as people or other foreground elements dotted around. Sparingly add some solid black areas to give weight to your drawing and provide contrast to all the white space.

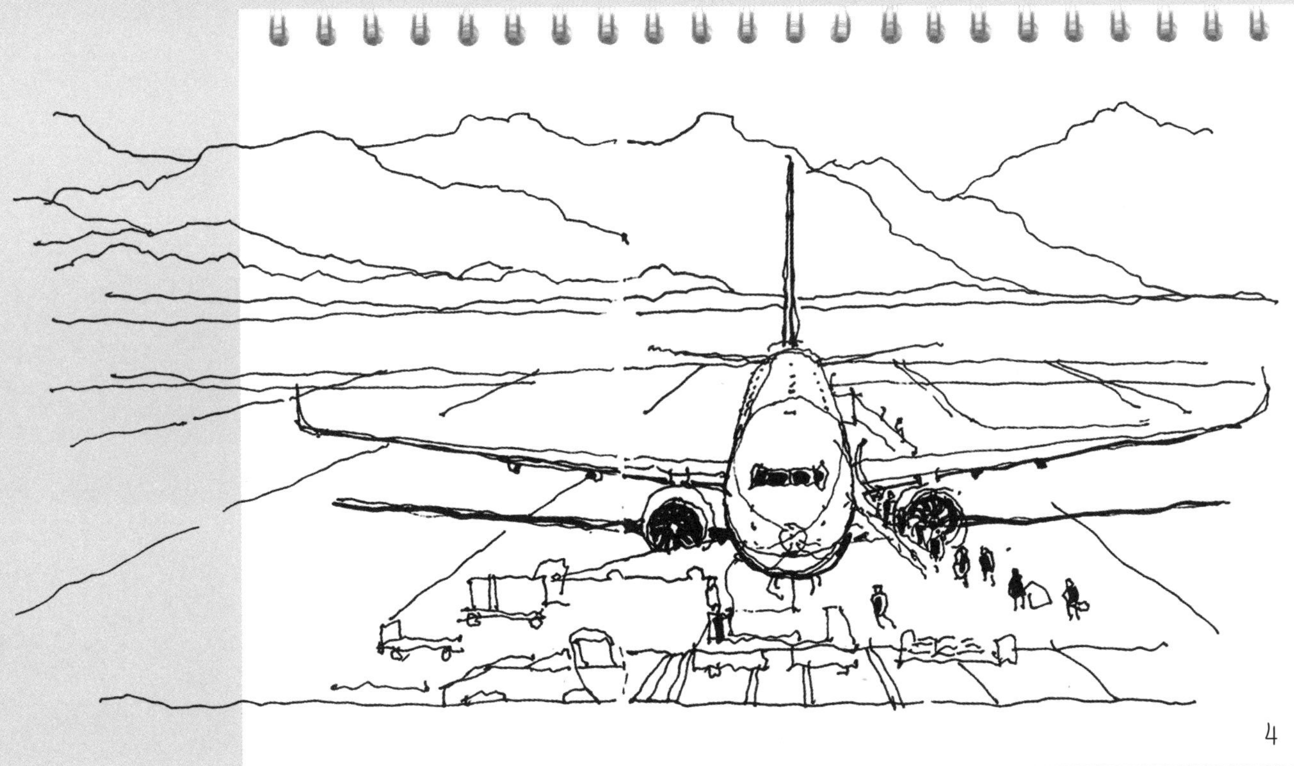

Format Exercise

Selecting the right format for a sketch is essential to ensure that you have the space you need to achieve your vision. It often comes down to the view and the sketchbook you happen to have with you – it can be nice to let this dictate how a sketch is tackled – but do leave yourself room to experiment. A more upright scene usually lends itself to portrait orientation, but don't assume this is always the case. Similarly, the expectation that a short, wide scene requires a landscape format is not always right. By choosing an unexpected format, you can create a surprising dynamic on the page, allowing for unique interpretations and potentially a lot of lovely white space.

- -

1. Select an extreme landscape or portrait view. Think about how you will include white space and also how the scene will work as a whole within your chosen frame. For this exercise it's best to stick to traditional wisdom – portrait orientation for a tall view or landscape orientation for a wide view. Lay down some main lines to anchor your focal points, using the measuring techniques we saw on page 34 to work out the basic proportions and angles.

2. If your scene is tall, focus on the main vertical lines of the building(s), and if it is wide, concentrate on establishing the horizontals that will anchor the scene. Start to add the details that reveal the height or width you are trying to describe, keeping your lines loose and gestural. If you're tackling something tall, don't worry about counting floors, but try to keep the window shapes recognizable and reasonably within scale.

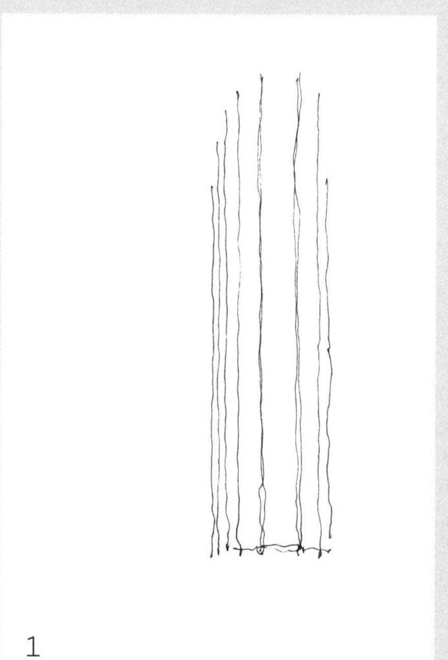

1

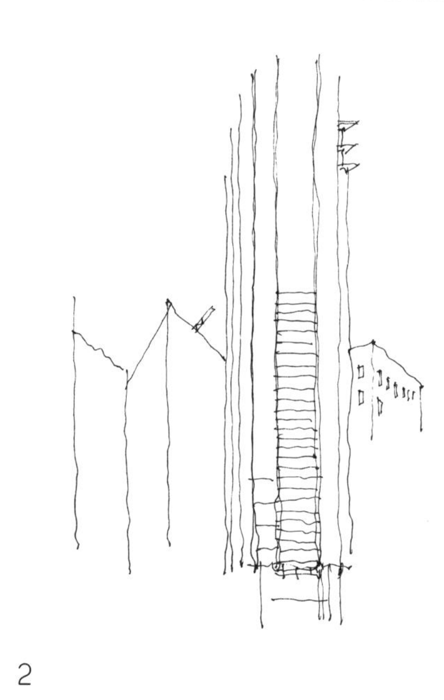

2

3. Emphasize extreme height by making your drawing tight and narrow, driving the eye upwards; and in landscape images this means stretching your composition out, in a cinematic style.

4. Choose some details that add to the tall or wide nature of the sketch. In my sketch, the majority of the details take the form of vertical lines, including the converging lines in the foreground, to keep the eye travelling up and down. Including a few people helps to give the scale of the monumental building. In a landscape image, focus on horizontal details, with perhaps a rolling bank of clouds or lots of white space in the sky.

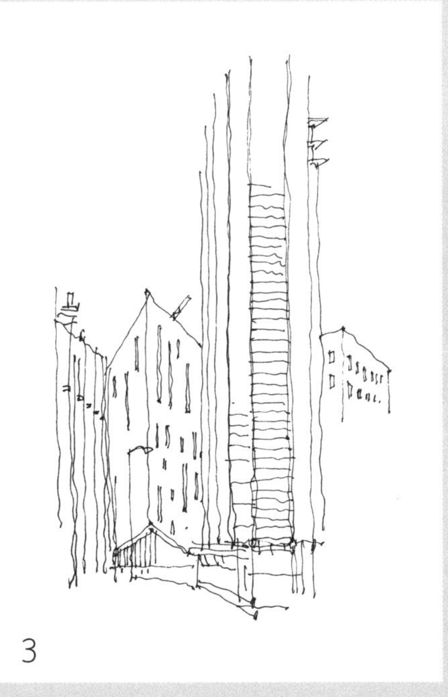

3

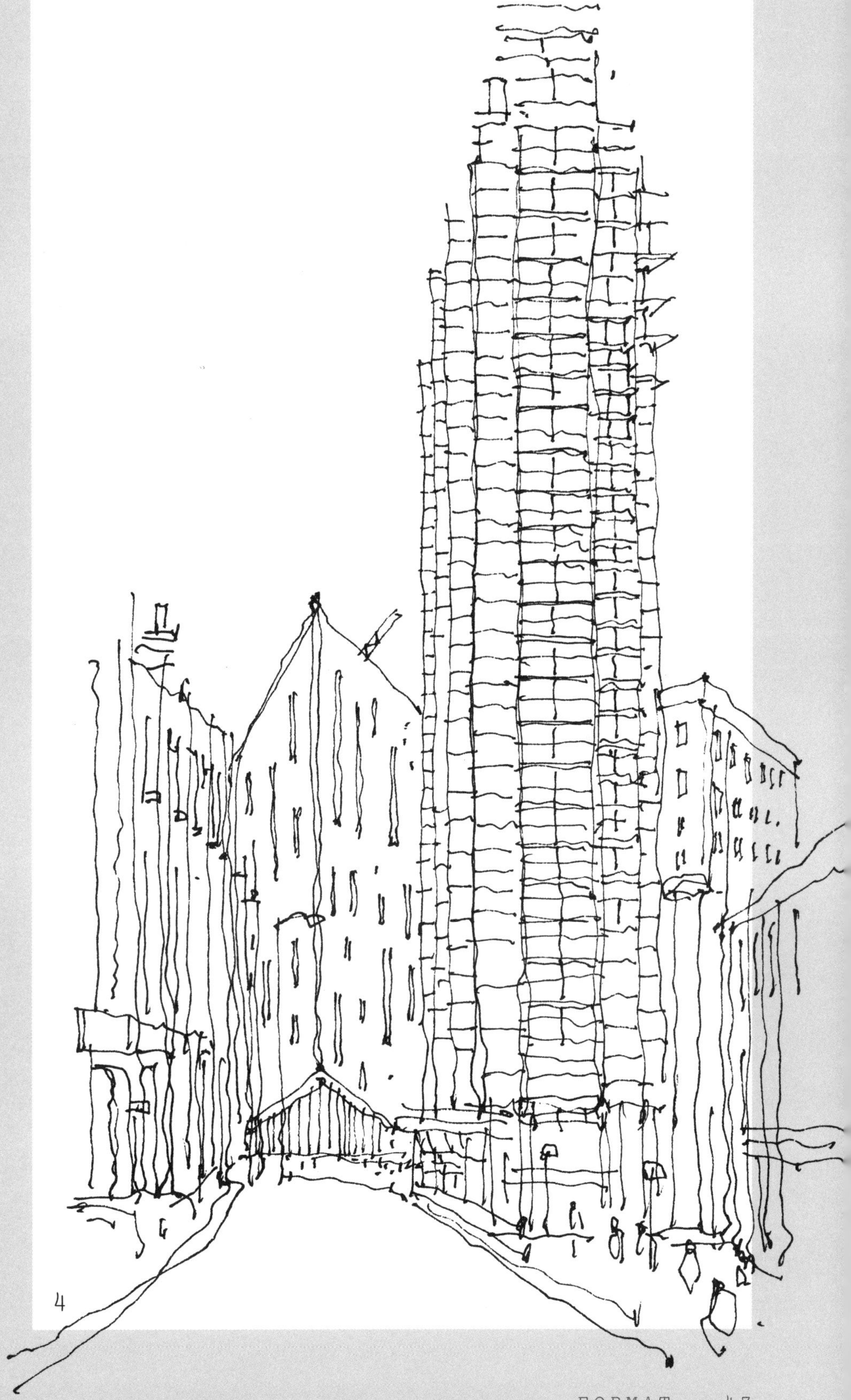

4

Perspective

The system of perspective used in much of Western art, called linear perspective, is thought to have been developed during the Renaissance period in Florence in the early 1400s. Linear perspective is a geometric system consisting of an eye level horizon line and lines that converge towards vanishing points to create the illusion of space and distance.

Perspective is the thing that urban sketchers often worry most about. Technical talk about one-point, two-point and multiple vanishing points, as well as foreshortening and diminishing, can be daunting, but in practice it's not difficult to get the hang of. There are many informative videos online for those who wish to delve deeper into perspective than I do here. British artist J.M.W. Turner is most famous for his landscapes but he was also Professor of Perspective at the Royal Academy of Arts in London for three decades – I recommend tracking down the fascinating drawings he made for this appointment.

My advice is to treat perspective with respect but don't let it completely rule your drawings. A grasp of perspective, along with a basic understanding of the laws of nature, is all an urban sketcher needs to capture effective scenes. Wonky perspective can also add character to a sketch, making it feel more authentic than a very technically accurate perspective drawing. The artwork comes into its own and you can see the decisions of the artist, rather than strict adherence to the reality of the scene.

However, it is only by understanding the basics of perspective that you will feel free to really experiment with it. Everything you draw will follow certain laws of nature and it's only when you truly start observing that you will see the principles at play. Once you start noticing perspective lines, it's impossible to unsee them.

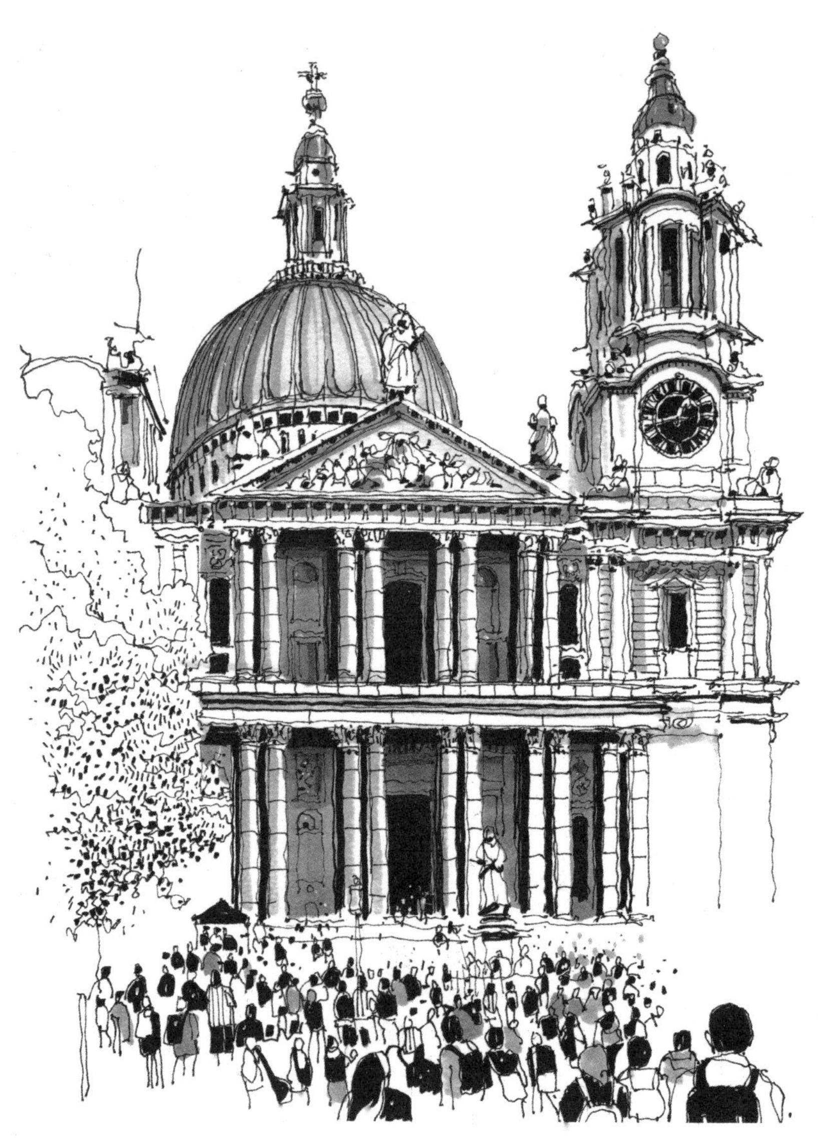

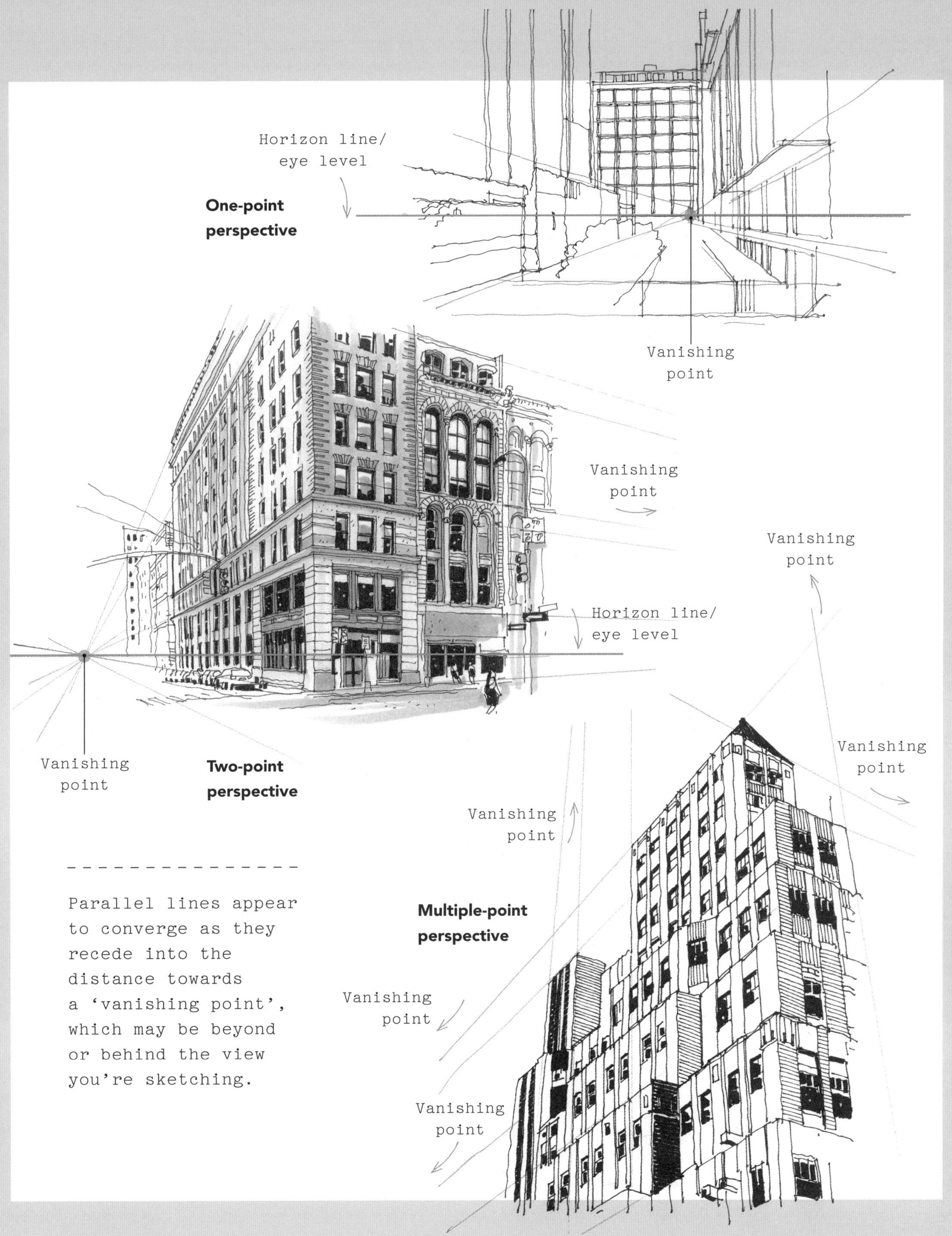

Horizon line/
eye level

One-point
perspective

Vanishing
point

Vanishing
point

Vanishing
point

Vanishing
point

Horizon line/
eye level

Vanishing
point

Two-point
perspective

Vanishing
point

Multiple-point
perspective

Vanishing
point

Vanishing
point

Parallel lines appear
to converge as they
recede into the
distance towards
a 'vanishing point',
which may be beyond
or behind the view
you're sketching.

Terminology

Horizon line/eye level

Classically, this would describe the line of the horizon in a scene, but bear in mind that in most urban scenarios you can't actually see the horizon because there are buildings in front of it. This line is also equivalent with your eye level: hold up a pen or pencil level with your eyes to judge where the horizon line lies in any scene.

Vanishing point

Whenever you look at a scene with any depth, all the parallel lines you see in that scene will appear angled towards each other, and if they continue far enough they will actually seem to meet at some point in the distance. The clearest way to see this for yourself is to stand in the middle of a long straight road – being careful of traffic, of course! The sides of the road and the lines painted on are parallel, but you will see how the centre line of the road runs straight ahead and the lines on either side angle in until all of them intersect. That point of intersection is the vanishing point.

View level

This determines whether you are looking at a scene from below, above, or at eye level.

- **Eye level** – the scene is in line with your eyes.
- **Bird's-eye level** – looking down on a scene from above.
- **Worm's-eye level** – looking up at a scene from below.

View angle

This is the angle at which you observe the subject.

- **One-point perspective** – looking at a view straight on, any parallel lines appear to recede towards one point.
- **Two-point perspective** – observing a view at an angle, lines appear to recede and converge towards two points on the horizon, to the left and right.
- **Multiple-point perspective** – observing a view at an angle and from a low angle (or, rarely, an extremely high angle), lines will appear to converge at a vertical point above, as well as at horizontal points to the left and right.

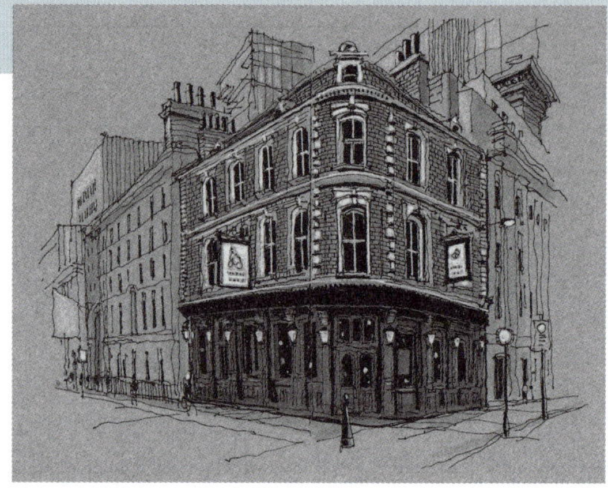

Eye level

As you can see from this London pub sketch, being at eye level drives only a one- or two-point perspective, on the horizontal converging lines.

Worm's-eye

When you sketch something from a low height, it can bring multiple-point perspective into play. If you extended all the vertical lines in the drawing below, you would find that they met at a vanishing point far above; the horizontal parallel lines converge more dramatically towards the left and right.

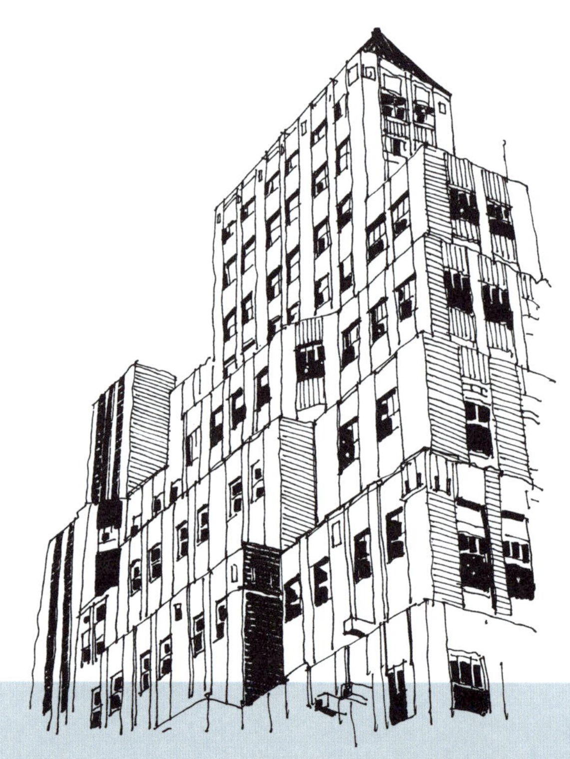

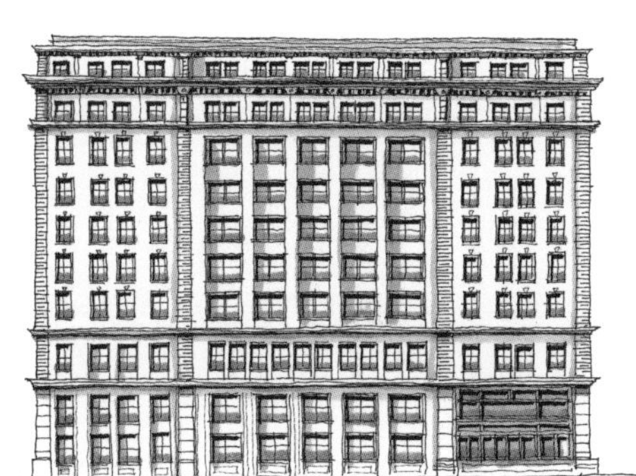

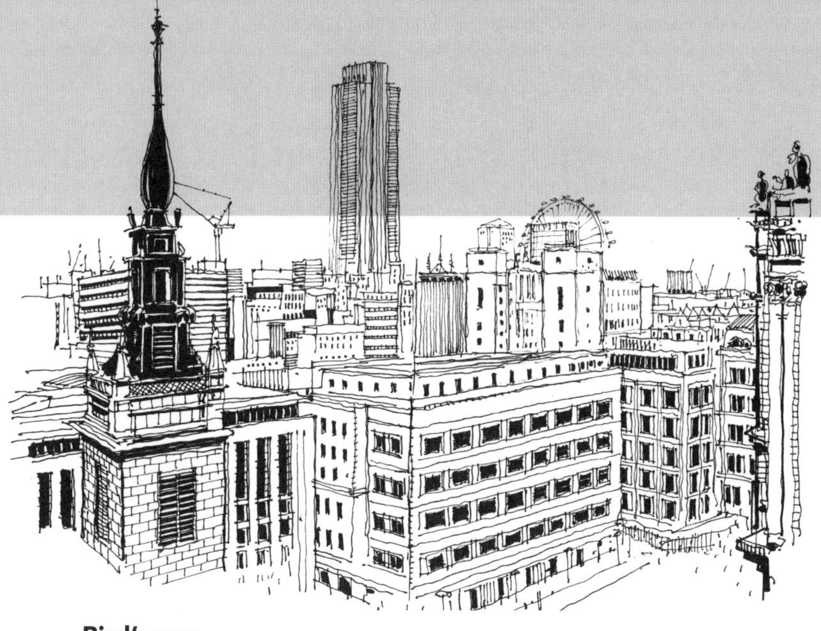

Elevation

When you draw one face of a building with no obvious perspective, this is known as an elevation. Since the building is relatively taller than eye level, however, you can suggest the perspective with a subtle convergence in your vertical lines.

Bird's-eye

This bird's-eye view typically provides less complex and dramatic perspectives. The scale of the scene means that the convergence towards vanishing points is less pronounced.

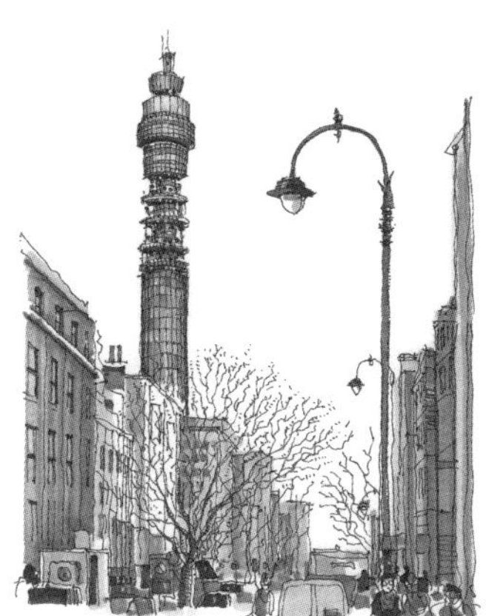

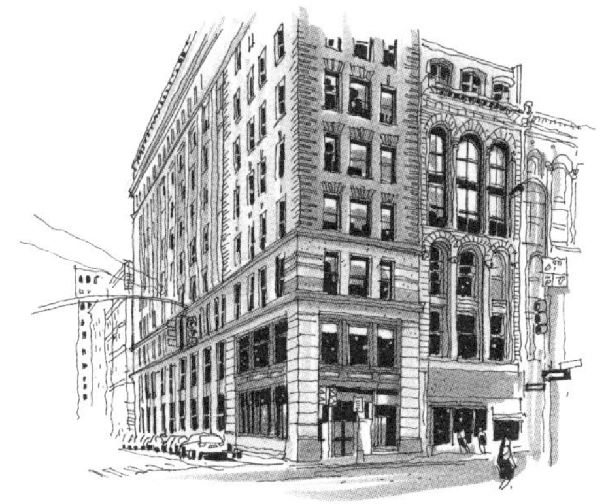

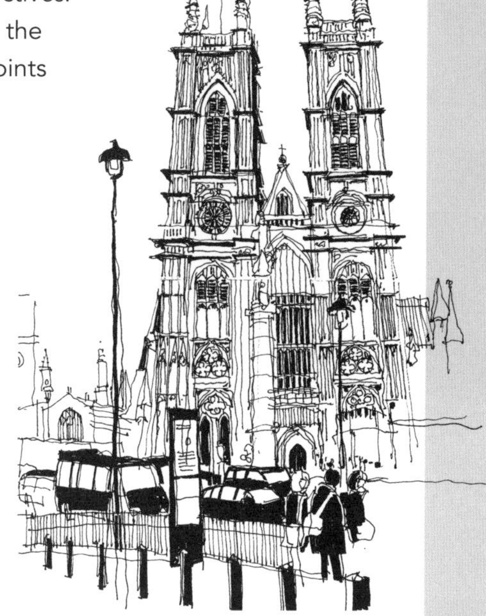

One-point

This London street scene uses one-point perspective lines for the buildings on the left and right of the drawing. If the tall tower was wider and a more regular shape, we might see some vertical convergence, but here this doesn't really apply.

Two-point

This New York sketch brings a two-point perspective into play, with two sets of parallel lines running in different directions from the corner of the building, converging at different points on the horizon line towards the left and right.

Multiple-point

This loose and lively sketch of Westminster Abbey in London uses multiple-point perspective, as it was drawn from a relatively low height – you will see the gradual vertical taper of the towers to the vanishing point in the far distance. Note the dramatically angled converging lines to the left of the building – this is due to my relatively low viewpoint and close proximity to the subject matter.

Vanishing Points
Exercise

This exercise has a one-point perspective with the main focal point being a building viewed straight on and from eye level. I suggest lightly sketching out your perspective lines and basic construction lines in soft pencil so that they can easily be erased before building your sketch up in a more permanent medium. The boxier the shapes of the elements in the scene, the easier they will be to translate along the lines of perspective. If you are just starting out, avoid more difficult, curved shapes like domes until you feel ready to tackle them.

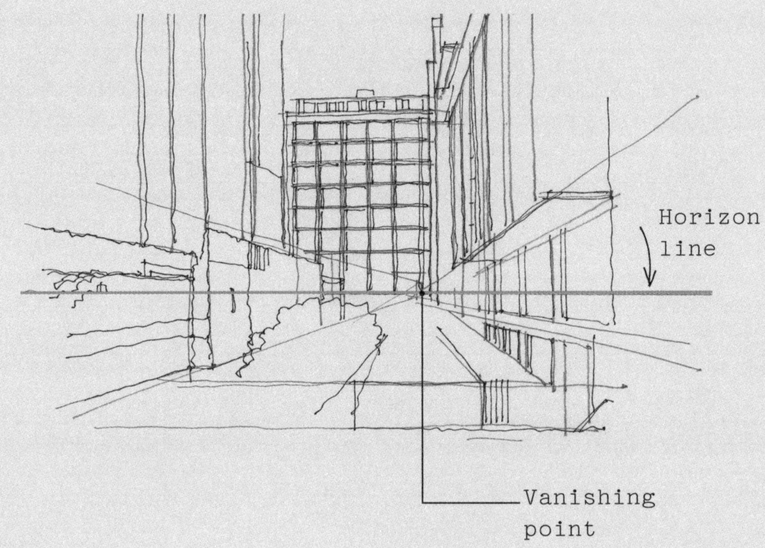

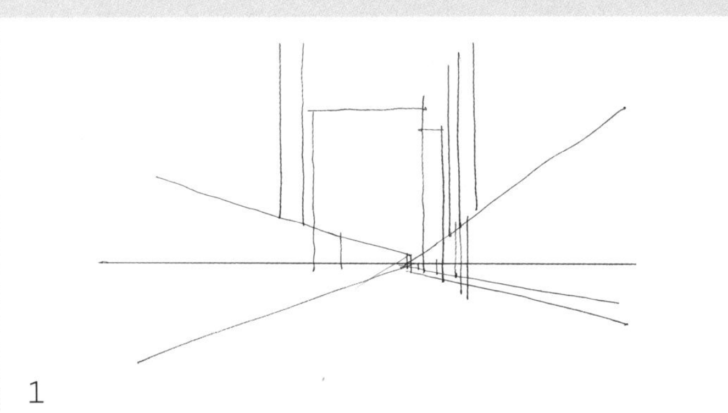

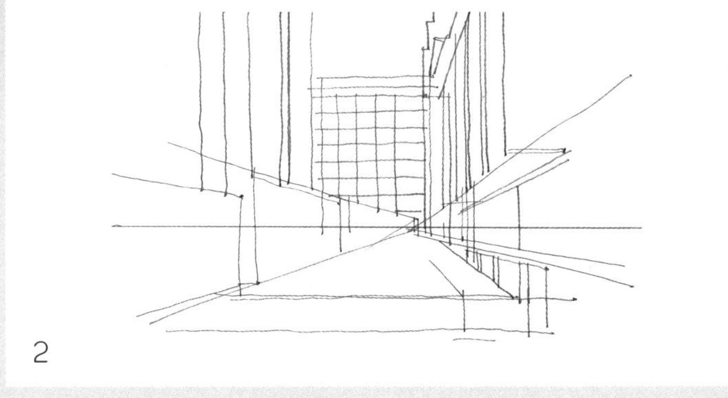

1. Find the horizon line by looking straight ahead and holding a pencil horizontally, level with your eyes. Use the measuring technique we looked at on page 34 to work out the angle at which any parallel lines in the scene converge at the vanishing point on this horizon line, and lightly sketch out these key construction lines in pencil. As we are dealing with a one-point perspective, keep all the vertical lines in your sketch parallel with each other.

2. Start to build up the basic lines of your buildings along the guidelines you have drawn. If you are planning to finish your sketch in pen, stick with lightly applied pencil for now, until you are confident of the basic construction.

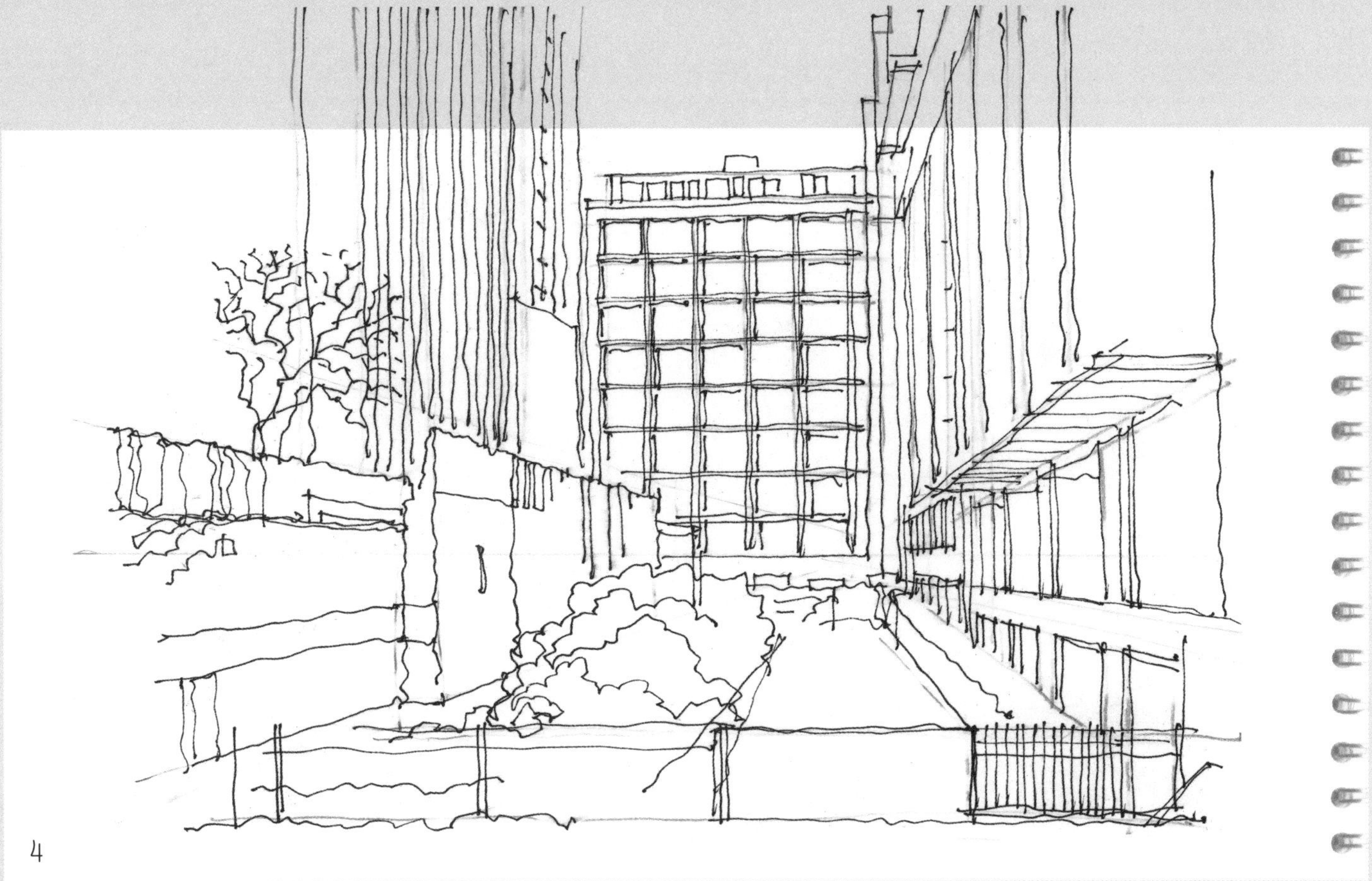

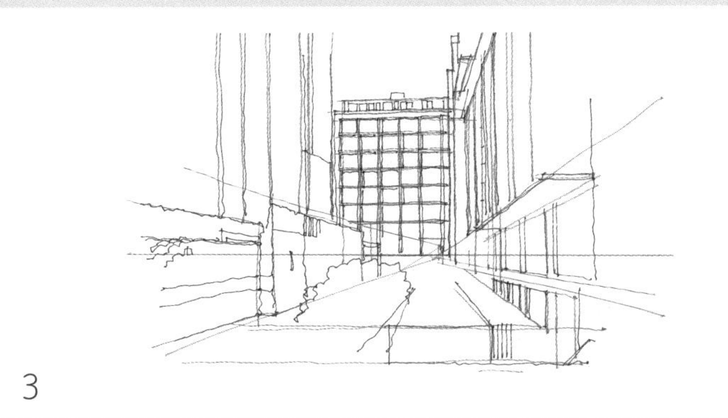

4

3

3. Once you're happy with the basic lines and shapes, you can move on to your preferred medium to finalize them. Add more detail to the scene by breaking down the big, basic shapes into their increasingly complex components. More confident sketchers may choose to add the detail in a less structured way, which often results in a looser, less precise but potentially more expressive image.

4. Erase the pencil lines using a kneadable eraser, taking care not to smudge the ink. Keep adding to the linework until you're happy with the image.

STARTING WITH A FRAMEWORK
Starting a sketch with a pencil framework should put you on very firm footing when it comes to developing an accurate image. Adopt this technique while you build up your confidence with urban sketching, and you will find after a short while that you no longer need to sketch out the pencil lines in as much detail to master the perspective in a scene.

Small-Scale Sketching

Urban sketching is not just about vast vistas and the large-scale drama of big cities — sketchers should always be on the lookout for the small details or moments, too. Train yourself to look for ordinary scenes that, when drawn, will become quiet artworks — a pocket sketchbook you can keep with you is perfect for catching the intimacy of details caught up close. These will contrast beautifully with the noisy, sweeping landscapes in your sketchbook, and tell more of the story of the town or city you are drawing.

- -

When working at smaller scales, use a fine pen or a hard pencil to make sure you can capture all the detail. Take care to observe the nuances of the subject – for instance, if you were sketching a chocolate bar, you would try to replicate the typography of the branding as closely as possible. Any unrealistic interpretations will be magnified at this scale, so it's important to take care over the details.

Architecture

Look up, closely observe the buildings all around, and you will discover exquisite details. Focusing on features such as beautifully carved stonework and ornate masonry and brickwork will give you lovely vignettes, and you will learn more about the buildings and the architecture of the periods when they were built. Internal features also make great subject material; look for intricate period details and interesting textures.

Travelling

Trips to another town or city are great opportunities for small-scale sketches. Focus on the details that make a place unique, whether that's a particular architectural style, a famous feature of the place, some telling graffiti, or anything else. Don't forget to record details on the way to and from your destination as well. Airports, train and bus stations and traffic jams are all ideal places for sketching.

Museums

Urban places often boast museums and galleries, and both are good places for finding unusual subject matter that you wouldn't usually see when you're sketching on the streets. Study interesting collections such as antiquities, ancient armour, pottery and sculpture.

Everyday mundanity

Entirely humdrum items, things that we don't usually notice, can look remarkable when sketched up close. Something as boring as an office hole punch can be transformed into an interesting device. A cactus in a small pot can become an intriguing shape. Try it and you will be rewarded with quiet vignettes of everyday life, as well as learning to see the things you take for granted in an entirely new way.

One small sketch a day

Sketching the smaller things in life is an easy way to get a routine going. Try drawing one small thing every day for a month. Don't put yourself under too much pressure; just pick a small, simple item and sketch it in as much or little detail as you fancy. The fact that the subject matter is small will help overcome any feelings of being overwhelmed and get you into a nice drawing rhythm. Give it a try and you will find your sketching invigorated.

A week's worth
of small-scale
sketching might look
something like this:

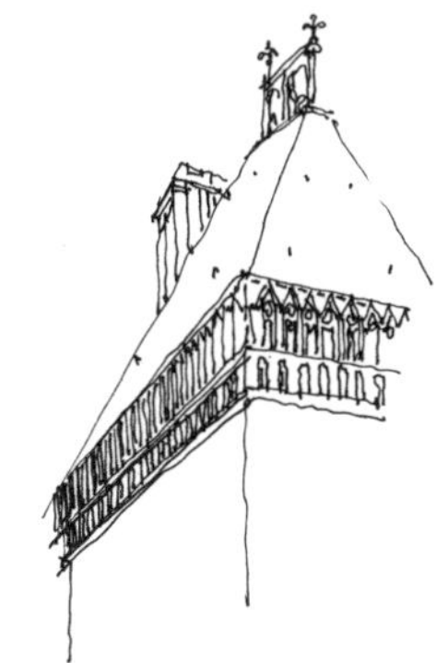

Inspiration for small-
scale sketching can be
found everywhere. Here
are some examples:

Architecture

▦ Day 1: On a bus,
sketch the design of
the seats or the
grab rails.

▦ Day 2: In the
office, sketch your
mobile phone on your
desk with an adjacent
chocolate bar.

▦ Day 3: At home,
sketch a cup of
coffee on the table.

▦ Day 4: In a café,
sketch a selection
of cakes or pastries.

▦ Day 5: In the
office, sketch
your pens in their
container.

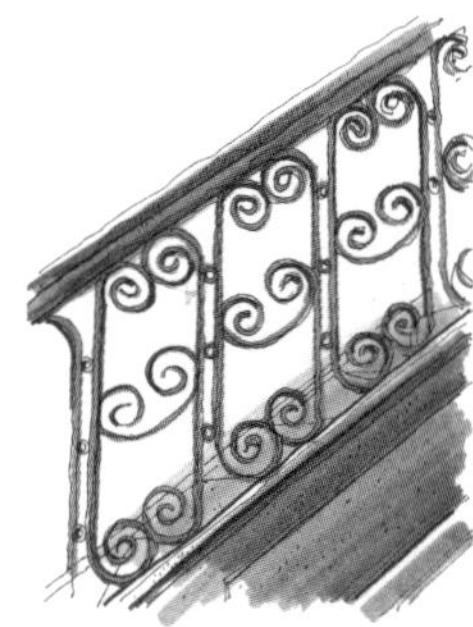

Ironwork staircase

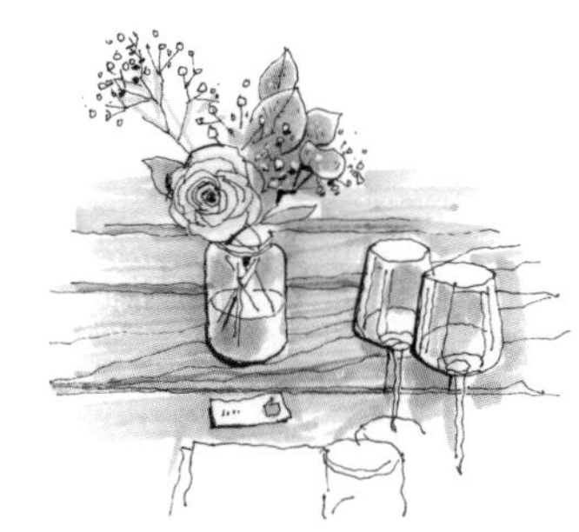

Table setting

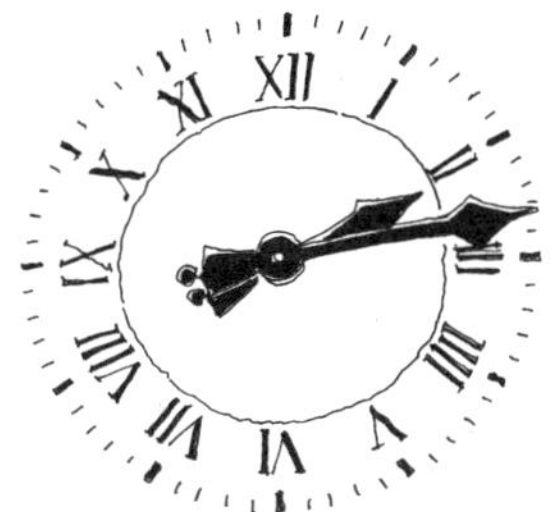

Clock face

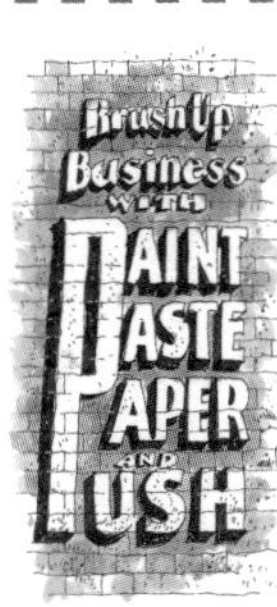

Typography

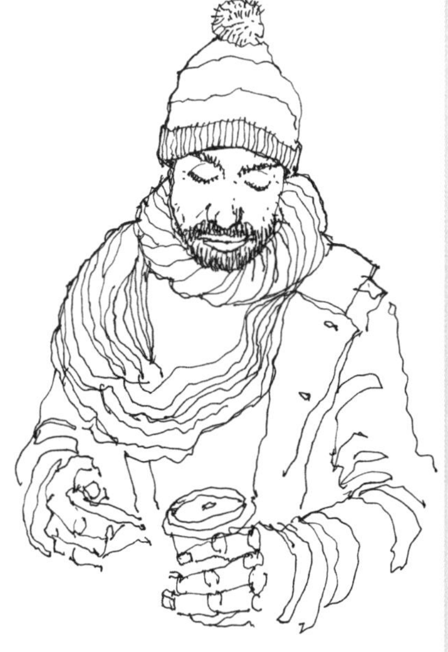

People

Doorways Exercise

Doorways are one of my go-to subjects when I want to capture the mood of a city and take some time to understand my location. In this exercise, I have chosen to create an intimate close-up sketch of a doorway at the Windsor Guildhall in England.

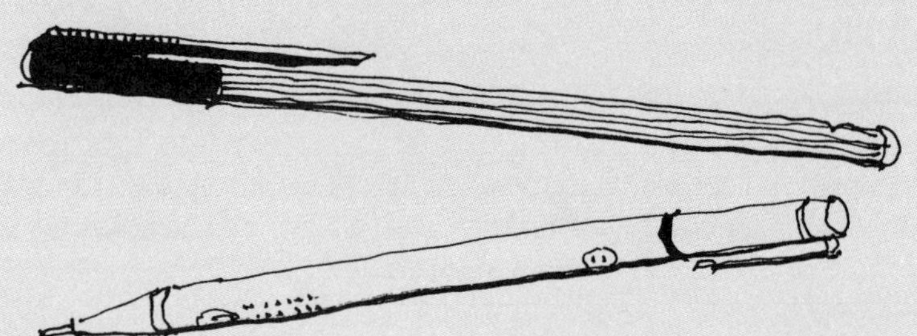

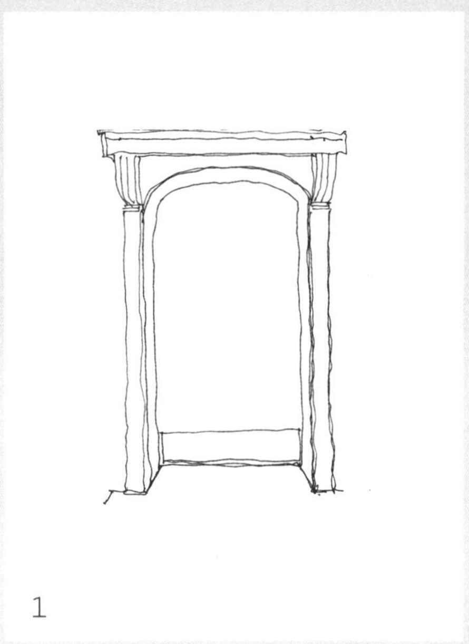

1

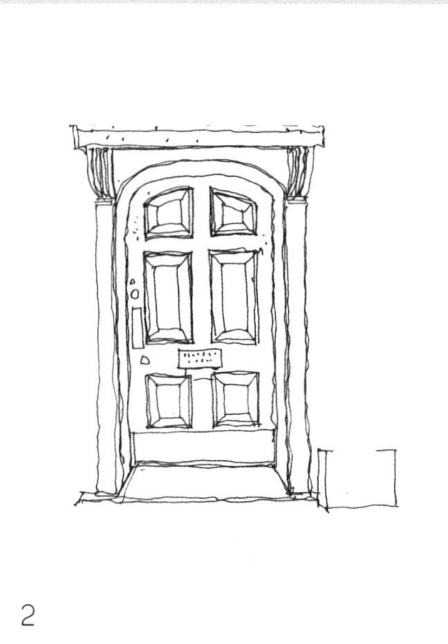

2

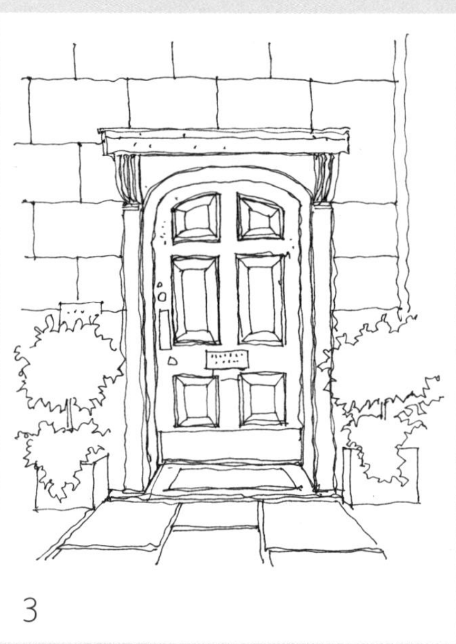

3

1. Start with the frame of the door to establish the basic structure of the sketch, focusing on getting the angles right. Doorways always look more impressive and architectural straight on, and they are much easier to sketch this way too. The shaky lines in my sketch are deliberate – they convey the age and character of the door I've chosen.

2. In close-up sketches, you have to pay attention to all the details. Look very closely and make sure you capture the detailed information that makes up the door: the bevel of the wood, the depth of carving and the architrave detailing, for example.

3. Keep working into the drawing. Loosely sketch any foliage surrounding the doorway and render the stonework or brickwork in more detail.

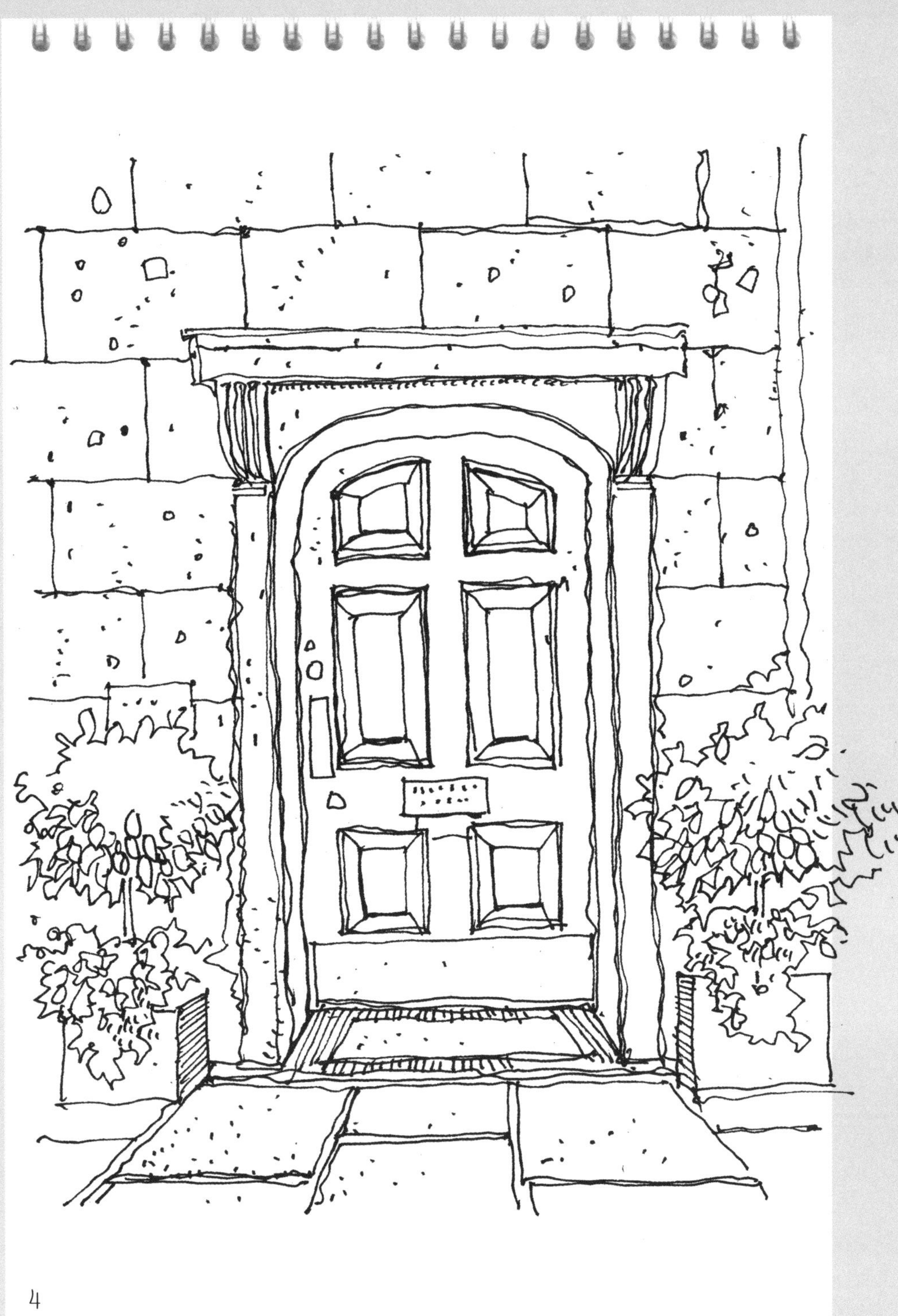

4. Be faithful to shapes, as I have been here with the bay leaves in the planters, but don't feel like you need to draw every single one. The stonework is quite old and battered, so I've used some delicate touches to add shadow and weight.

Sweeping Scale

This section is all about getting up high to capture a vista. City rooftops are magical subjects to work with, and offer great practise for tackling perspective, scale and multiple shapes. Rooftops that are open to the public can be hard to find, especially ones where you can sit peacefully for an hour or two, but search them out in your city and you will be rewarded many times over. Before you get started, make sure that the rooftop you are on is safe and legal for sketching.

Sweeping cityscapes lend themselves to large formats, so for something like this, try sketching on very large pieces of paper. For urban sketching, I advise against a full easel setup, as their size and weight makes them quite limiting. Instead, find a drawing board to fit the size of the paper (they are widely available in art stores, or you can use a piece of plywood cut to size by a local wood merchant). Work on fairly thick paper (150gsm is a good weight to start with) as thinner weights are more easily damaged at larger sizes. While it is possible to work in a large pad or sketchbook, a board gives you far greater stability that you will appreciate when working at a larger size.

With a larger scale comes the possibility of using bigger drawing materials. Chunky pens work well, as do graphite sticks instead of pencils. Avoid starting your sketch out too small – we're aiming to use the whole 'canvas' of our paper – and remember the principles of composition we saw from page 40, as they are just as important at this enlarged size.

Secure around ten sheets of paper to your board with board clips or masking tape to give you a few spare sheets to work with. Practicalities are important when working at this scale and so you'll need to find somewhere where you can rest your board, as the weight will be too heavy to comfortably hold over a prolonged period of time.

Don't be intimidated by the size of the paper. Begin by faintly drawing in your skyline, planning your sketch just as you would on a smaller format. The one thing you will immediately notice when you're perched above the street is that there are many challenging angles and shapes, most of which will be strangely cut off by other overlapping forms. Simplify the complexity of the view by thinking of the buildings as a collection of simple geometric shapes. By reducing them to their most basic physical construction, you can put them together like a jigsaw puzzle, and you may even be inspired to sketch in a more abstract way.

Belgian urban sketcher Gérard Michel's incredible cityscapes provide inspiration for any artist thinking of challenging themselves with a complex rooftop view. His technique is architecturally considered and technically very accurate; he says the secret to his drawings is measurement.

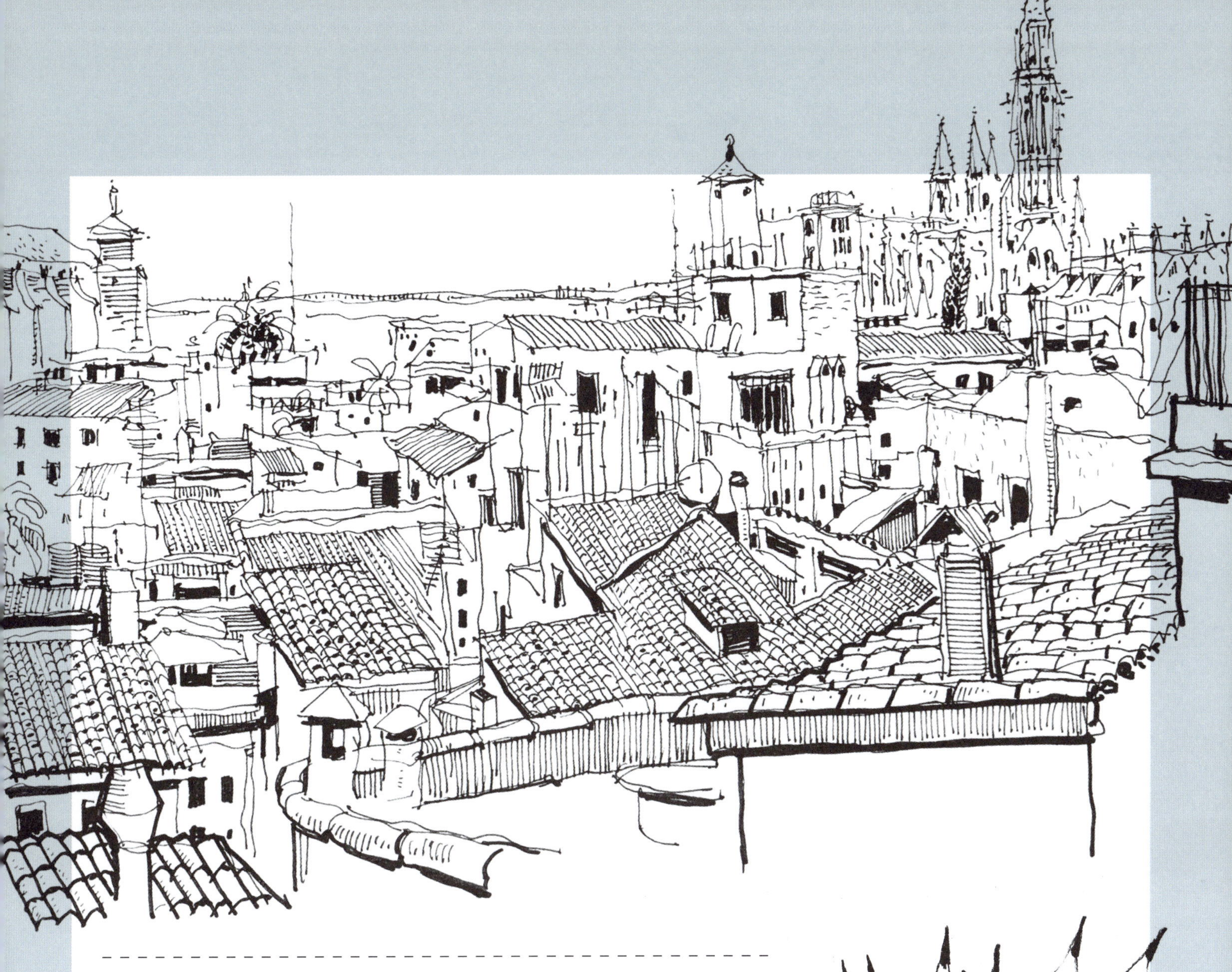

PENCIL TIPS

If you want to create an entire large-scale drawing in pencil, make sure you have a good selection ranging from H to 4B to ensure you can use different line weights. Keep your pencils sharp so that your lines are clean and accurate throughout. For longevity, it's best to use a craft knife or scalpel and a sandpaper block to keep your pencils sharp. Pencil sharpeners tend to make your pencils vanish before your eyes!

Sketching on Rooftops Exercise

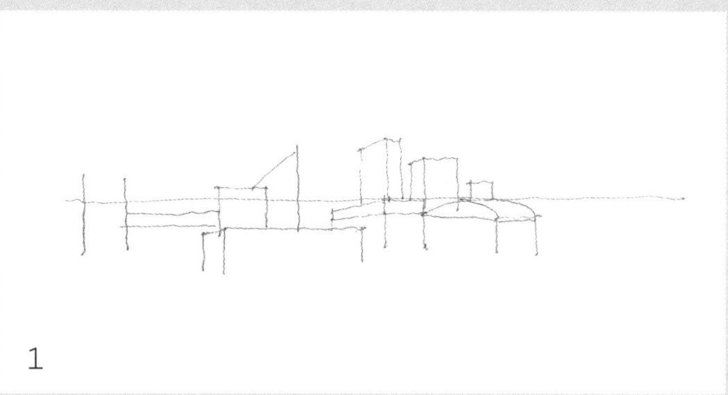

1. Lightly sketch out the horizon line and begin to build your scene from there. Allow for plenty of white space above to represent the sky, but don't be tempted to add clouds at this stage. I used a fine HB pencil initially and then built on top using pen later, but you can use whichever medium you prefer.

2. Block out the key shapes of the scene in pencil to make sure that you can fit all the main elements you want to include on the page. Use the space you have on the page well, and don't feel like you have to fill every square inch of it.

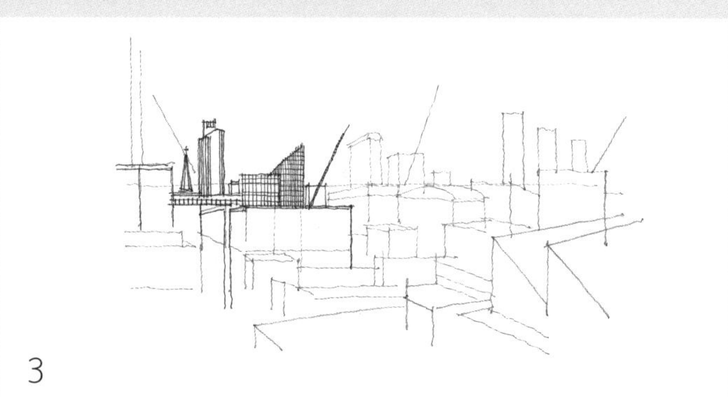

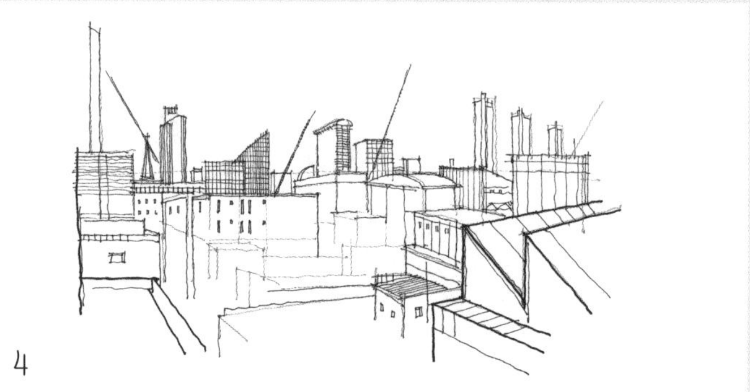

3. If you are using pen, start to draw over and work into the basic pencil shapes. Keep your linework loose and free, and don't put too much detail into subjects that are a long way off, instead add gestural details that suggest the forms of what you're seeing.

4. For elements that are closer, add more detail and use bolder, thicker lines to give a sense of solidity (things in the distance appear less defined). As the aim is to convey the sense and shape of a cityscape, don't worry too much about what's going on in the foreground.

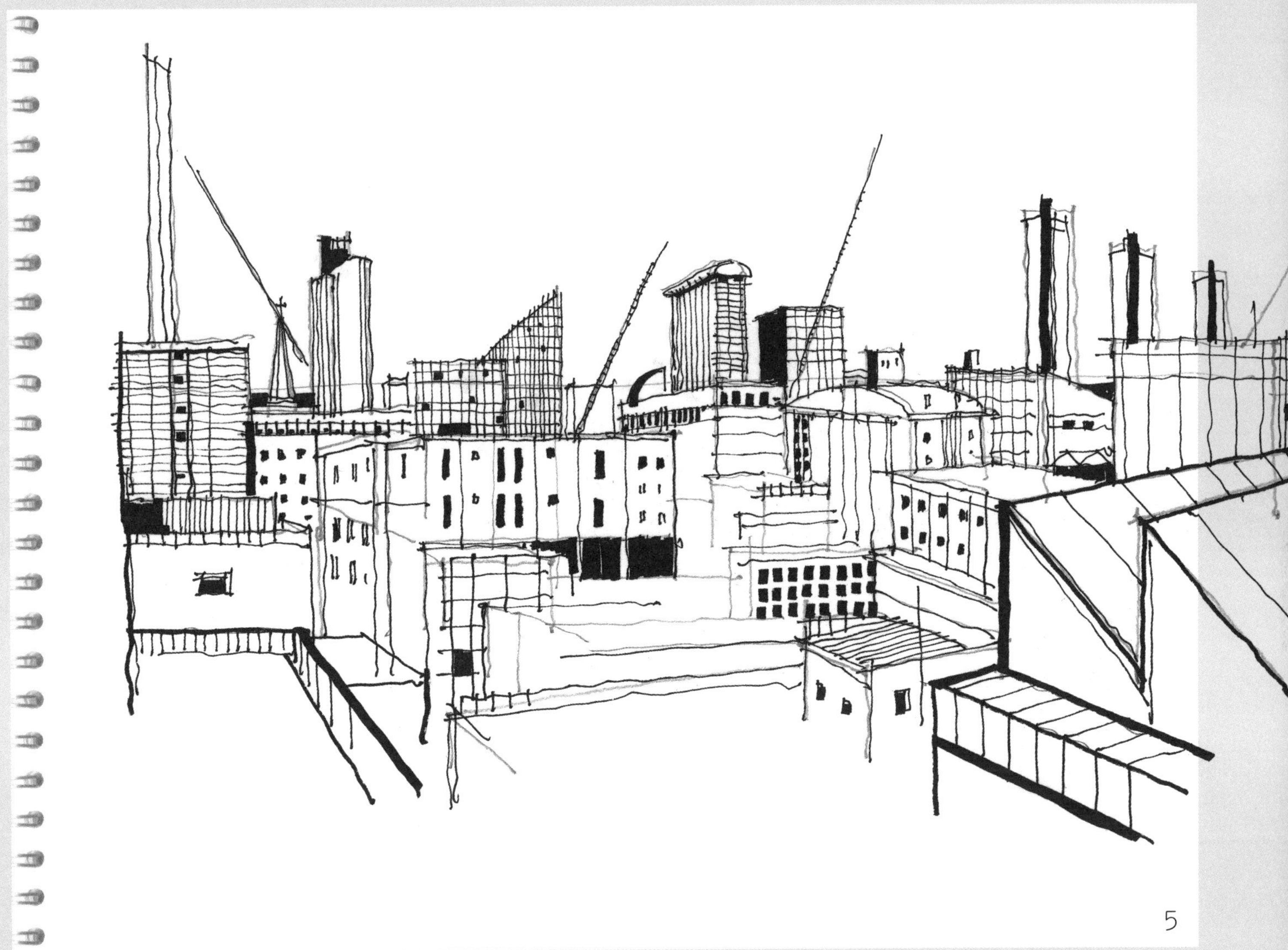

5. Add little touches of solid black to represent windows or heavy shadows. These areas contrast with the finer, more delicate lines, which helps your sketch achieve more visual interest and balance; but be judicious with the use of heavy ink if you want to retain a light and airy feel to your rooftop vista.

LESS IS MORE
It can be tempting to try to fill the page with detail. Remember that less is often more, and white space is necessary to balance a busy scene.

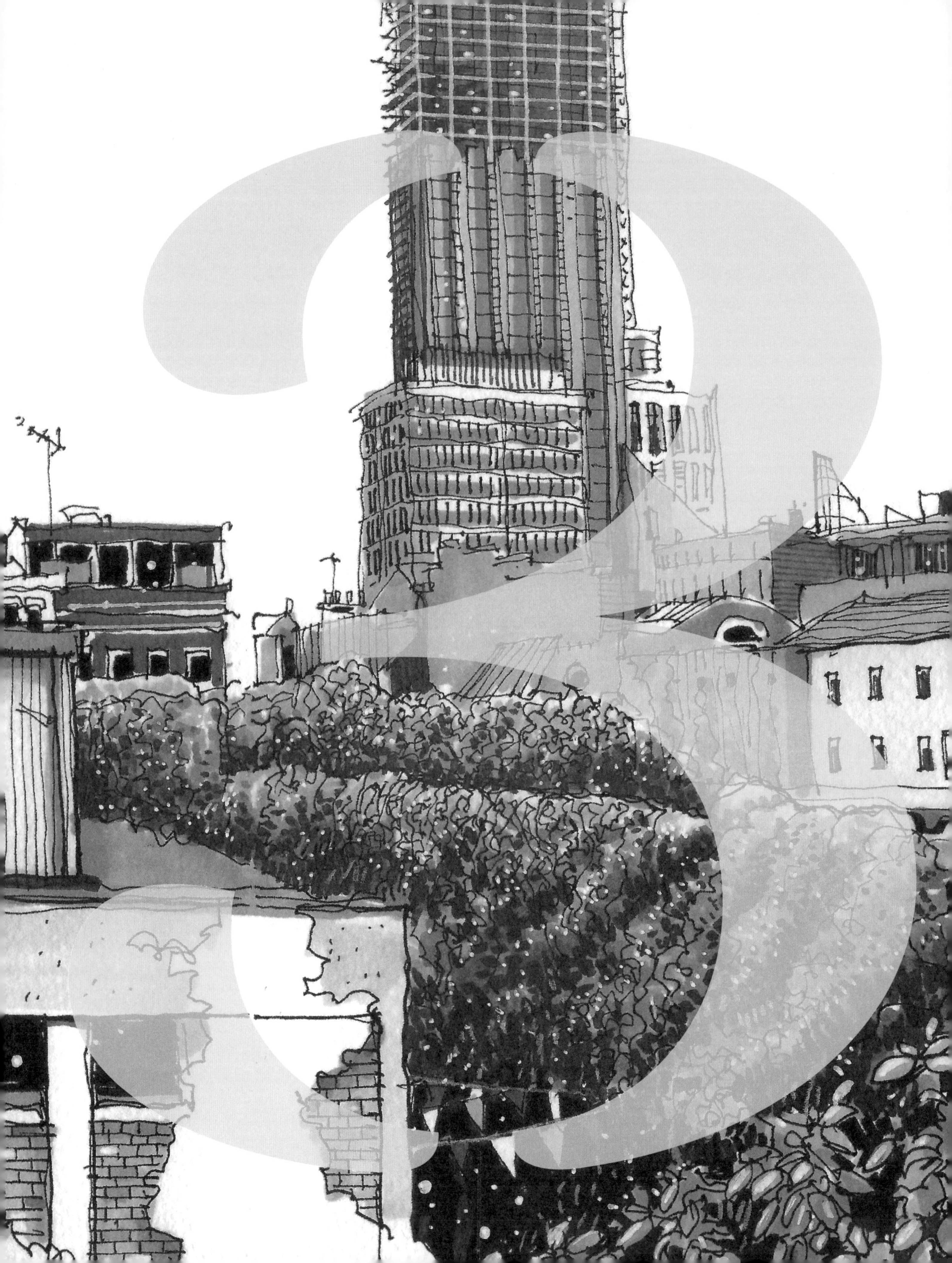

Tone and Contrast

While I love the cleanness and space of a well-executed line drawing, there is a lot to be said for the power of tone to really bring a sketch to life. This chapter explores how to add tone and contrast to your sketches through a variety of techniques, from adding punchy blocks of solid black to contrast with fine linework, to subtler, graded shading to increase realism and depth.

The first two exercises demonstrate the effectiveness of graphic black-and-white drawings that utilize different line weights and solid blacks, which we've already seen some examples of in the previous chapter. This is a really easy and striking way to bring dimension into your work. The second two exercises explore complex tone in more detail, showing you how to work into your images, build up layers and add texture to take your sketch to the next level.

Tone

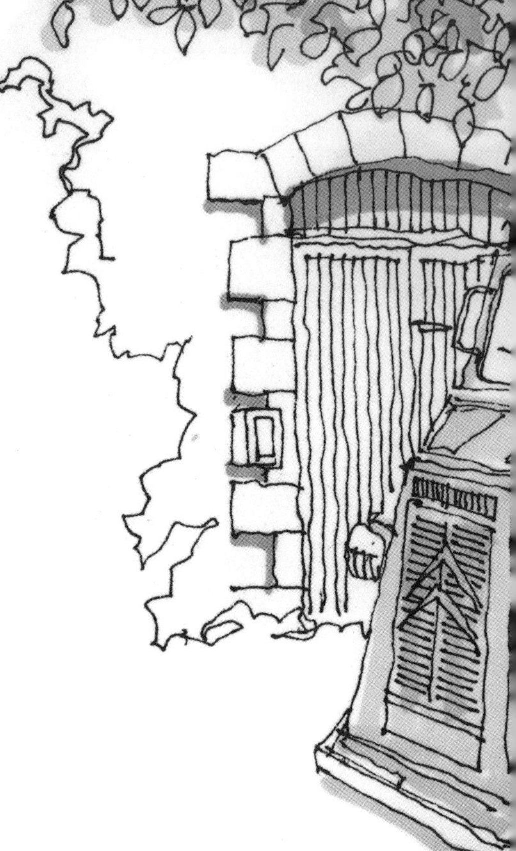

- -

Line drawing purists would disagree, but I believe that a brilliant drawing can usually be improved further by adding tone – and there are many ways of doing this.

When you are thinking about adding tone to your sketches, it's useful to ask yourself the following questions:

- Is the sketch complex and would it benefit from the addition of tone to denote detail?
- If the sketch is simplistic, would tone add extra interest?
- Would tone bring extra realism to the sketch?
- Are there details in the scene that could be brought to life in your sketch using tone?

Tone can be added using pencil, marker, ink, watercolour, charcoal and pastels, and many other mediums besides – it all depends what you are trying to achieve and what is suitable for the subject matter. I would recommend when possible to add tone live on location, because it will be harder to replicate the particular qualities of light and shadow in a scene when it's not there in front of you. That said, it is not always possible to add tone in a quick session, in this case I recommend simply taking a photo on your phone to remind you of the light when you return to the sketch at home.

When you are adding tone to sketches, it is useful to create a reference scale to help you work out what shade you need to use. Using the paper that you would normally sketch on

– as different papers take tone differently – create a scale with swatches of tone from light to dark. The scale opposite is a marker and pencil scale, but you can make them using other materials, such as watercolour and coloured pencil.

Here are some examples of the transformative effect tone can have on drawing:

Minimal tone

1. Only two shades of cool grey markers were used on this sketch from a wedding in France. The initial line drawing was lively and evocative of the event, and marker was used to denote simple blocks of colour that help the eye see the scene more clearly. Identify key areas in your sketch that dominate the composition and add tone to those. Markers were used in this case, but a similar treatment could be applied using watercolour.

Tinted paper effect

2. This row of scooters on an ordinary street in Spain looked fine as a line sketch, but when tone was added to accentuate the effect the light was having on the trees, it turned into something else. Using mid-tone tinted paper, as I did here, means that the lighter and darker shades will work harder against the tint of the background. You can also add whites using pastel or gouache.

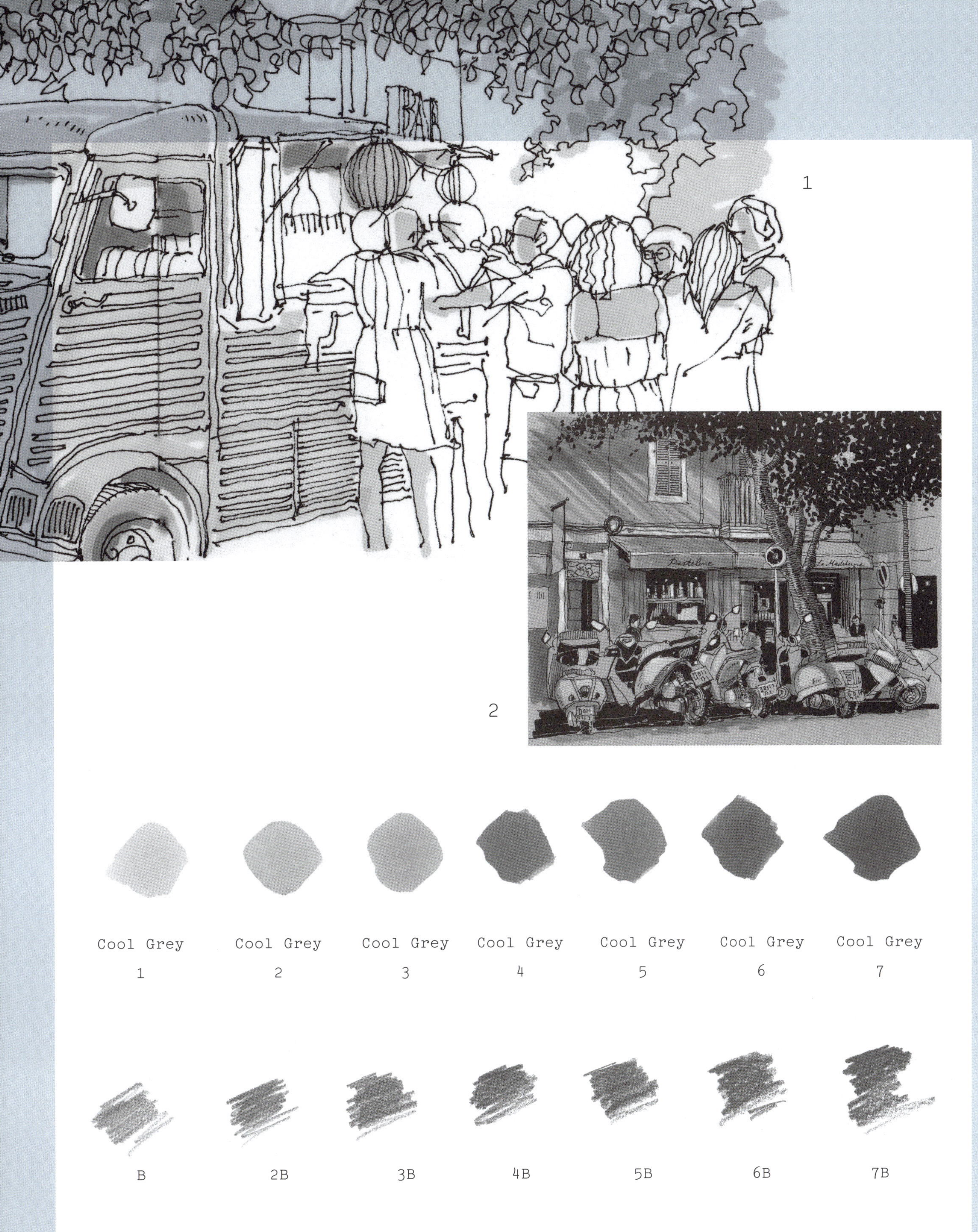
1
2
Cool Grey
1
Cool Grey
2
Cool Grey
3
Cool Grey
4
Cool Grey
5
Cool Grey
6
Cool Grey
7
B
2B
3B
4B
5B
6B
7B

Simple tone

3. While this loose and urgent line drawing of a pub in London's Soho was charming, it needed the addition of simple tone to breathe life into it. It was sketched on brown kraft paper and only two shades of tone were added, along with some white gel pen. I created a few dark areas where there were shadows and used the same tone to pick out striking features like the blinds. Resist the temptation to add too much – the key is a limited application of tone. I digitally desaturated the colour after scanning the sketch to make it monochrome.

Complex tone

4. The beauty of tone is that it can be built up for more complexity. This sketch of Shoreditch in East London, is a great example of a multi-layered urban scene where complex shading really adds to the narrative. I used marker, pencil and gouache to add depth and texture to a fairly mundane architectural view. Without the tone, this drawing looked unremarkable, but with the addition of shading, it was transformed. Always be on the lookout for uninspiring sketches you have made that might be taken to another level by the addition of a little tone.

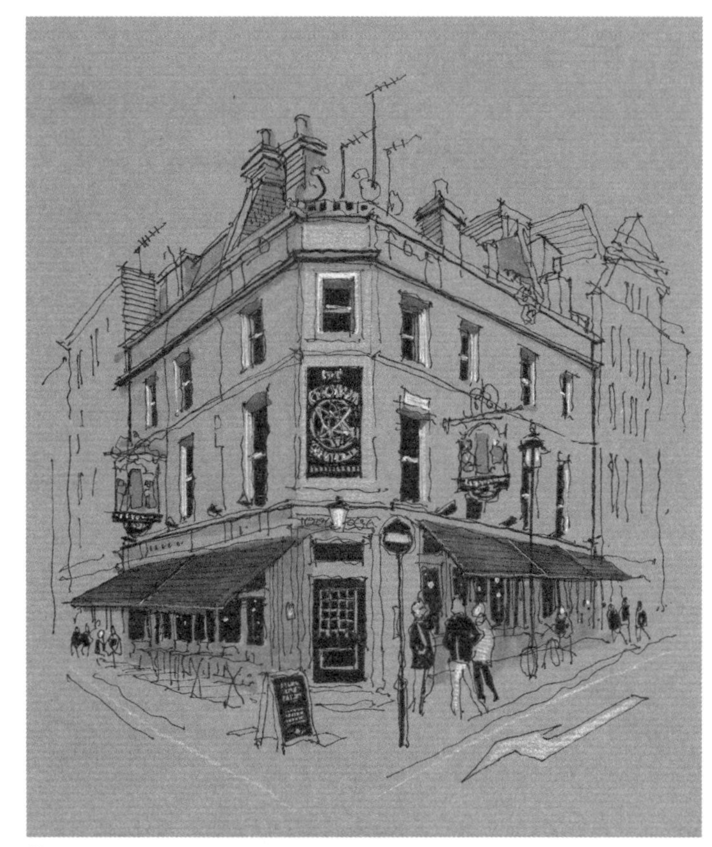

3

4

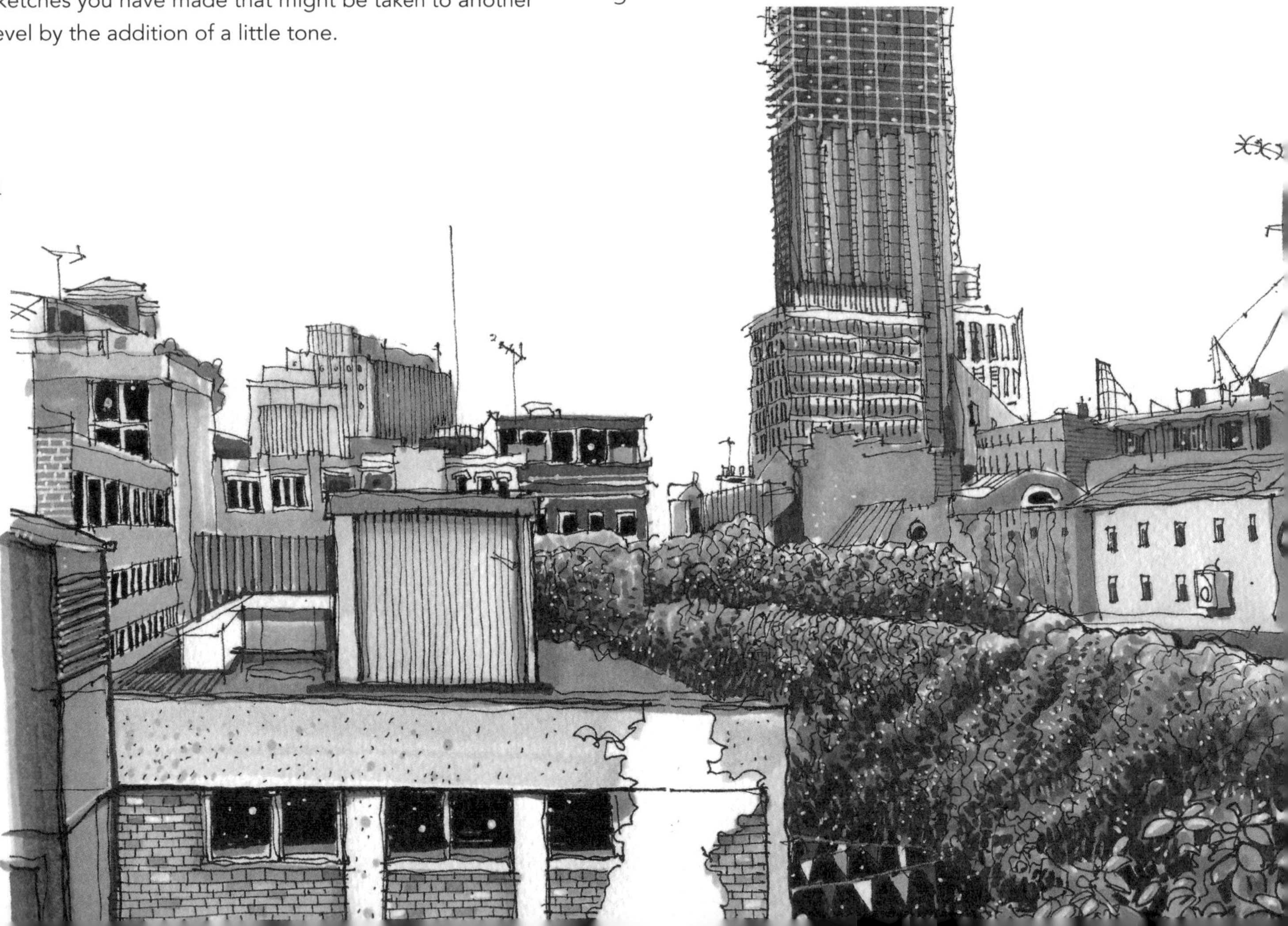

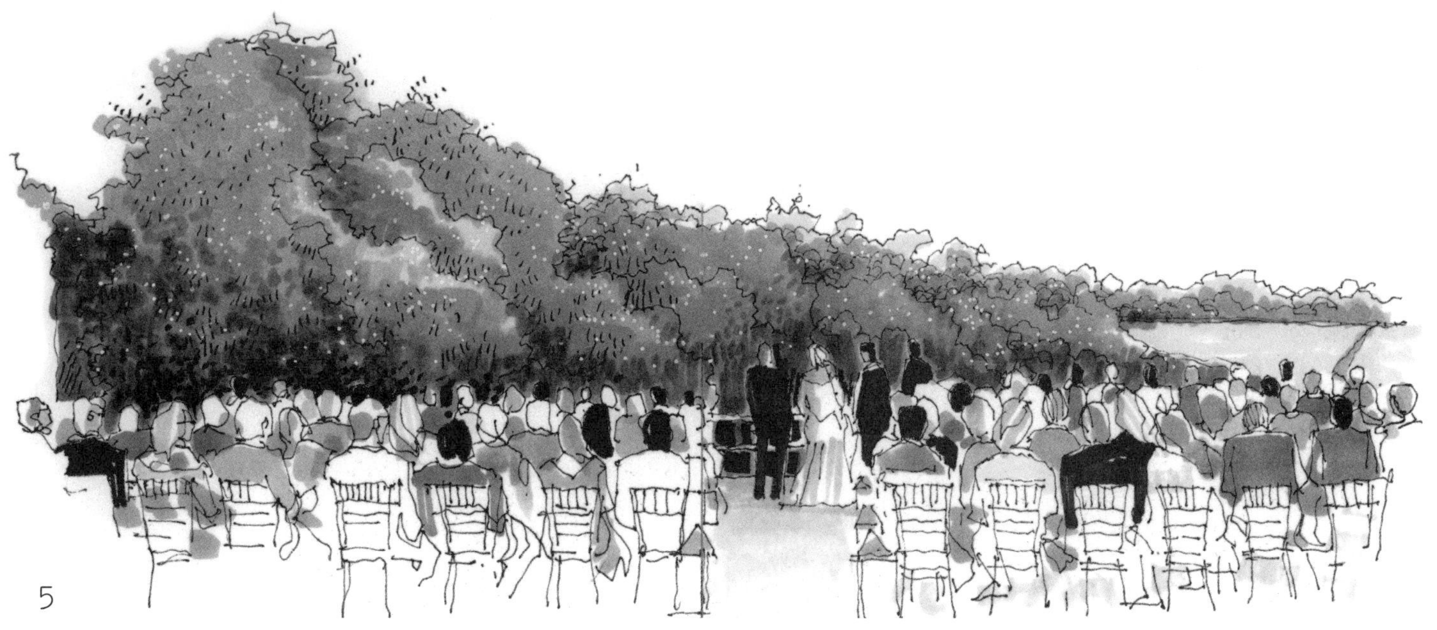

5

Graduated tone

5. Graduation is the subtle build-up of tone to create a soft shading effect, rather than a flat or blocky tonal finish. Here, graduated tone is used primarily in the trees to create a dramatic backdrop to a wedding ceremony in Dorset, in the south of England. I started with the lighter shades of the trees and built up gradually to the darkest tones. When working with marker, as I was here, it is important to work quickly while the ink is wet on the paper to blend the shades and avoid hard edges in the graduation.

6. In this sketch from Sicily, Italy, I gradually built up to four tones of shade to capture the subtlety of the shadows and the full, sculptural effect of the pillars and ornate stonework. Graduated tone gives this sketch a more realistic look.

Tone using different media

7. Watercolour is a lovely medium for adding subtle tone to a sketch. The effect is delicate and traditional and definitely worth exploring. I would advocate a less-is-more approach with watercolour. In this sketch from Clerkenwell in London, the watercolour is added with the lightest possible touch.

8. Pencil and charcoal are wonderful media for adding immediate tone to a line sketch begun in the same medium. This sketch in Tribeca, New York, uses bold layers of charcoal tone in the foreground, built up fluidly and organically. In this medium you can work back into the dark tones with erasers or white chalk to add highlights. I left the other parts of this sketch clean to contrast the heavy shading.

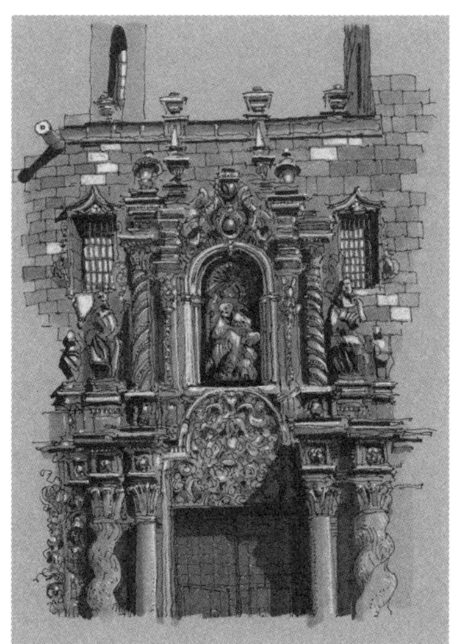

6

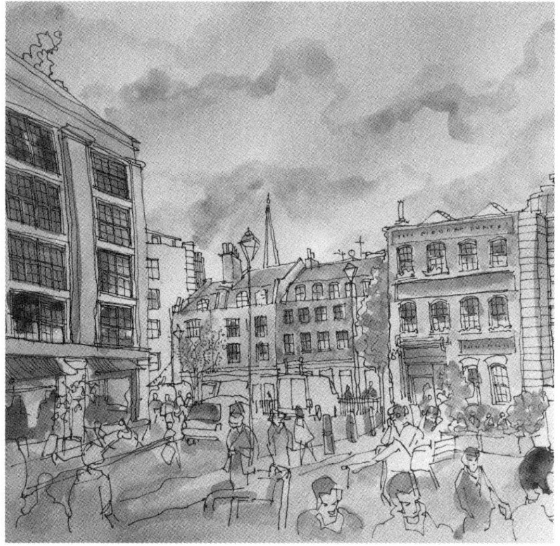

7

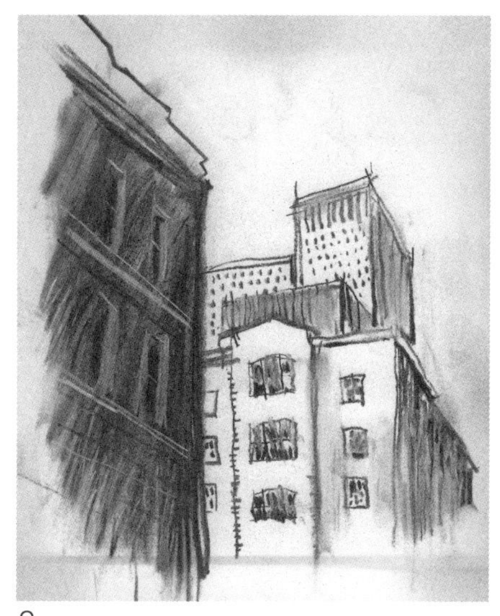

8

Contrast Using Solid Black Exercise

Simple black-and-white line sketches with a variety of line weights can be powerful. This exercise is best embarked upon when the sun is shining and creating a lot of hard, dark shadows – the natural contrast will help when you come to add the solid black areas. This scene in Malaga, Spain, contains lots of interesting graphic shapes due to the angle of the sun, which is what first attracted me to it. I recommend using a chisel-tipped pen to help you keep your edges sharp.

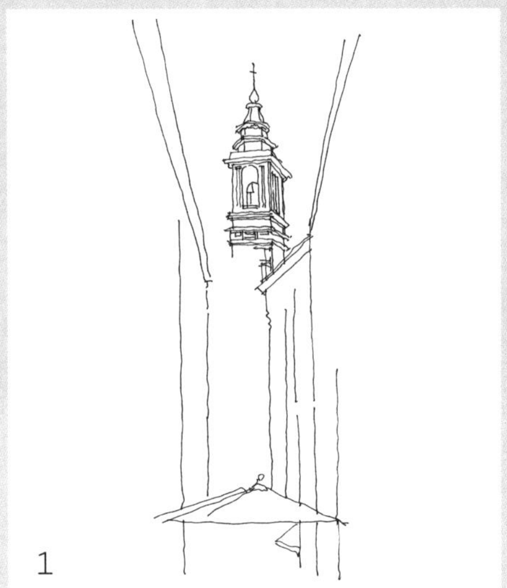

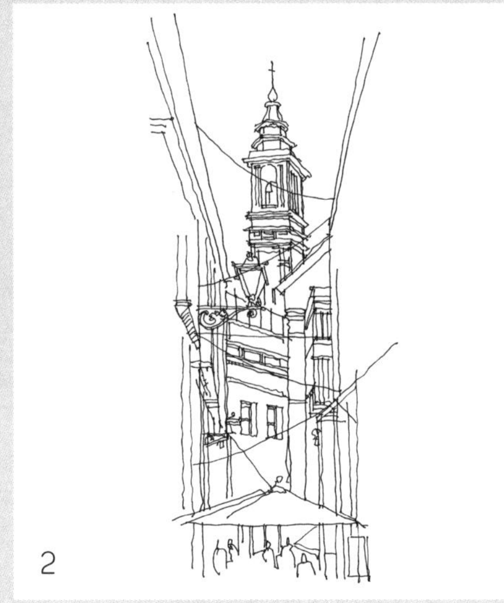

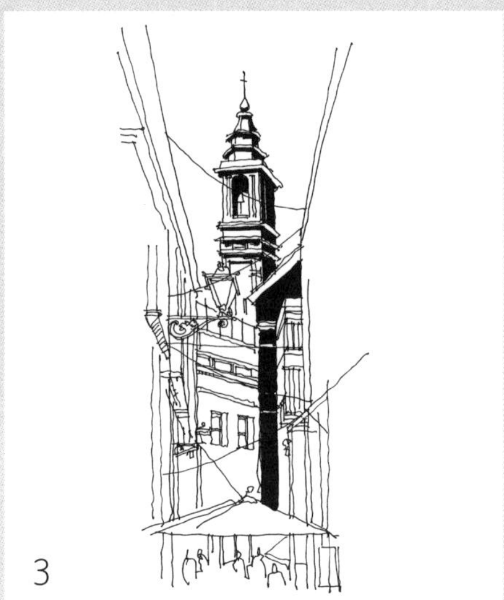

1. Find a cool and shady spot where you can see the details of your scene clearly and not be dazzled by the sun. Begin your sketch as you normally would and focus particularly on the structure of the buildings. Remember to use perspective and measuring techniques as you work.

2. While you concentrate on building up the linework, look out for deep shadows, noticing where they strike the surfaces. Don't worry too much about the accuracy or straightness of your mark-making, as the dominating black shadows will overpower any shaky lines, and sometimes cover them up.

3. Once there is enough information on the page, start adding some solid blacks. Start blocking in the shapes on the buildings, paying attention to the position of the sun (in my example it would be at the top left of the page). Inconsistently placed shadows will make the scene look strange and unrealistic, so keep observing and place them where they naturally fall, rather than inventing areas of shade.

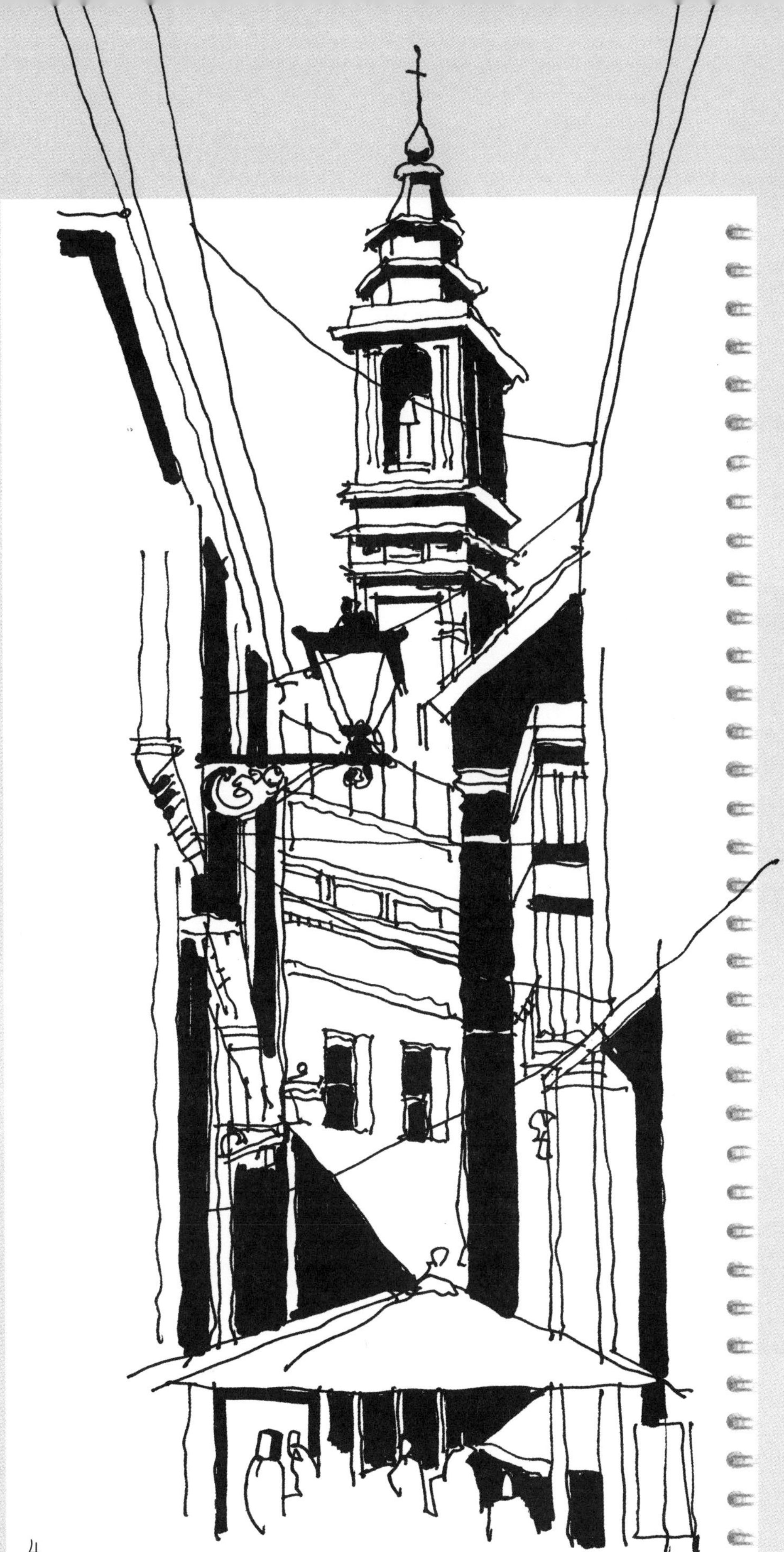

4. Build carefully and don't forget about the composition of your drawing on the page. When adding lots of solids, the white space around the sketch becomes even more important to balance the picture. Break up large areas of shadows with small details left white to suggest angle and depth – look for areas in your linework sketch to see where this will be effective before you start adding the solid black. The contrast in the resulting image lends real atmosphere to the sketch.

Varying Line Weights Exercise

Using different thicknesses of line is a great trick to denote depth and scale. This exercise can be done in pen or pencil, but if you can, it is worth trying it with a few pens of different-sized nibs to help you achieve the thickness you're looking for immediately. As a general rule, the lines of objects closer to you should have a heavier treatment than those farther away, as subjects in the distance appear to recede. Using a heavier line weight can also be a very effective way to pick out a feature in the composition that you want to draw your viewer's attention to.

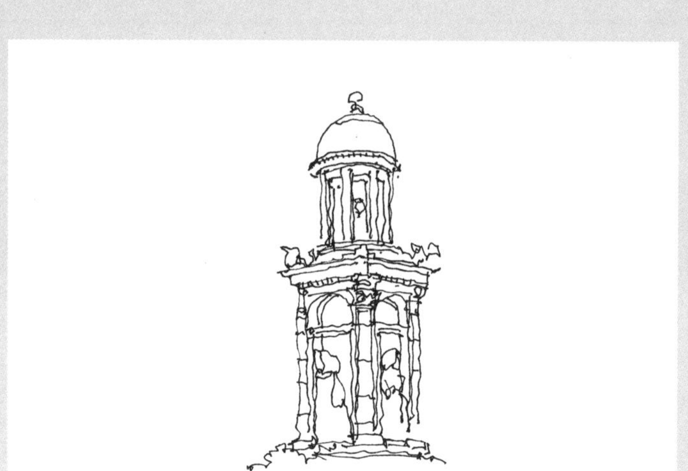

1

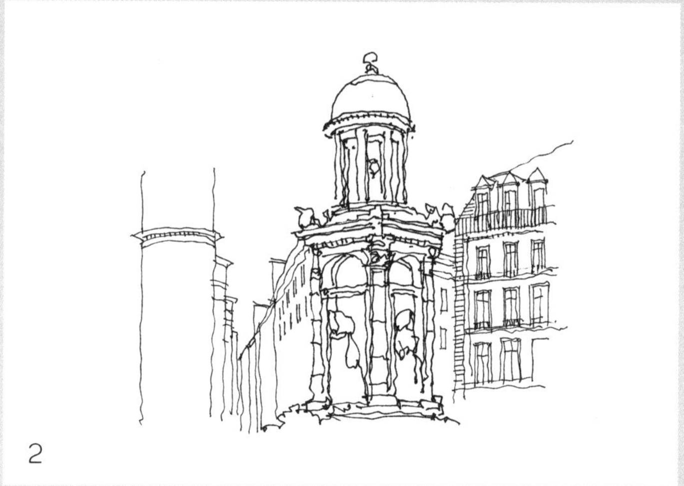

2

1. Begin by drawing the main feature of your sketch, which should also be nearest to you, using a medium fineliner (for me, 0.5mm). In my scene, the fountain sculpture is the most obvious place to start, and it sets the scale for the sketch and the surrounding buildings. Also remember that objects closer to you should have more detail than those in the background, so make sure to capture this.

2. Using a narrower fineliner (in my sketch, 0.3mm), add the surrounding buildings to your sketch, starting with larger shapes first to construct the composition, then working into detail. The lighter weight of line will give a sense of depth to your image, and you might want to use an even finer pen for details farther in the distance. Use the pen technique (see page 34) to measure any angles and to make sure your lines of perspective are true. You can leave the edges of the sketch unfinished, with a few straggling lines to suggest more buildings.

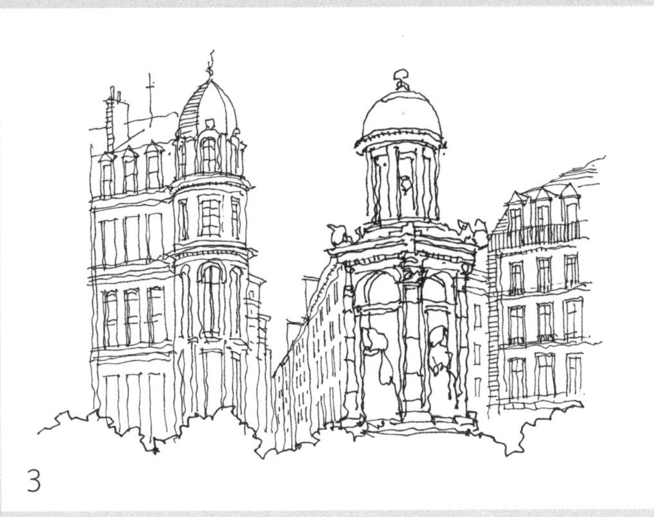

3. To give the sketch a sense of scale and depth, add some further foreground details using the medium pen so that the foreground appears closer than the surrounding background buildings. Here, I've added some shrubbery.

4. If you are feeling bold, try using a sign pen or a brush pen to add an even heavier line to details of your key and supporting foreground features, where this contributes further scale and depth. Use solid black sparingly to suggest the shadows on your main feature.

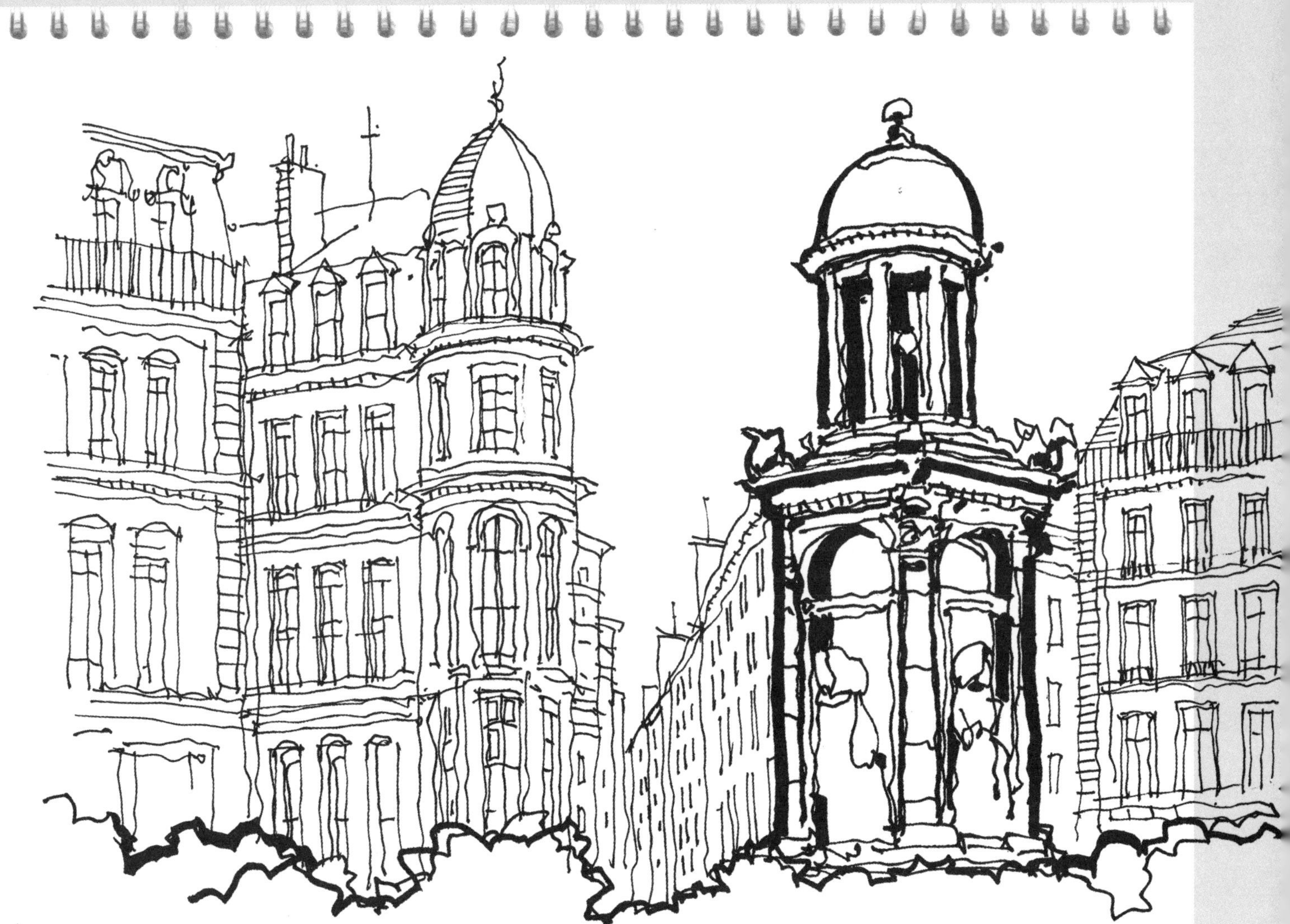

Simple Tone to Add Texture Exercise

This exercise demonstrates how simple tone can elevate an artwork. In my example, the line drawing was detailed and controlled but I thought that the addition of some tone would add interest to a fairly simple building. If you are adding tone while sketching live, start by filling in the bold shapes that dominate the scene. It is advisable to build tone from light to dark, but if adding tone live, as I was here, I recommend beginning with any dominating blacks from shadows in case the light changes.

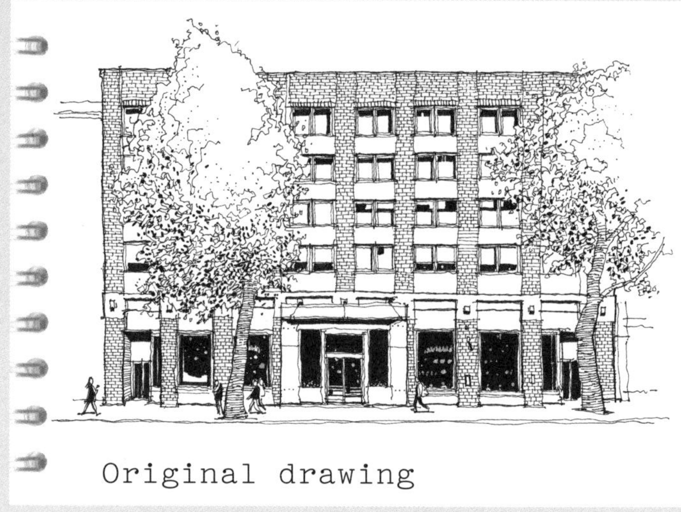

Original drawing

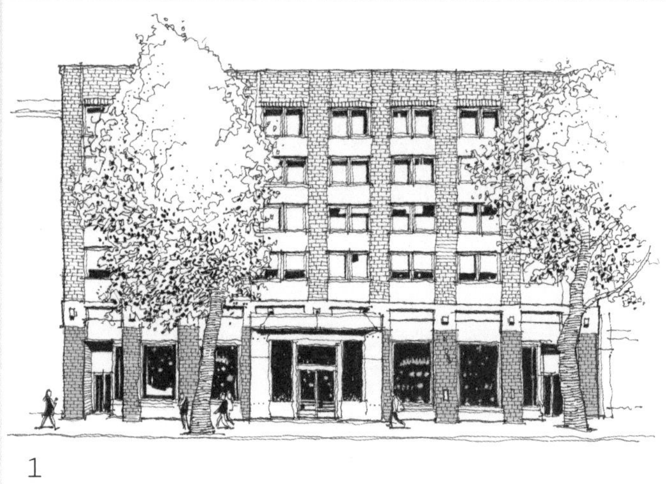

1

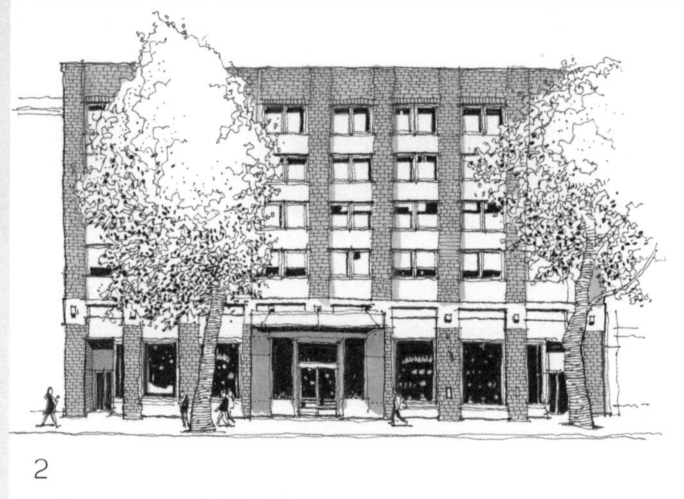

2

1. To add tone to this line sketch, I used a set of Cool Grey Winsor & Newton ProMarkers as shown on page 65. With a Cool Grey 2 marker, starting at the bottom, I filled in the brick sections of the building first. They were the obvious place to start because they dominated the building.

2. Build the tone out from the place you started. With a Cool Grey 4 marker, I added some selective shadows on the windows to denote the depth of the brick columns. The alcoves and recessed doors are also in this darker shade. Keep your strokes very tight to deliver a controlled feel to the tone.

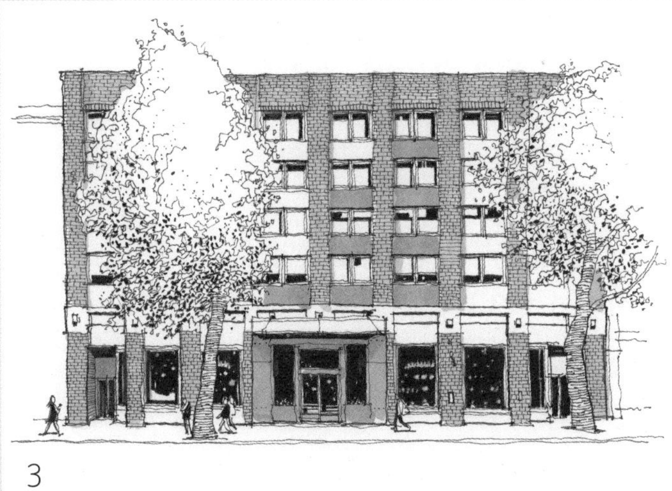

3

3. Still using the darker grey, I filled in the panels below the windows, taking care to keep the tone within the lines for a crisp finish. Go over key areas to add an additional layer of tone on the shadows. I decided to keep the windows white to contrast with the textured brickwork.

4. At the outset of the sketch I chose to keep the trees predominantly white, allowing me to use darker shadows on the building so that it would remain the centre of attention. To create just a suggestion of shadow on the trees, I added some dappled texture using the chisel-tipped end of a Cool Grey 1 marker to add a solid grey that contrasted with the dotted shadows.

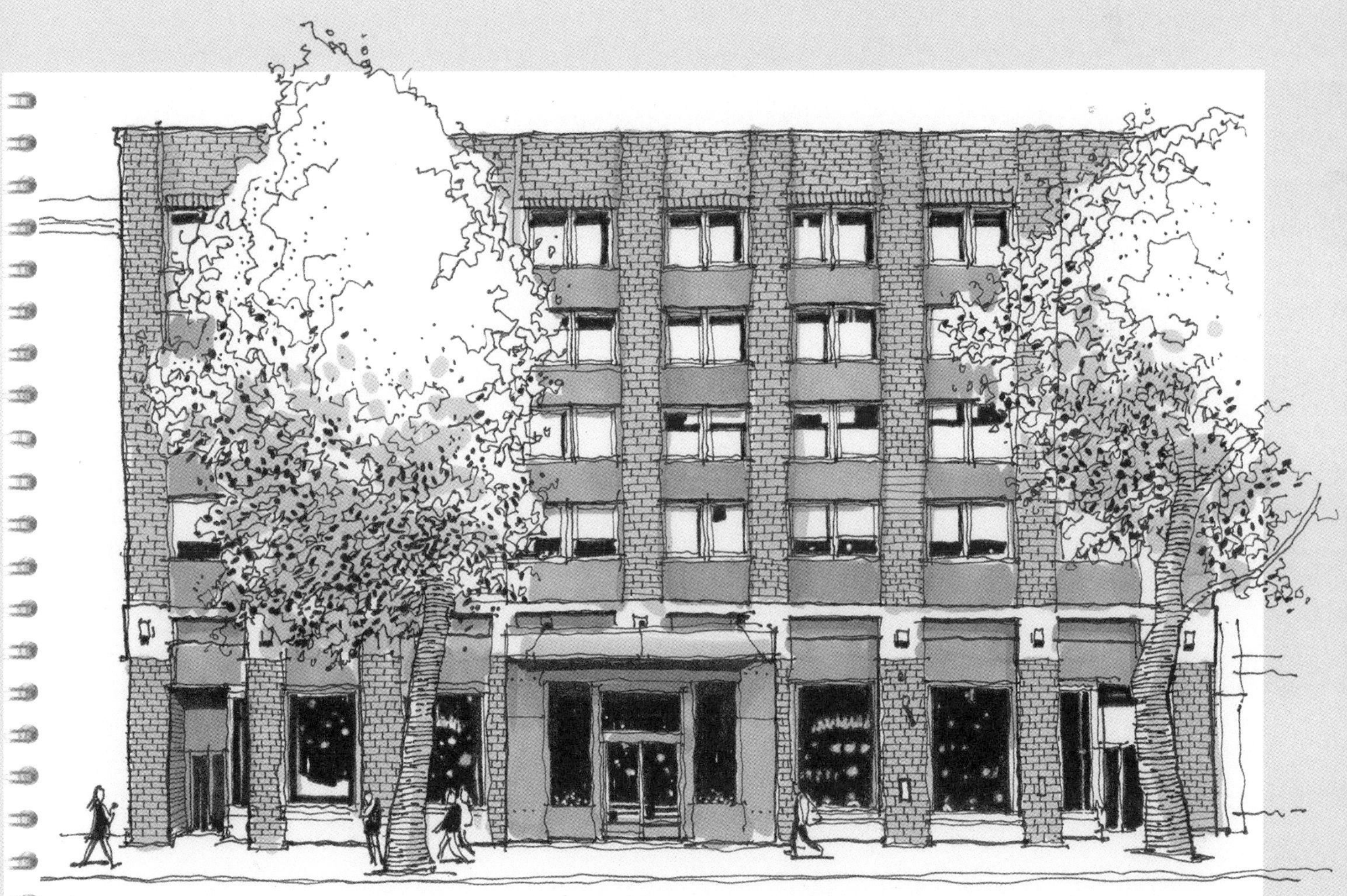

4

Building Layers with Complex Tone Exercise

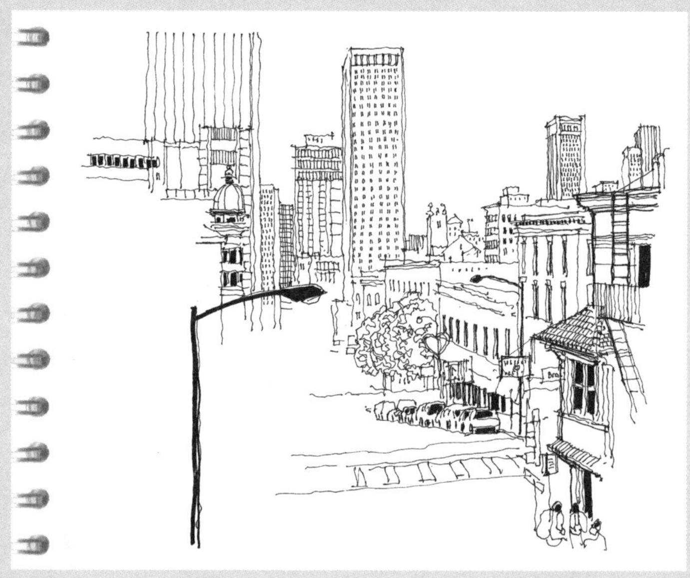

Building up layers of tone using markers is a very effective way to add depth and detailed texture to a complex urban scene. In this sketch of a street in San Francisco, I kept the shading quite free and relaxed because it adds character to the predominantly boxy architecture. The darkest areas were added first, and then I used a set of Winsor & Newton Cool Grey markers for a flat and illustrative finish and a contrast between tonal buildings and white space.

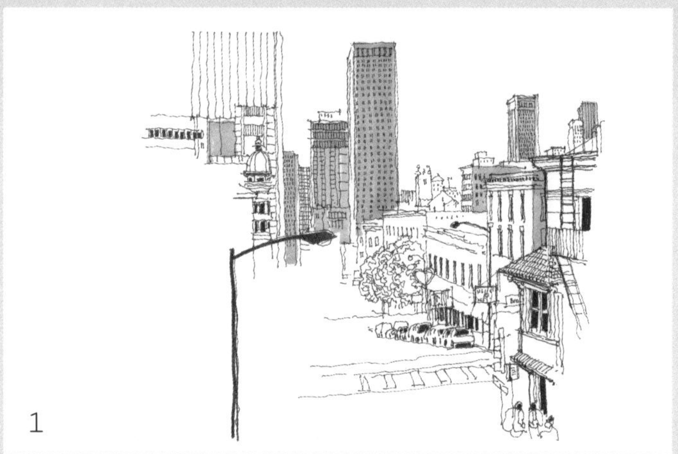

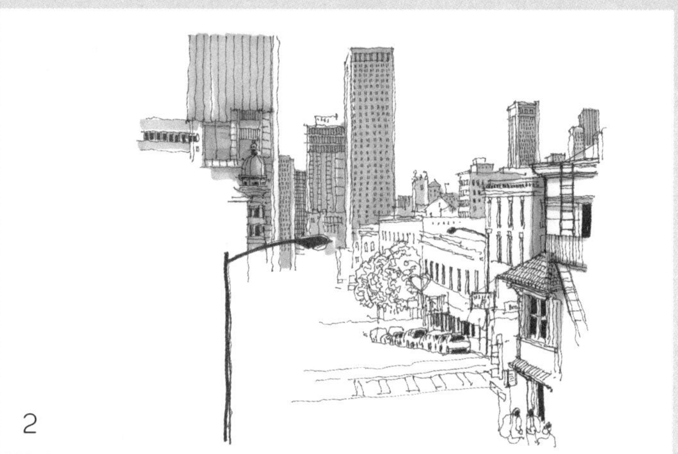

1. Look carefully at where the shadows naturally fall and add them consistently. In this sketch, the sun was fairly low on the horizon on the left of the page, which is where I chose to start. Using a light marker (here, Cool Grey 2), I blocked in the skyscrapers in the distance and some deep shadows in the foreground.

2. Start to layer the tones, building on top of the lighter tone you have already laid down with darker pens to add a little more dimension to your buildings. I used two medium markers (Cool Grey 3 and 4) for this.

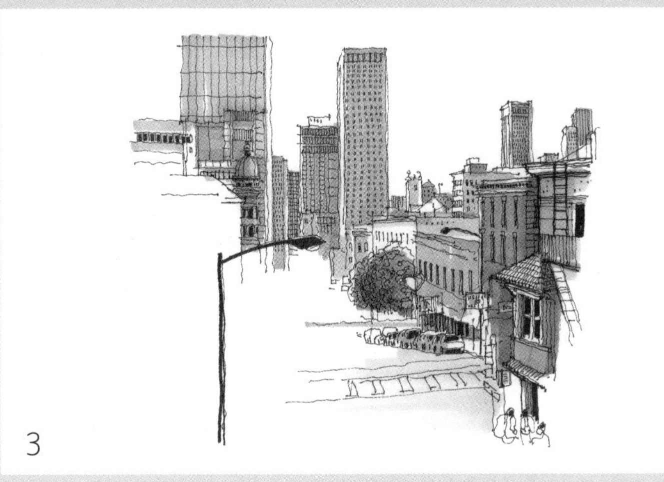

3

3. Alternating between a lighter pen and a darker pen (I used Cool Grey 2 and 4), continue to build up the layers of tone. Layering tone rather than going straight in with a darker pen gives you more control over the strength of the shading, enabling you to make subtle marks, so you can add realistic details to foreground features.

4. Finishing touches can be made with black and white pencils to add further texture to the tones already laid down. White gel pen can also be used to provide some highlights. Try to add these where the sun would naturally hit the subject. Don't add too many highlights, as they can start to look like snow!

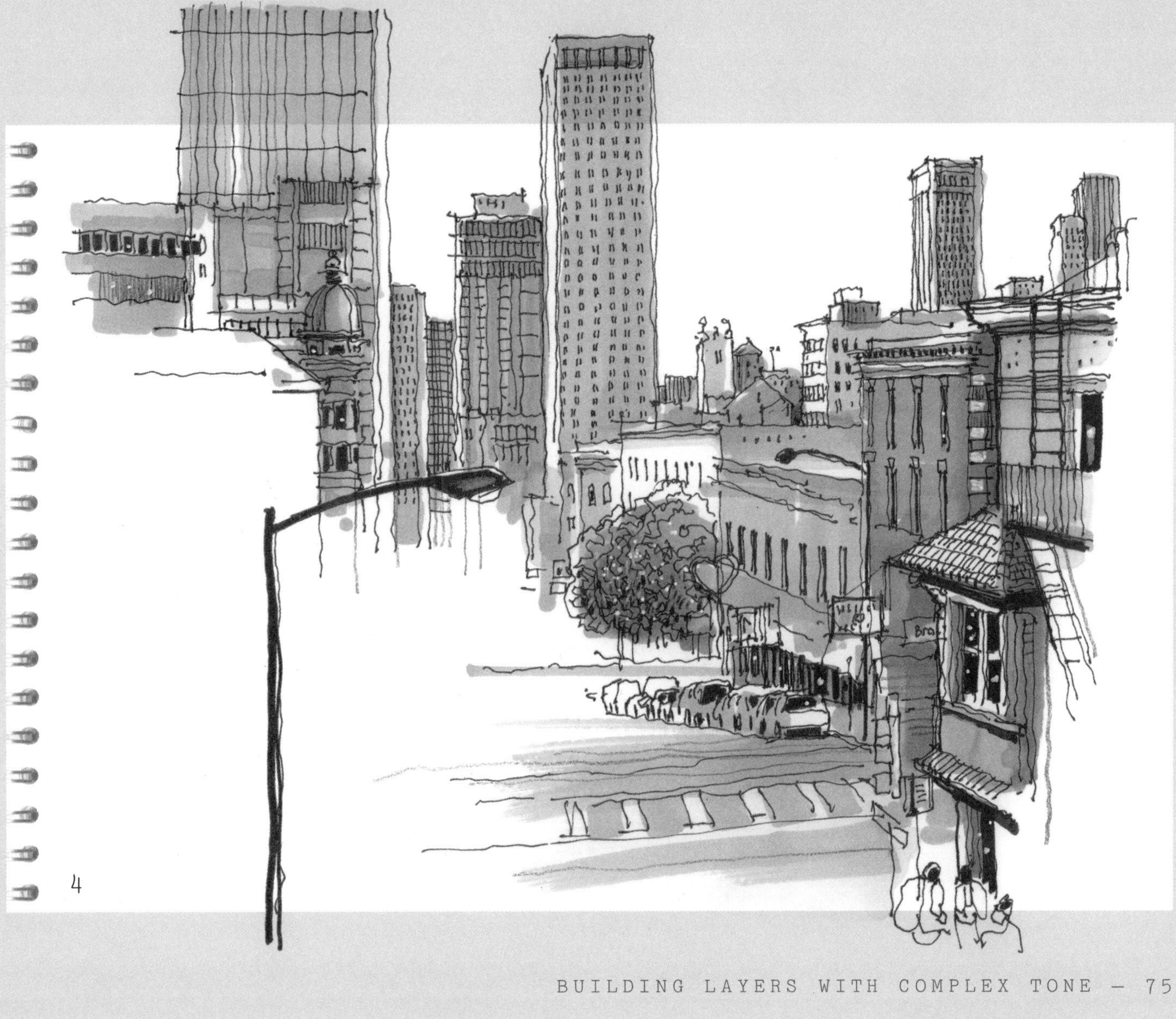

4

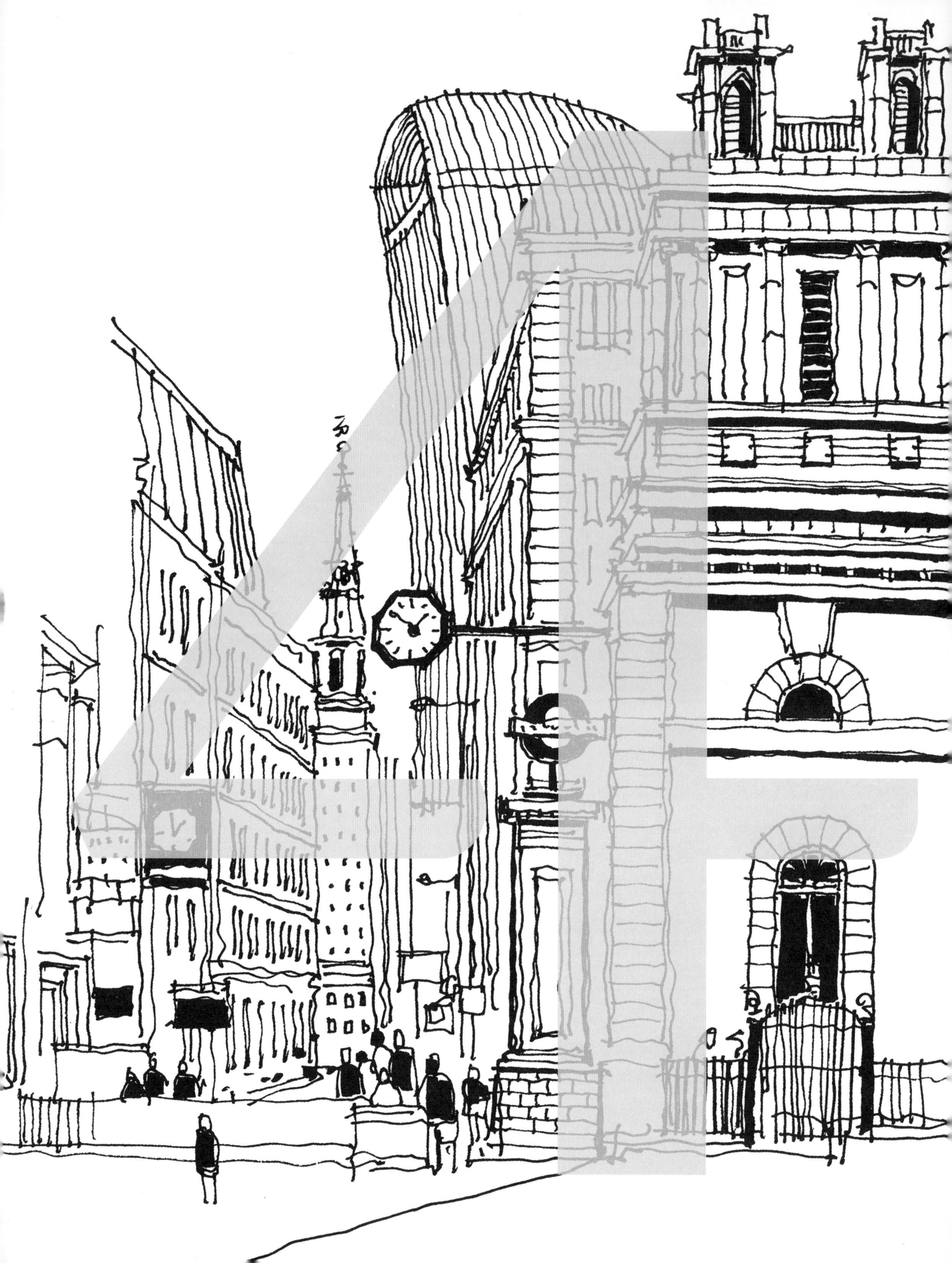

Taking it Further

This stage of the sketching journey is all about taking your sketches to the next level. But what does that really mean? It's about focusing on the incremental changes and making the extra effort in your approach. It's about challenging yourself to add detail and complexity to your sketches, and seeking ways to improve your images without overworking them.

Now that you understand the basic principles of urban sketching and are hopefully getting lots of practise, you have the foundation to explore new and exciting ways to transform the work you produce. There are many ways to enhance a basic line drawing and, in this chapter, I'll take you through a few of my tried-and-tested techniques to help turn your drawings into artworks.

We'll look at incorporating people into your artwork, which can bring life, vibrancy and energy to a sketch. We'll also look at deciding how close to reality your drawings should be, and explore ways to push the boundaries of your sketching and think more laterally about interpretation. We'll then look at how the addition of colour at the end of a work can be truly transformative.

People

When you're starting to practise drawing people, try adding them gradually to your sketches. Remember that they're not there to be the centre of attention, but to support your overall composition. When people are just background characters in your scenes, you don't need to be concerned with anatomical accuracy. In the first instance, just look to capture the essence of the form. You will soon find that you develop a default 'people style' for certain scenarios; quick gestural lines for busy crowds or simple line-and-dot marks to denote very small human forms, for instance.

When drawing a very large subject such as a skyscraper, try adding people to convey the scale of the scene. Even if they look like ants, they will help sell the sketch. If the people are a bit more substantial and you can't get away with little dots, measure them carefully against the other elements in your scene. A simple check using the thumb-and-pen technique (see page 34) is enough to make sure the scale of your people makes sense within the environment.

When sketching people close-up, start by loosening up with the exercise on page 28. Once you are used to getting your sketches started, find a quiet corner in a coffee shop and experiment by sketching a few static people. Build up your confidence gradually by applying the measurement techniques we looked at earlier to human proportions. The key is to look at your subject as much as possible.

It is worth taking inspiration from how other artists draw people in their sketches so that you can see how diverse the possible methods and styles are. The people drawn by British artist David Gentleman, for instance, have a beautiful economy and energy to them. A master of capturing people in minimal brushstrokes is L.S. Lowry. The workers in his urban environments are delightful in their brevity. Take note of how both artists merely suggest the human form without overworking the human figure, and try something similar in your next street scene.

Incorporating people into your sketches will do the following:
- Bring vitality, life and energy to a static scene
- Provide a wonderfully soft contrast to hard, architectural edges
- Give scale to the buildings and other elements
- Draw the viewer in to the sketch

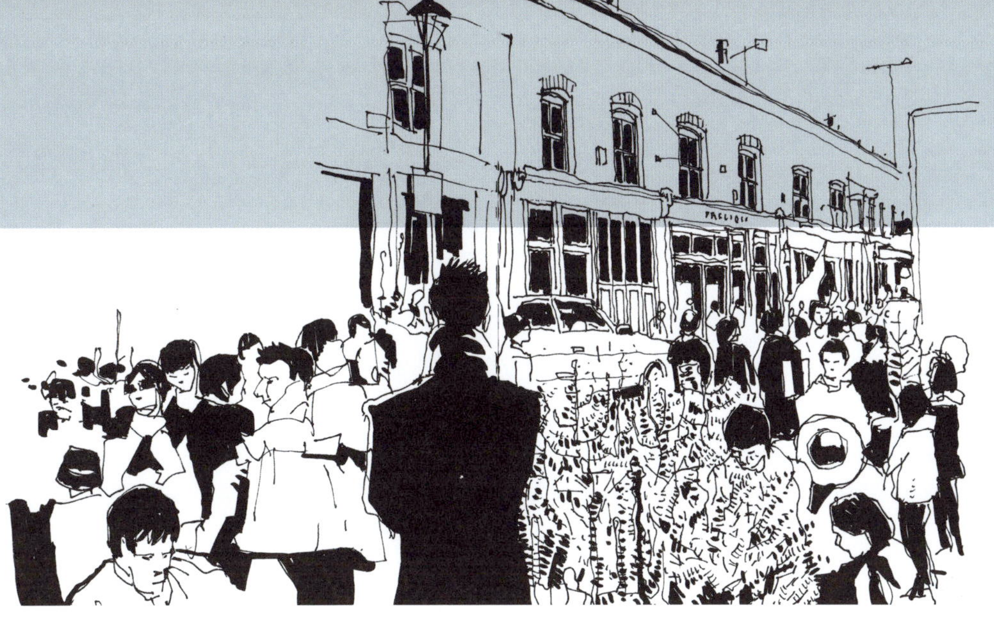

Bringing
energy to
a scene

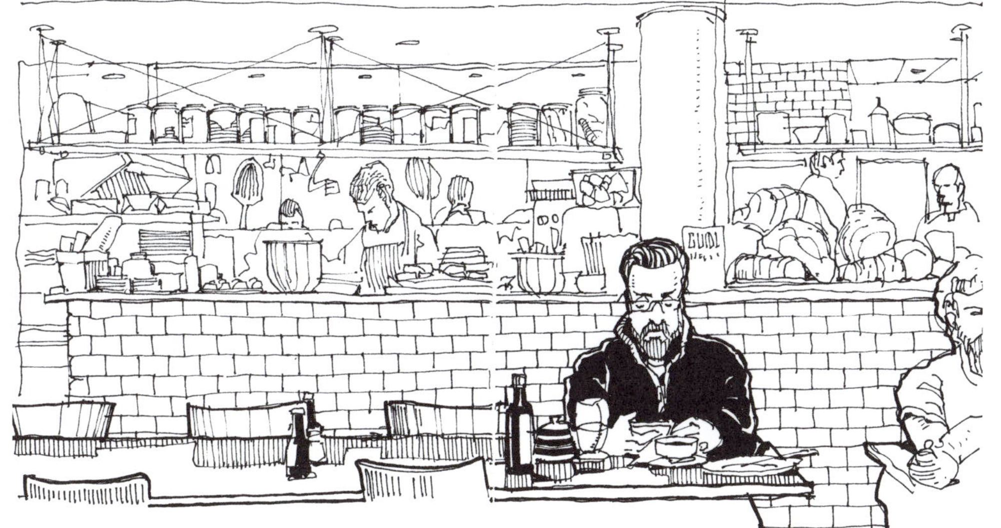

Developing
sketching
confidence

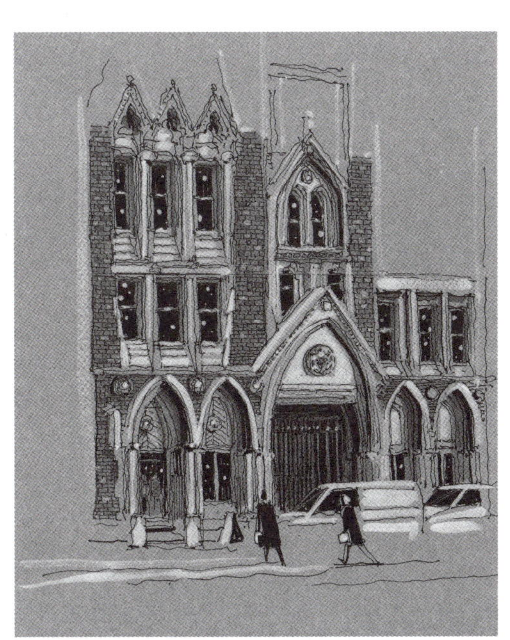

Adding
scale

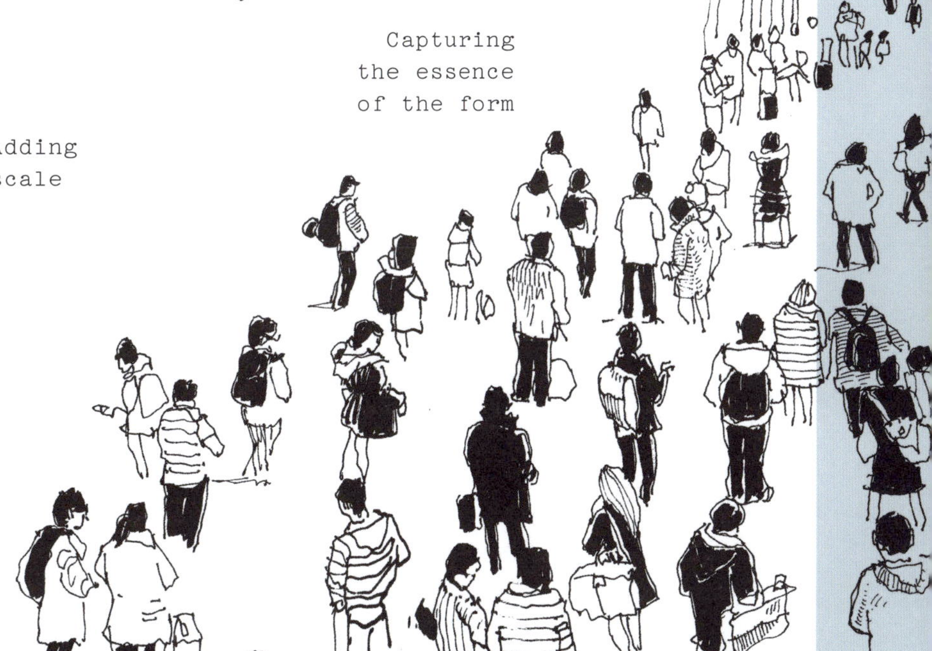

Capturing
the essence
of the form

Adding People to Enhance a Scene Exercise

For this exercise, find a busy street scene with interesting architecture and buildings that aren't too tall. You don't want the scale between the size of the people and the buildings to be too dramatic.

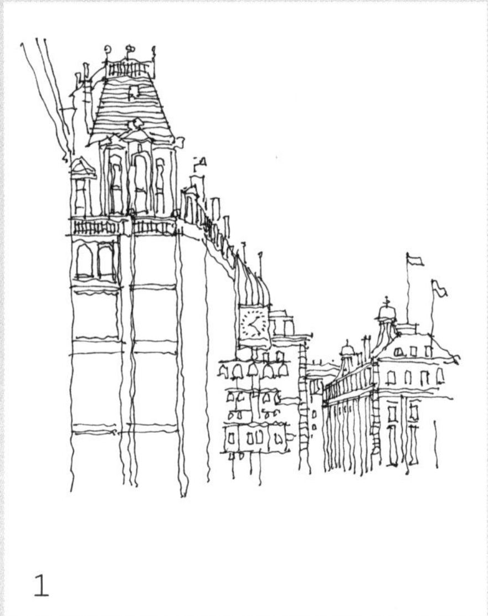

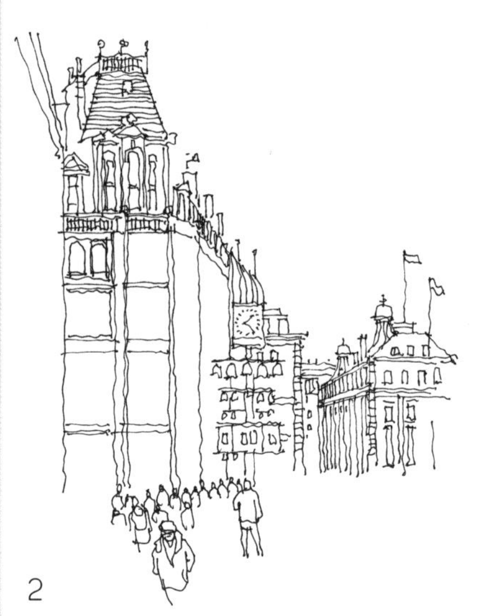

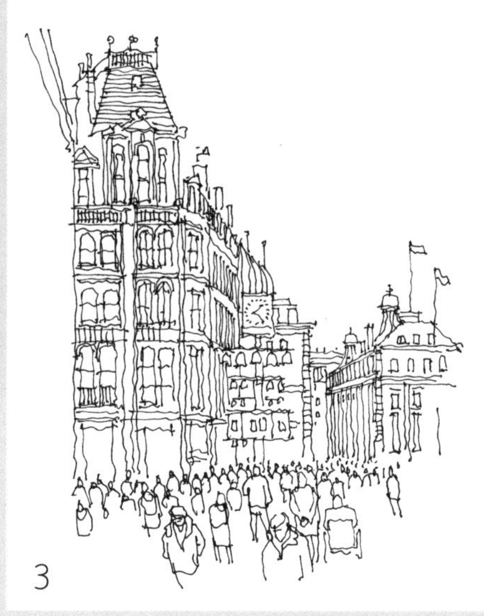

1. Start by drawing the buildings, and remember that they are still the star of your show. I drew freely and fast here in the same way that I will later add the people. Loosely drawn people can also be used to complement tightly drawn architecture, but in this instance I wanted the entire sketch to be fluid to reflect the busy scene I was capturing.

2. Build up the scene and start adding suggestions of people at street level. People farther away should be quite vague in shape – here I used a basic head-and-upper-body shape to suggest their form. People closer to you should be larger and more detailed, just as with the architecture. You will have to work quickly to capture people as they rush past you.

3. Alternate between the architecture and the people to keep your sketch balanced as it develops. Rather than adding every detail of a person, look for the little details that make them believable – backpacks, hats, coats, wheelchairs, dogs. Don't completely fill the scene; we're not looking for a football crowd in this sketch, but just enough activity to bring the street to life. The people farthest away are simply tiny flicks of the pen.

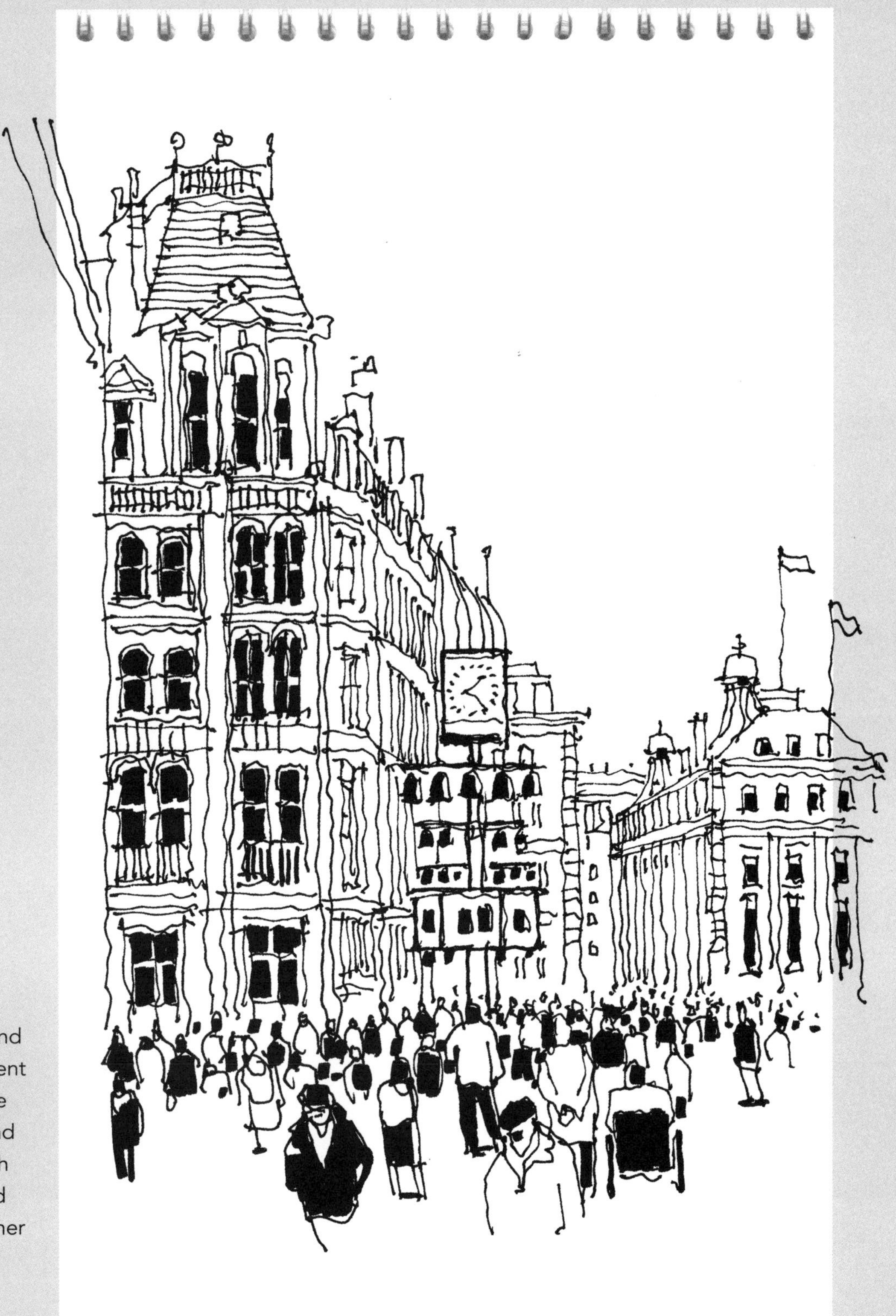

4. Select a small chisel-tipped pen and block in some dark shapes to represent dark fabrics, shadows and hair on the people in the scene. Be selective, and be careful not to fill all the space with solid black. Here, I added some solid black to the windows as well for further contrast and balance.

People in Detail
Exercise

In this exercise we zoom in on people in more detail, so it is best conducted indoors in a location where you have more time to observe and sketch with more control and comfort. Coffee shops, bars, airport lounges and hotel lobbies are all prime locations for taking time to observe and sketch people when they aren't dashing around. This doesn't mean they won't move (in fact, they certainly will), but you will have a better chance of capturing a great drawing of people if they are sitting down.

Choose a small group of people and find a quiet corner nearby so you can observe the scene unobtrusively – what we are looking for is reportage sketching, not posed scenarios.

I used pencil, which is a great medium for sketching people, as the softer lines it produces are very forgiving. I wanted to primarily use line with minimal tone and so I used a Koh-I-Noor 3B pencil for the foreground and a Staedtler HB for the background detail.

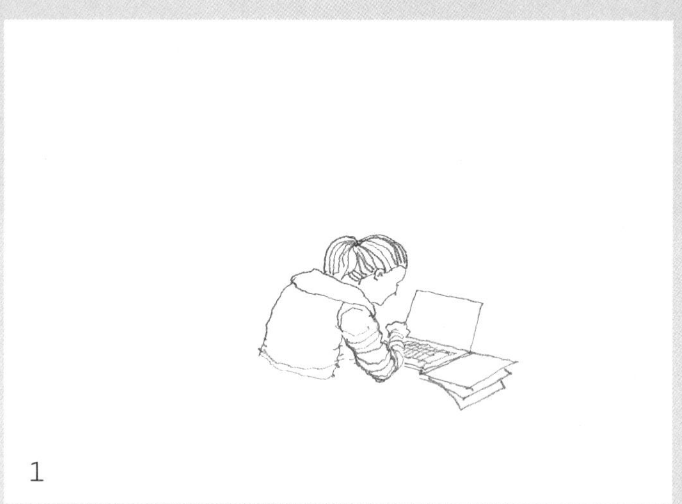

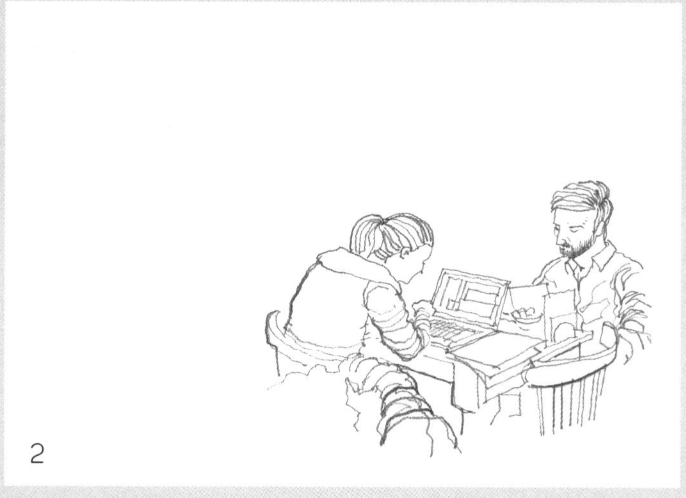

1. Start with the person nearest to you to set the scale for the drawing. Remember to be measuring constantly to make sure everything else you fill in is in proportion with this first person. People that are looking away from you as you sketch are a good place to start. Faces are often daunting, but remember that in sketching scenarios like this, there's only ever time to get a quick impression, and you can keep it as simple as you like while you gain confidence.

2. Build the sketch outwards to incorporate other people nearby, capturing as much of the surrounding detail as you can – coats hanging over the backs of chairs, papers spread on a table – as these all help bring the sketch to life. Be conscious of the non-people shapes in the scene – for instance, the laptop screen and the tabletop – and use the angle-measuring technique from page 34 to ensure they are an accurate size.

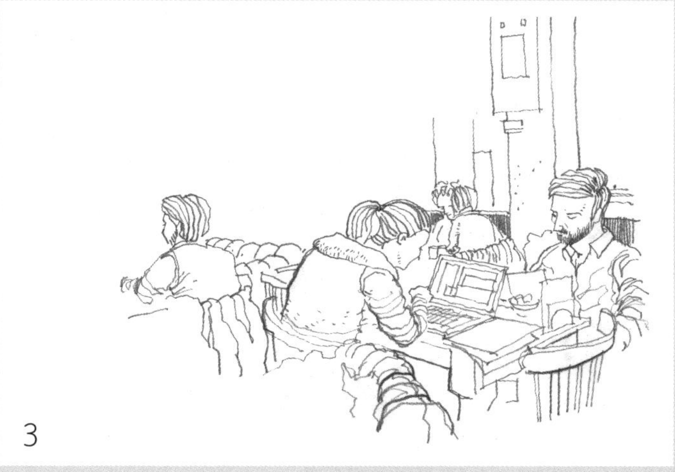

3. Vary the weights of your pencil lines on the subject in the foreground and take time to look at the folds and textures of their clothing and the way the fabric falls. Use your marks to suggest the creases of the material and the shape of the body beneath. Add in the background details closest to you, including other figures, to build up the scene.

4. Once you have sketched the people, you can focus on the background and surrounding elements at your leisure since they aren't in any danger of moving. Take your time adding the finishing touches that complete the story, using a lighter pencil for things that are farther away.

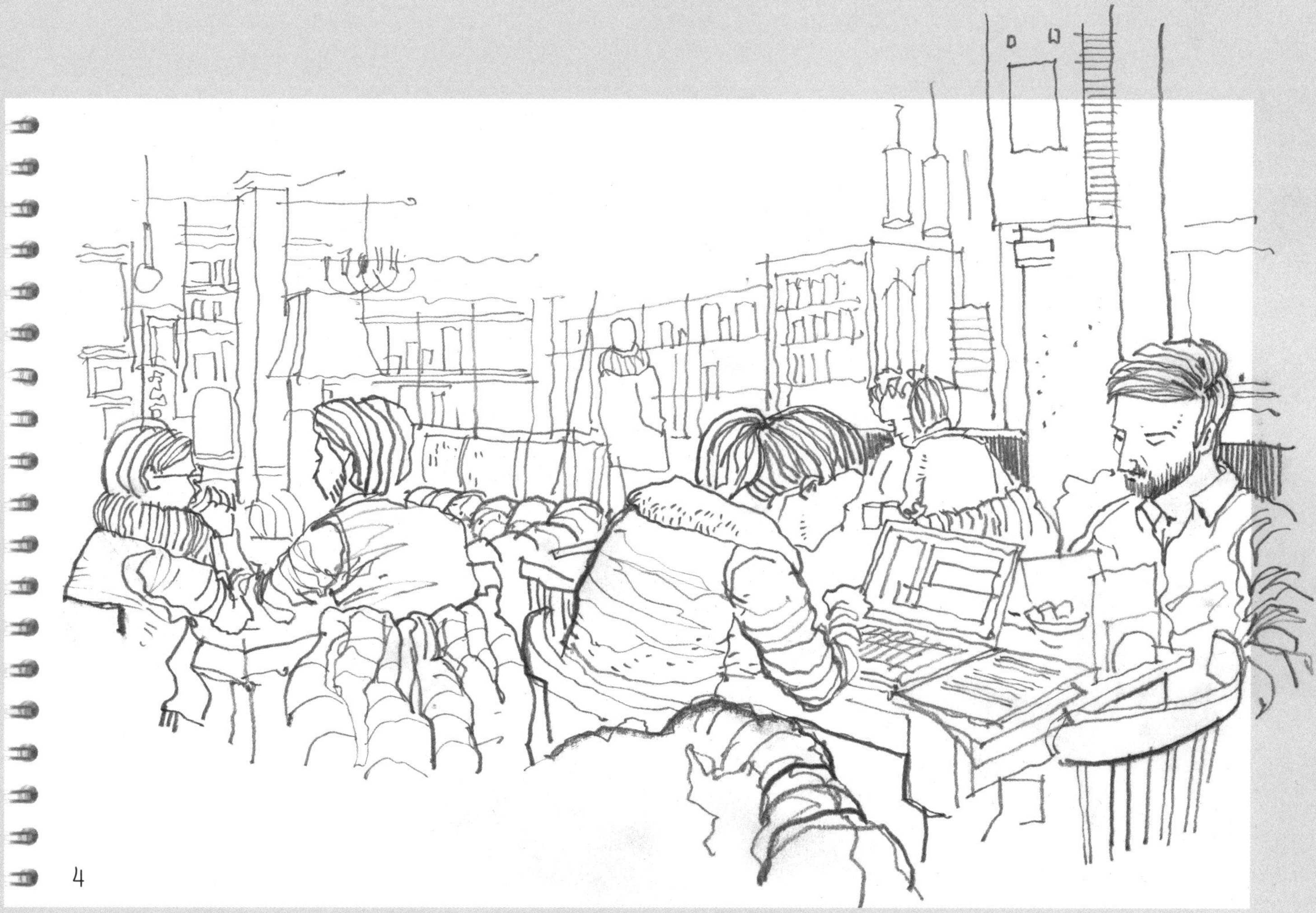

Creativity

In a recent sketching workshop that I ran, one of the participants moved a railway bridge about 50 metres so it sat next to a building because she thought it looked better. At first, I was shocked at the anarchy of her thinking, but on reflection I conceded that she was well within her rights to move the bridge — it was her drawing and she was free to do what she wanted. As urban sketchers, we can get too hung up on making every detail accurate, and I encourage all sketchers to use whatever means they like to produce great work that they are proud of.

- -

I tend to be fairly 'old school', and for me, using creative licence might be skipping a row of windows or knocking a floor off a building so it fits on the page. While it doesn't exactly constitute a sketching rebellion, I am able to bend the rules to suit my particular style or get what I want out of a scene. As I have already said, if you want an entirely faithful representation of a scene, take a photograph.

Creative licence can take many forms. It could be something practical like leaving something that doesn't fit your vision out of a sketch, remedying a mistake you have made by changing the structure of a scene or repositioning a key element to make sure it is included. Because urban sketching is a documentary exercise, creativity usually tends to be born out of necessity or the desire to make a drawing work harder. But you can push it as far as you want, creating a cityscape all of your own and unrecognizable to any inhabitants of the area, if you like.

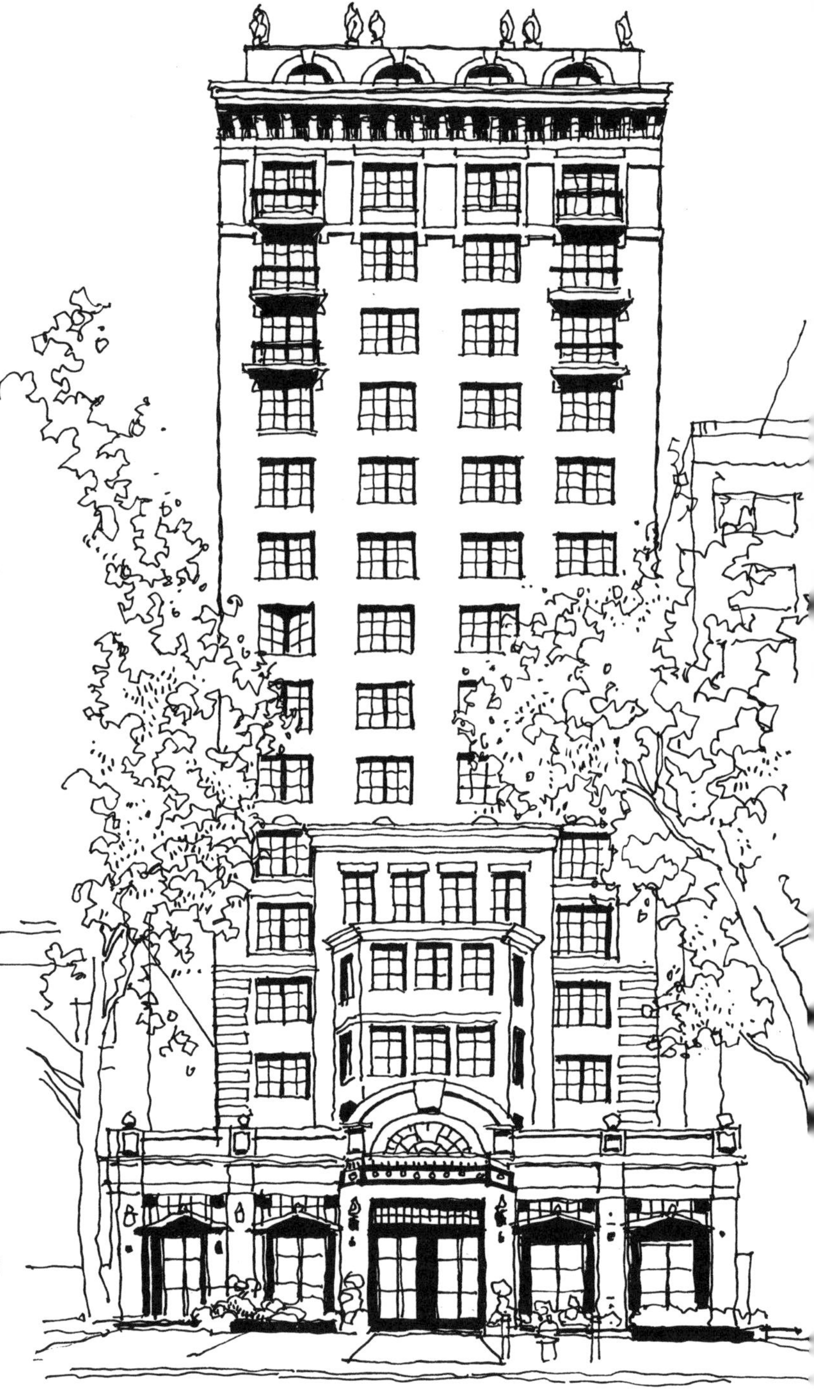

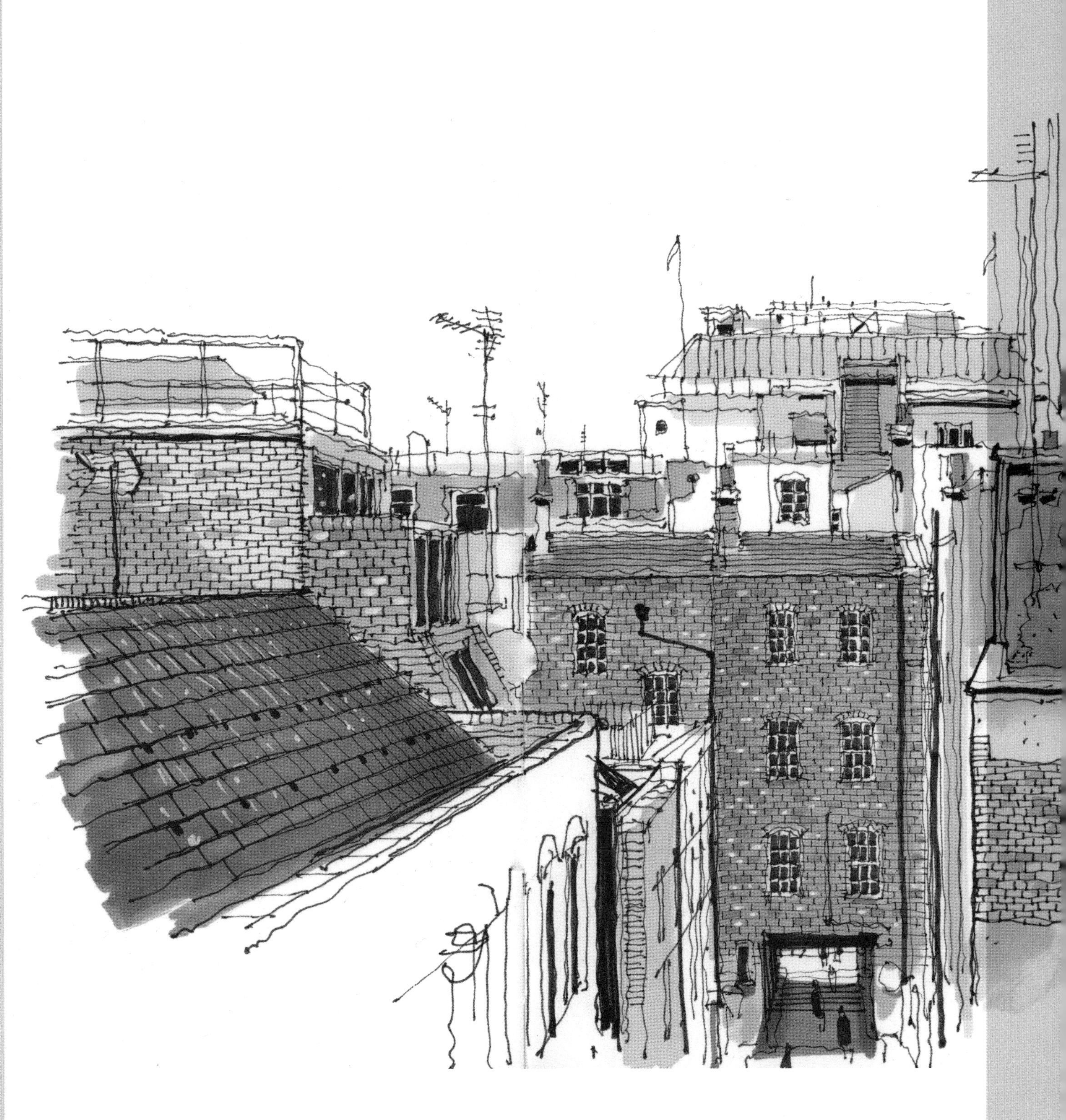

Creative Licence Examples

Here are some examples of sketches where I have deliberately changed elements in a scene or adapted the subject to deliver what I envisioned for the finished artwork. Some of the artworks are deliberately unreal to serve the aesthetic purpose of the drawing.

- -

1. Less accurate style

This street scene in London has been consciously drawn in a cartoonish style with little regard for realism. The linework is loose and jaunty, while the perspective is deliberately 'off'. The black linework was drawn on grey Canson paper using a fountain pen, and the black tone was added with a chisel-tipped pen. Note how I have left details out of the scene, such as most of the brickwork, and left buildings unfinished to serve the overall composition.

2. Modernist New York

This drawing was inspired by the vibrant New York drawings of American modernist painter Abraham Walkowitz. Seeing his work made me want to interpret the New York skyline in an unusual way. Armed with a photographic reference, I used charcoal of different widths to create an uncanny view of the city. I worked into the sketch with white chalk, smudging and blending with my fingers. This is a great example of where a scene does not have to be realistic to be effective. Creativity is to be encouraged!

3. Skewed perspective

The linework in this sketch does not represent a normal perspective of the buildings, nor does it faithfully follow the lines of the shapes. I wanted to create a light-hearted version of the scene with little regard to accuracy. The awkward angle of the spire and the skewed oval perspective of the church sets the tone and allows everything else around it to be interpreted in the same way.

Meanwhile, the unfinished building represented by just a rough outline on the left-hand side adds to the slightly unreal feel.

4. Cubist London

I have sketched this view in London many times. The contrast of modernist architecture and classic buildings creates a pleasing view for sketching. Inspired by 1920s cubist painter Robert Delaunay, I thought it would be interesting to interpret this scene with a different approach. I drew in all the main shapes, paying little attention to the rules of drawing, using black pen and ink on tinted paper. I then added blocks of white gouache at the end. The architectural details are represented simply – there is an energy and freedom to working this way.

5. Breaking traditional sketch conventions

This internal view of an old building plays havoc with perspective and contains virtually no straight lines. It breaks traditional sketch conventions but delivers a playful interpretation of what would be a mundane scene if drawn 'correctly'. The key to working in this way is to commit to the effect – decide you are going to try to achieve it before you start and follow through till the end. Combining curved ceilings and off-kilter walls, and adding uneven, inaccurate detailing creates an uneasy feel. Tone is used simply to denote planes within the room and help balance the sketch with a touch of realism.

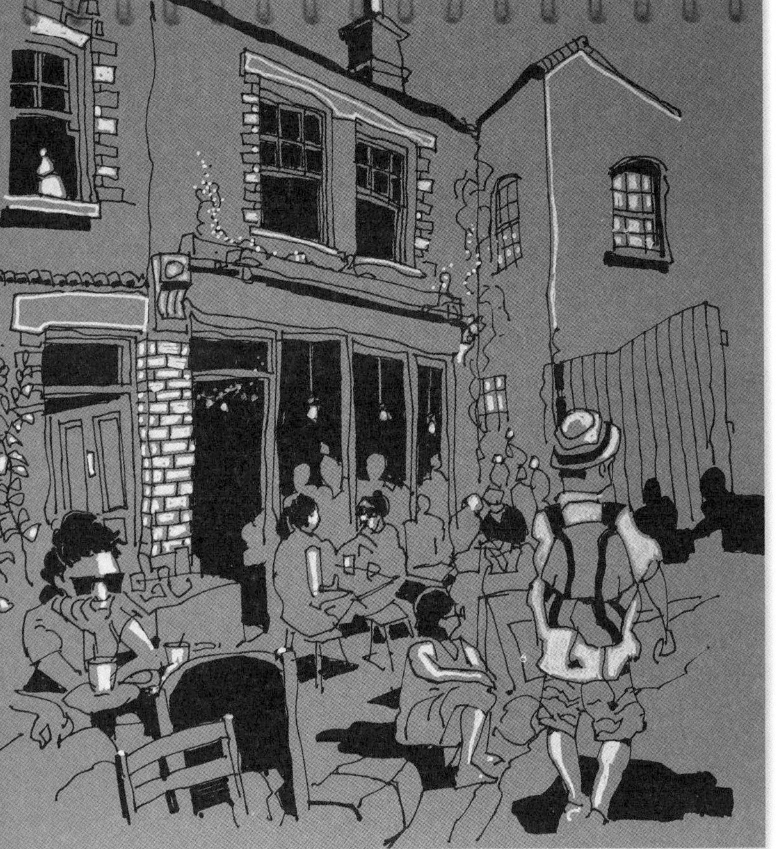

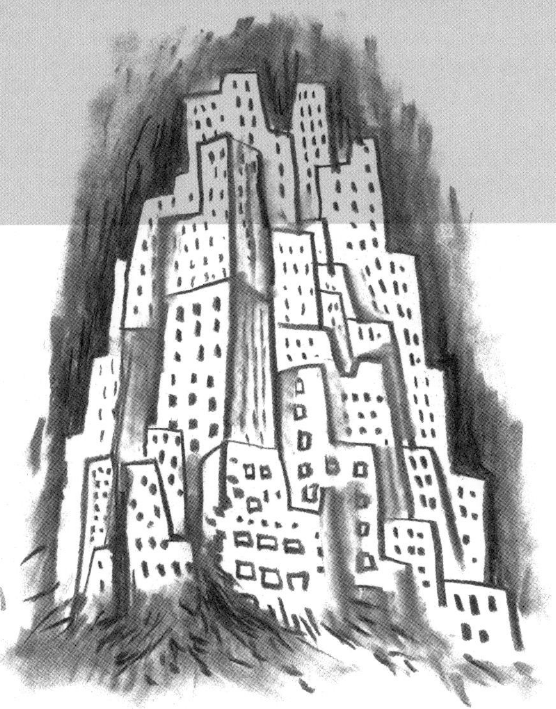

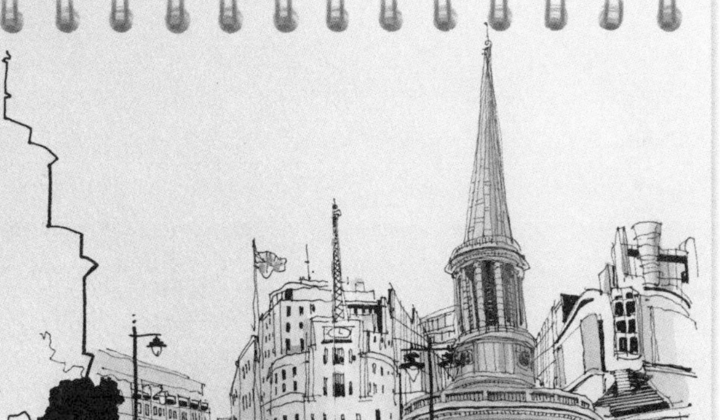

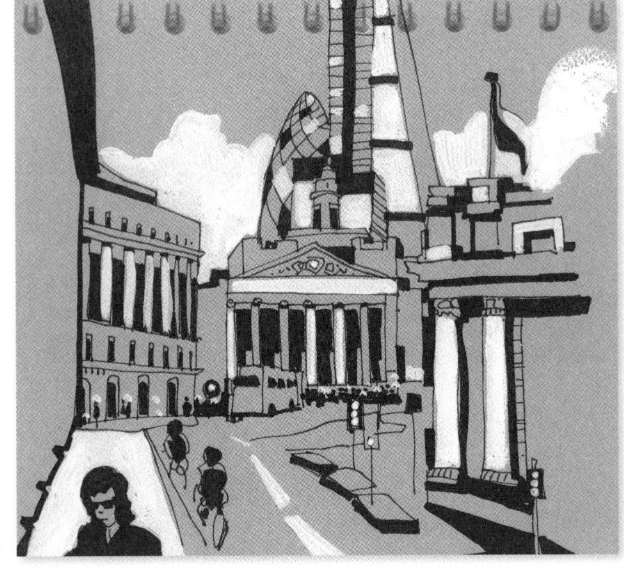

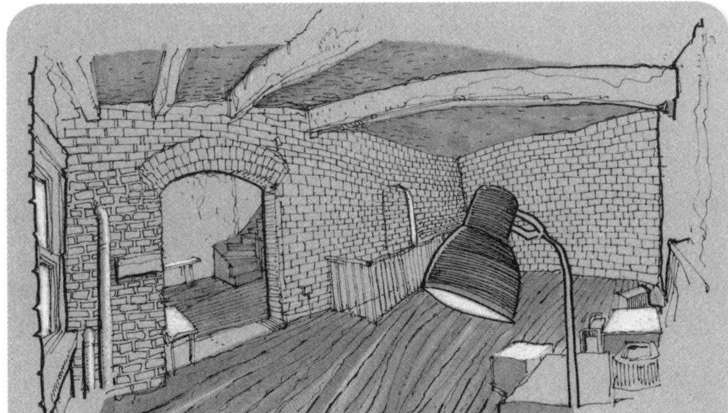

How to Use Creative Licence Exercise

The aim of this exercise is to show how editing your vision of the scene in front of you can produce a more effective sketch. At each stage, I explain how I have used creative licence to make the sketch tell a story. Every single drawing you produce will contain some version of artistic licence and I encourage you to embrace that.

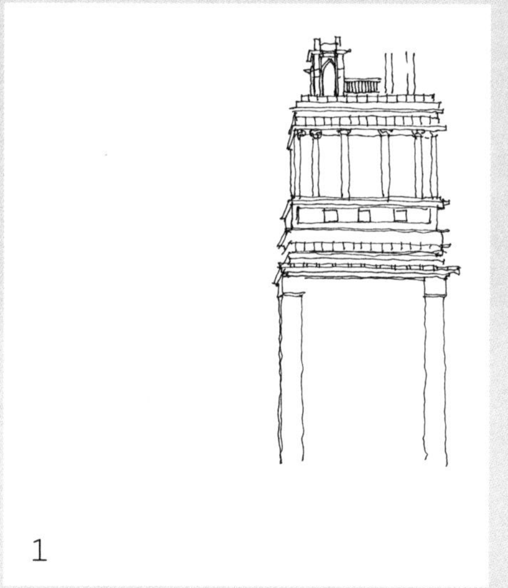

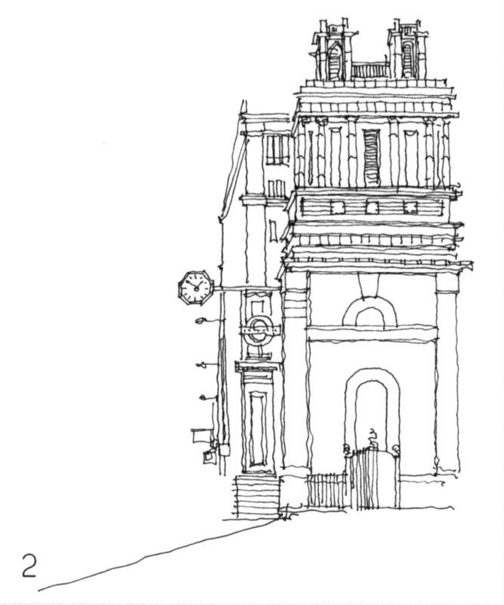

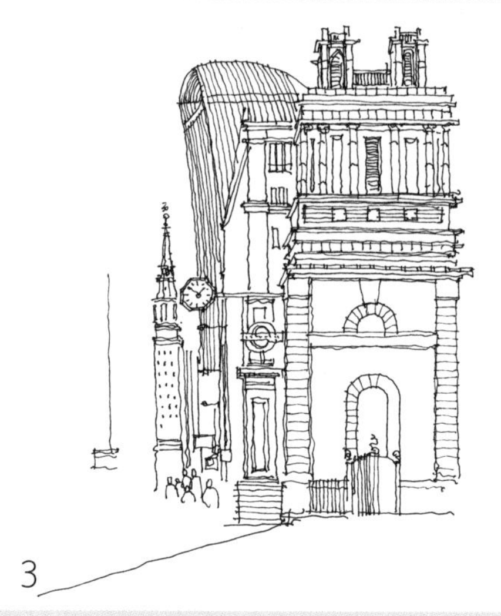

1. Begin your sketch with the key building or monument you want to include. In my example, while I captured the basic structure of the church, I did not count every single block. Get the basic structure right, and then use your eye to add the detail as you go.

2. Start taking artistic liberties by selecting details you want to include in your image and deciding what you would prefer to leave out. In my sketch, I moved the clock to the left so that it stands out more and I slightly adjusted the height of the column in the foreground. You can reposition items to suit your composition.

3. Look at the rest of your scene and decide what other elements you want to include. In my sketch, the large, curved skyscraper in the background (known to Londoners as the 'Walkie Talkie') has been moved to the left as it wasn't originally in my line of sight. To sketch it, I changed my view slightly before returning to my original position. In this montage of views, I also moved the church a little away from the buildings so that it could be seen.

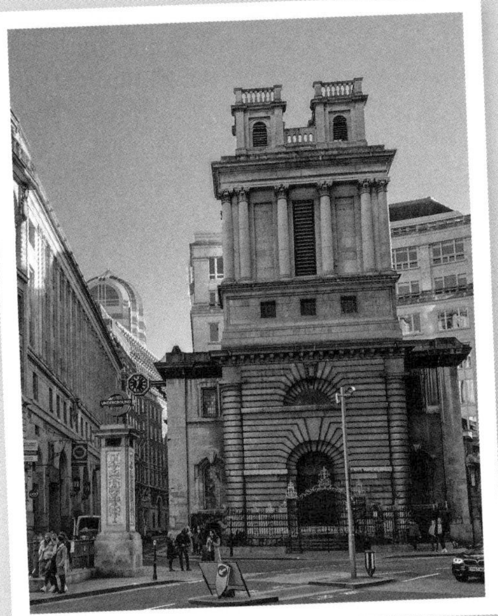

Photograph of the actual view

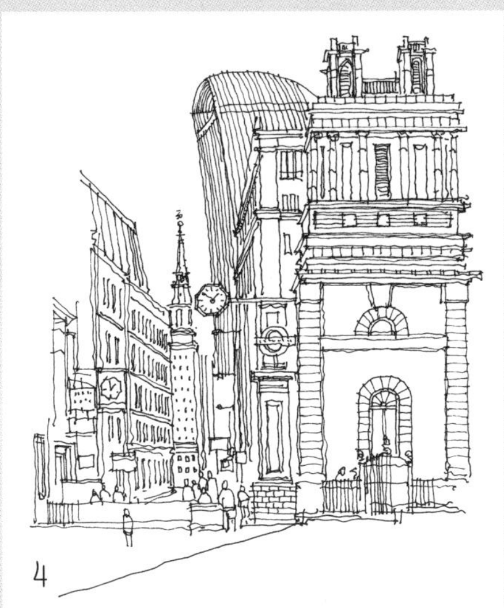

4

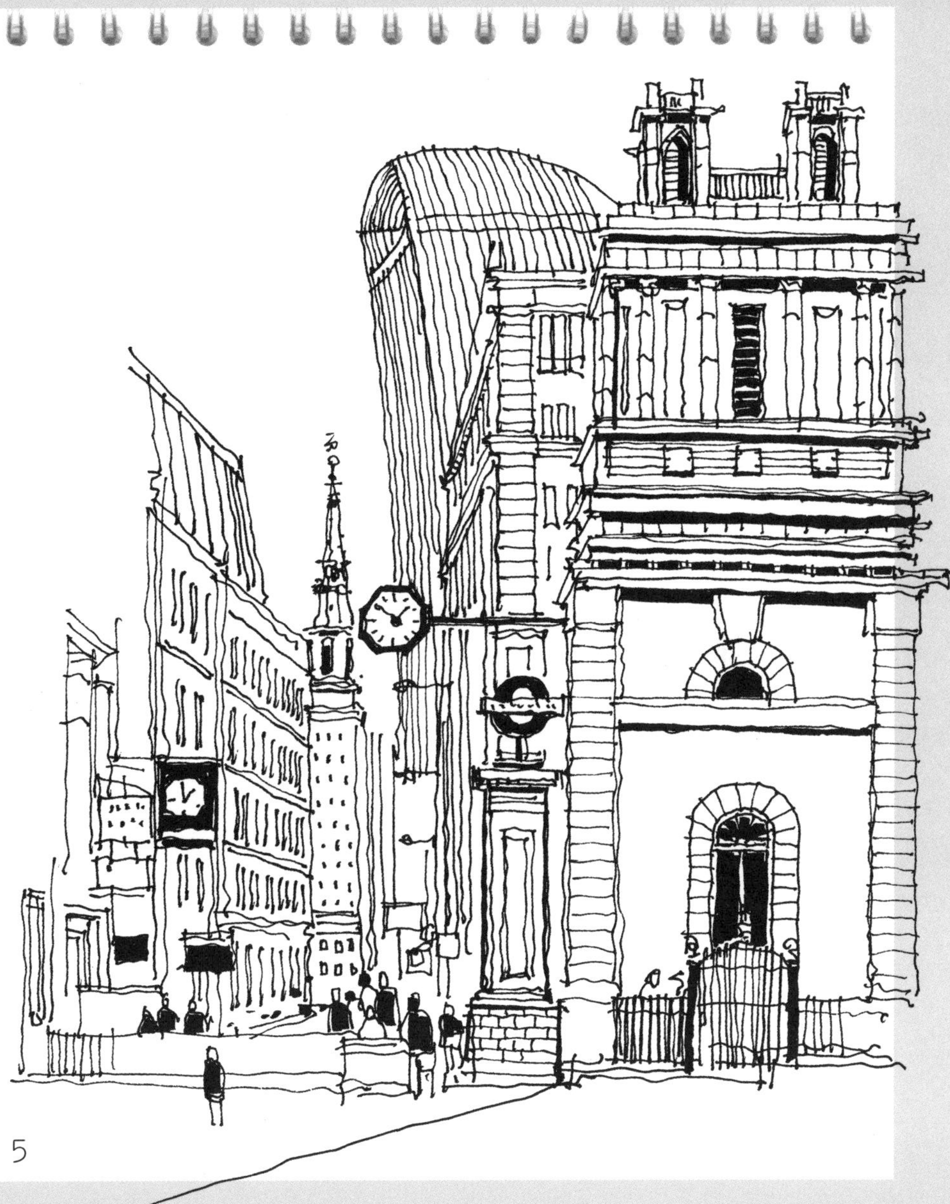

5

4. As I built the sketch out to the left, I added people that weren't really there to give scale, as well as additional signage to add to the story of the street scene. Think about the tweaks you can make to balance your artwork and don't worry if these elements aren't present in real life. I've also left out a huge chunk of stonework detail in the foreground because I think the scene works well without it.

5. Add some tone or contrast to balance your sketch and make it look good, as opposed to realistic. I've added solid blocks of black that are vaguely representative of the subject matter but not entirely true to life. Artistic licence has been pretty extensively used in this sketch, but in subtle, believable ways. It's not necessarily about making things up that are not there, but making the subject matter work well in the finished composition.

Details

Urban sketching is not always about detail. Often, the
simplest line drawings can capture the flavour of a scene,
and some of the most satisfying sketches are drawn quickly
with light detail. The question for every sketcher is, can
my quick capture be enhanced with the considered application
of more detail? So: when does a sketch need the extras and
when do you leave it alone?

The key is to look at your sketch and think about what
could be added to develop the story and add texture,
depth and interest. If the drawing has enough personality
as it is, maybe don't meddle with it. If you feel that it
doesn't work hard enough, then consider adding some
more detail.

Here are some examples where the addition of detail has
transformed the original sketch:

Crowds – the original sketch of this cricket match was
mainly just the bare bones. It has been greatly enhanced
and brought to life by the addition of detailed crowd texture
using pen and marker.

Reflections – this hotel sketch from Chicago was satisfactory
as linework, but drawing in the reflections of the trees in the
windows adds significantly more depth to the scene.

Brickwork – a perfect illustration of how adding textural
lines to represent the character of a building can elevate a
sketch's authenticity. Brickwork requires patience, but the
more carefully the bricks are drawn, the better the finished
result will be.

People – we have already looked at how human activity can
be used to great effect as storytelling details. This sketch
uses a few key people in the foreground and a larger mass
of indistinct people farther off to give scale and movement.

Trees – it can be painstaking, but take the time to add
detailed renderings of the leaves, trunks and branches
of trees. This autumn sketch highlights the tonal texture
to the leaves, which brings a richness to the finished piece.

Tone – this rooftop sketch from France looked very plain
until the addition of tone took it to another level. It uses
marker and pencil to breathe life into this potentially
mundane artwork – the rooftops and foliage work
particularly well together.

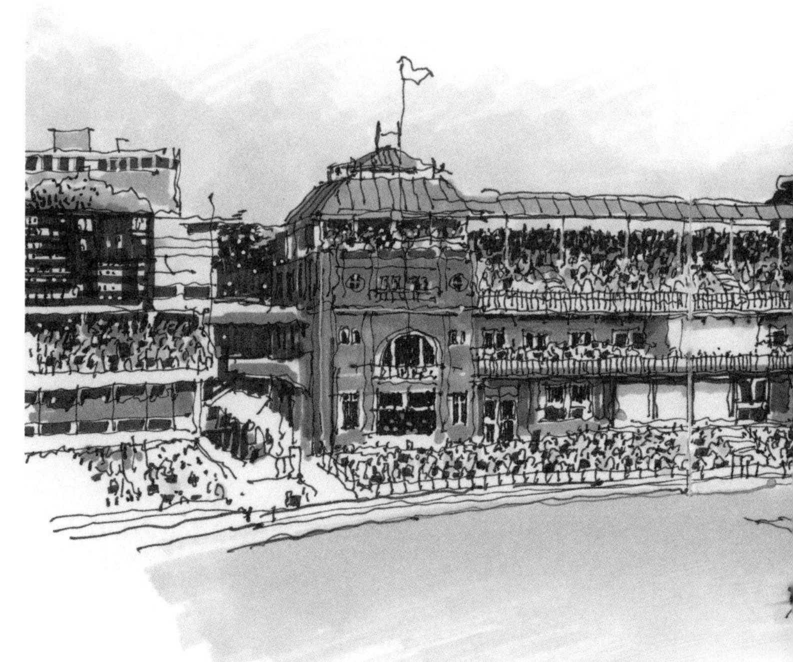

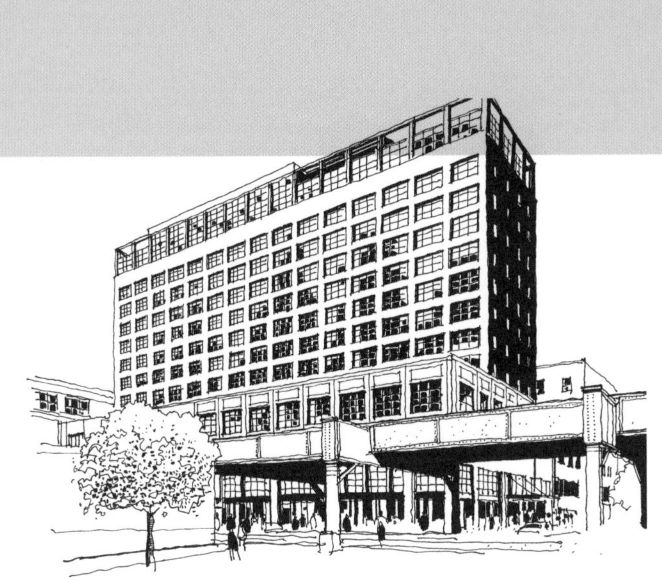

Reflections

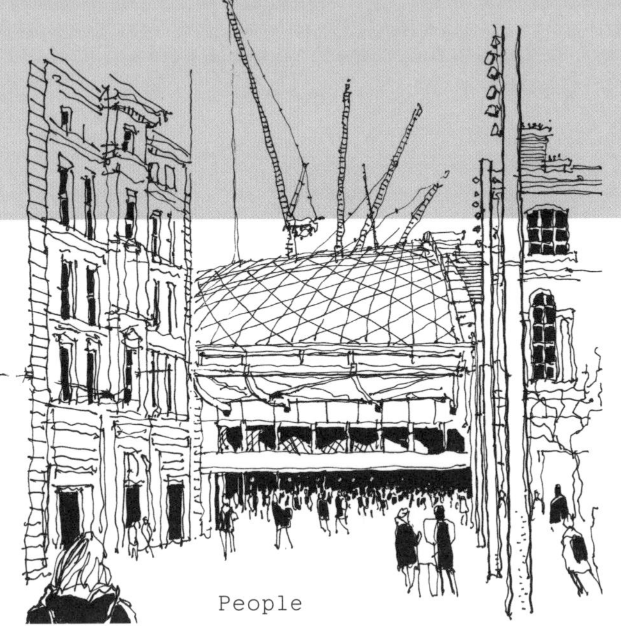

People

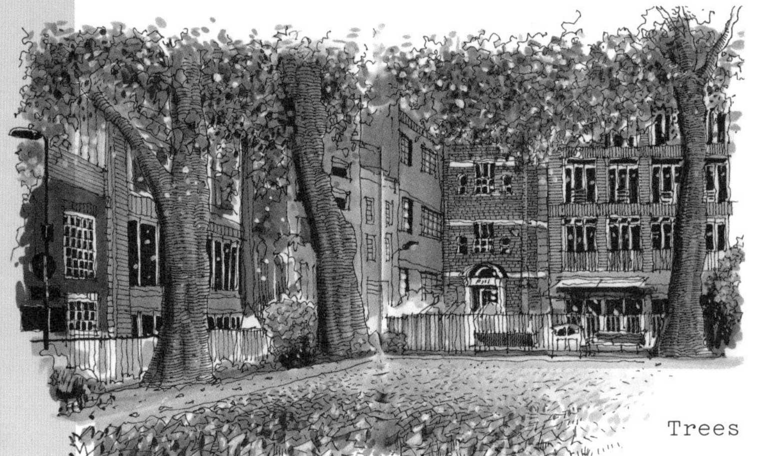

Trees

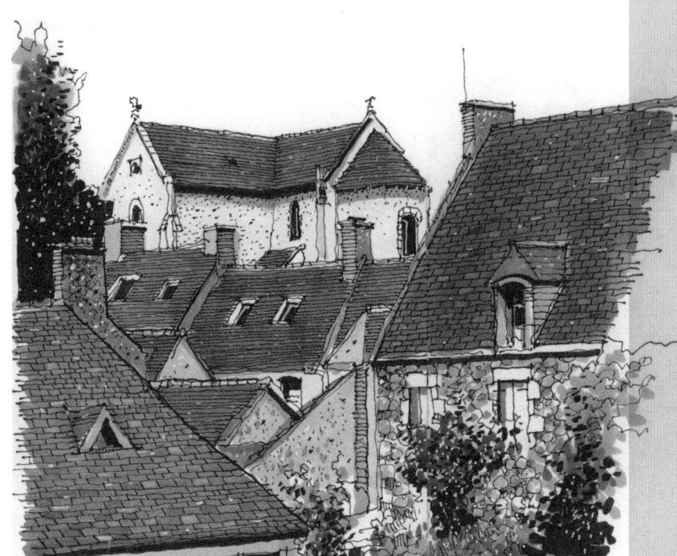

Tone

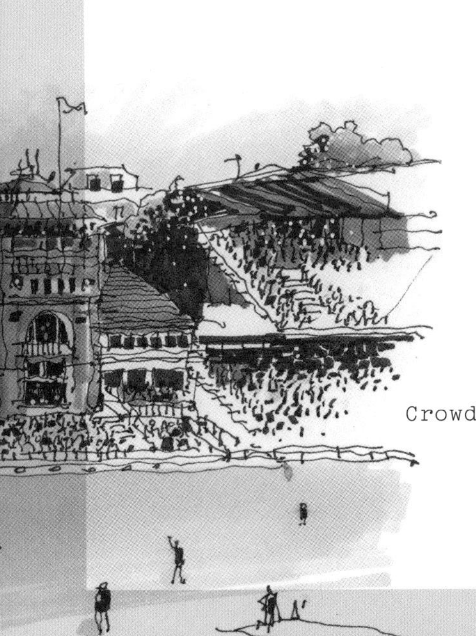

Crowds

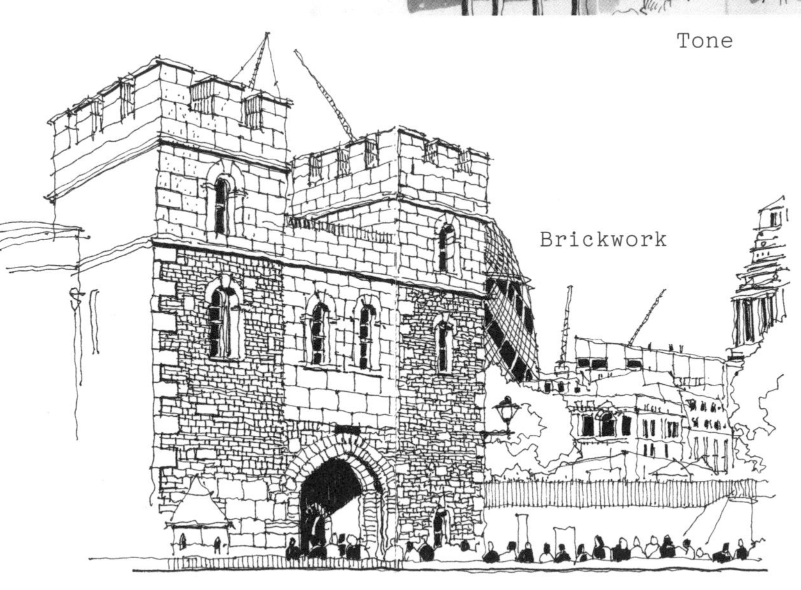

Brickwork

When to Add Details
Exercise

This exercise starts with a simple line sketch and finishes with a more interesting and enticing finished illustration, in marker, gouache and pen. Choose a line drawing of your own that you feel could do with a bit more love and attention – this is when it's good to have saved a reference photo.

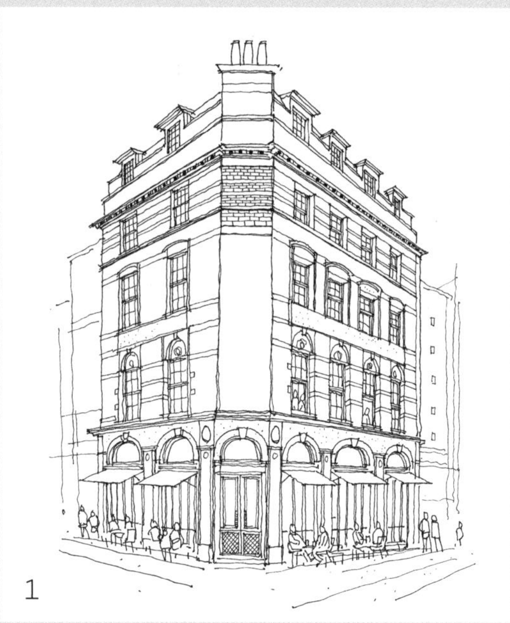

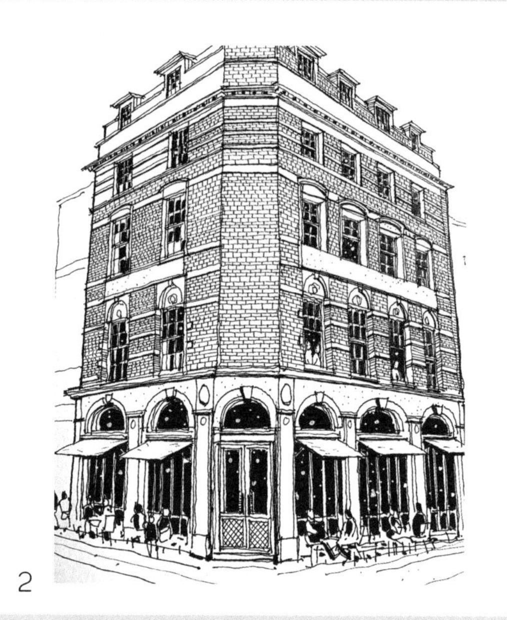

1. The outline of this pub in East London was drawn using a 0.3mm fineliner pen. It is an elegant and strong building, but the sketch is crying out for more detail. As it stands, not including all of the Edwardian architectural features is a missed opportunity, and there is much colour and texture that could be added, which would not be possible using just pen.

2. To begin with, think about the building materials and the different textures in your scene. In my case, what stood out was the classic brickwork. Using a thin fineliner pen (I used 0.02mm), I carefully filled in the texture of the bricks. Each brick must be dealt with individually, with the pattern of bricks drawn accurately. When adding brickwork, be mindful of the perspective and try to follow the lines of the building. There are different ways to draw brickwork, but the quickest and by far the most effective is to set up some guidelines for the layers of bricks at the top, bottom and middle, and work from them.

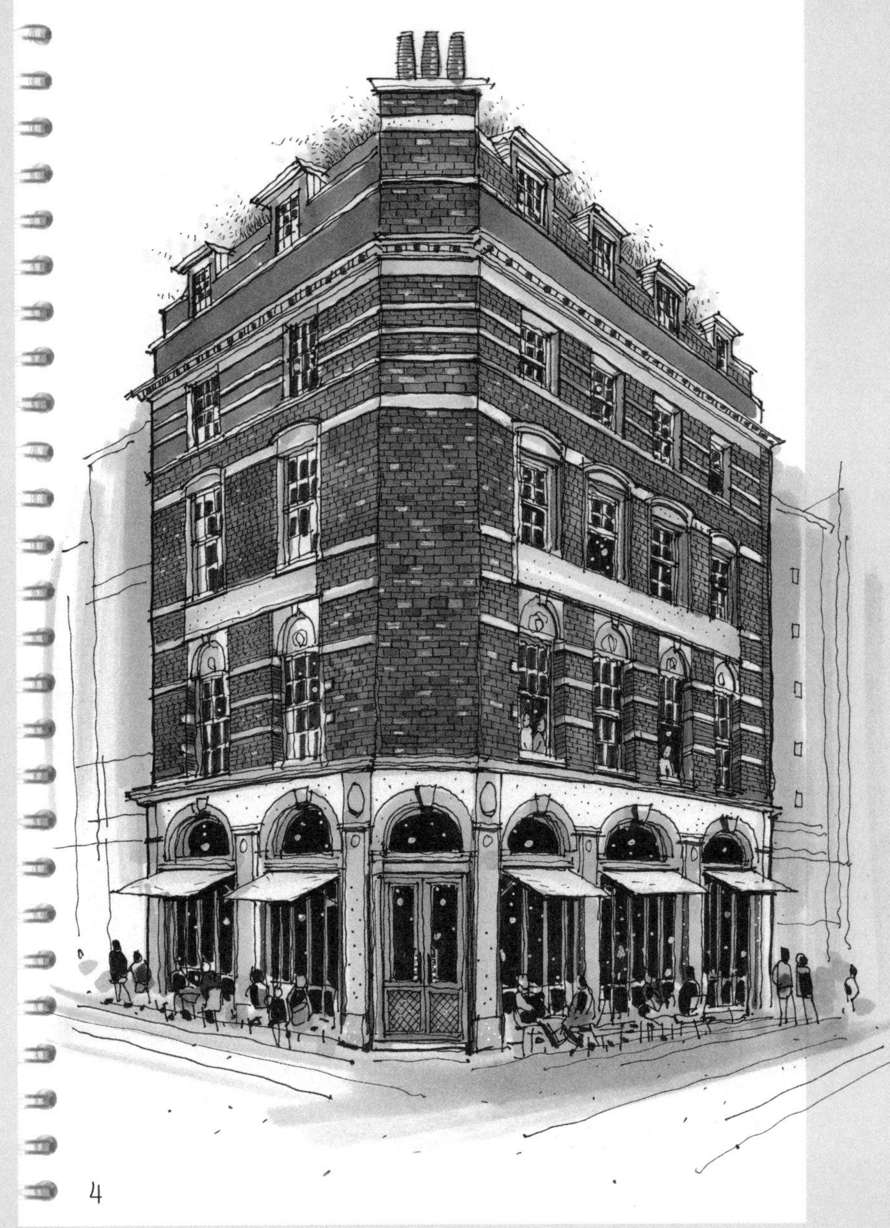

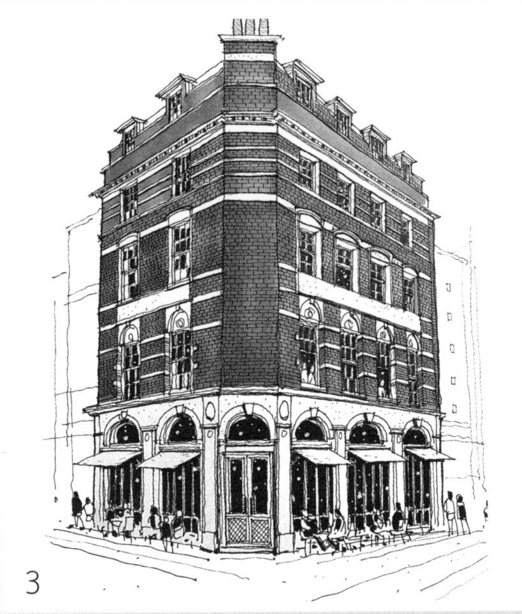

3. The next stage of detail is to add some tone. I used a Winsor & Newton Cool Grey 5 brush marker to lay the colour flat across the texture of the bricks, and then I used the point of the brush to get the ink into the corners of the windows. As you add marker tone, keep an eye out for linework that needs refining. Use a white gel pen or white gouache to add lighting inside windows to give the building an occupied feel.

4. Finally, add highlights and dark areas across your piece. I used the thin end of a Cool Grey 5 marker to randomly add some darker bricks, keeping within the lines for a controlled feel. Don't be tempted to overdo these darker elements as it can make the overall effect too heavy. Using white pencil and white gel pen, dot in more highlights – in my case, paler bricks to complement the darker ones in equal measure. Finally, I used Cool Grey 1 and 2 pens to softly blend in peripheral shading on the pavement and adjacent buildings, and I finished off with tiny flecks of black ink for final textural flourishes.

Colour

Colour can be used in a way that works to improve the realism and believability of a sketch, however, it can also be used in a more creative way to complement the qualities or composition of a sketch. Fundamentally, urban sketching is not about photorealism and therefore any colour you add to your sketches doesn't need to exactly resemble the scene you are looking at. Remember this when you begin to explore a more complex use of colour with your sketching.

- -

I love the use of colour by the 18th-century Venetian painter Canaletto in his cityscapes – the way light hits the buildings is lush and atmospheric. He applied an artistic interpretation to the cities he painted and I appreciate his meticulous detail, yet willingness to stray from total accuracy for the sake of creating a masterpiece.

For the urban sketcher, colour can come in the form of different media, including watercolour, marker, pencil and gouache. While adding colour on location requires an array of materials and a degree of preparation, it is completely doable. It can, however, be a lot easier to add colour when back at a desk, using photographic references. Another benefit of this is that you have more freedom to experiment with colour combinations before you commit to them. This process also works well for artists who set out on a sketching mission not really knowing where they will end up or what they will be sketching. Packing materials to cover every eventuality means carrying a cumbersome bag around, which is not very practical in the urban environment.

When adding colour to a sketch, think about how it can be selectively added rather than applying full colour to every part. Most of the time, it is the colours of architectural features – surfaces such as stone, brick, concrete and wood – that vary from place to place and dominate the urban landscape, setting the tone for the overall palette you use.

The sketch opposite provided the perfect opportunity to add colour in a highly selective way for maximum impact. The original drawing of this central London scene was a pleasing architectural study, but it was transformed by the addition of a single colour to mark out the capital's famous red buses. If you think a clean line sketch could be improved by minimal spot colour, think about the context of the sketch and what is significant in that city or view. It could, for example, be gold edging on a monument, the wine in a glass or a brightly coloured piece of clothing.

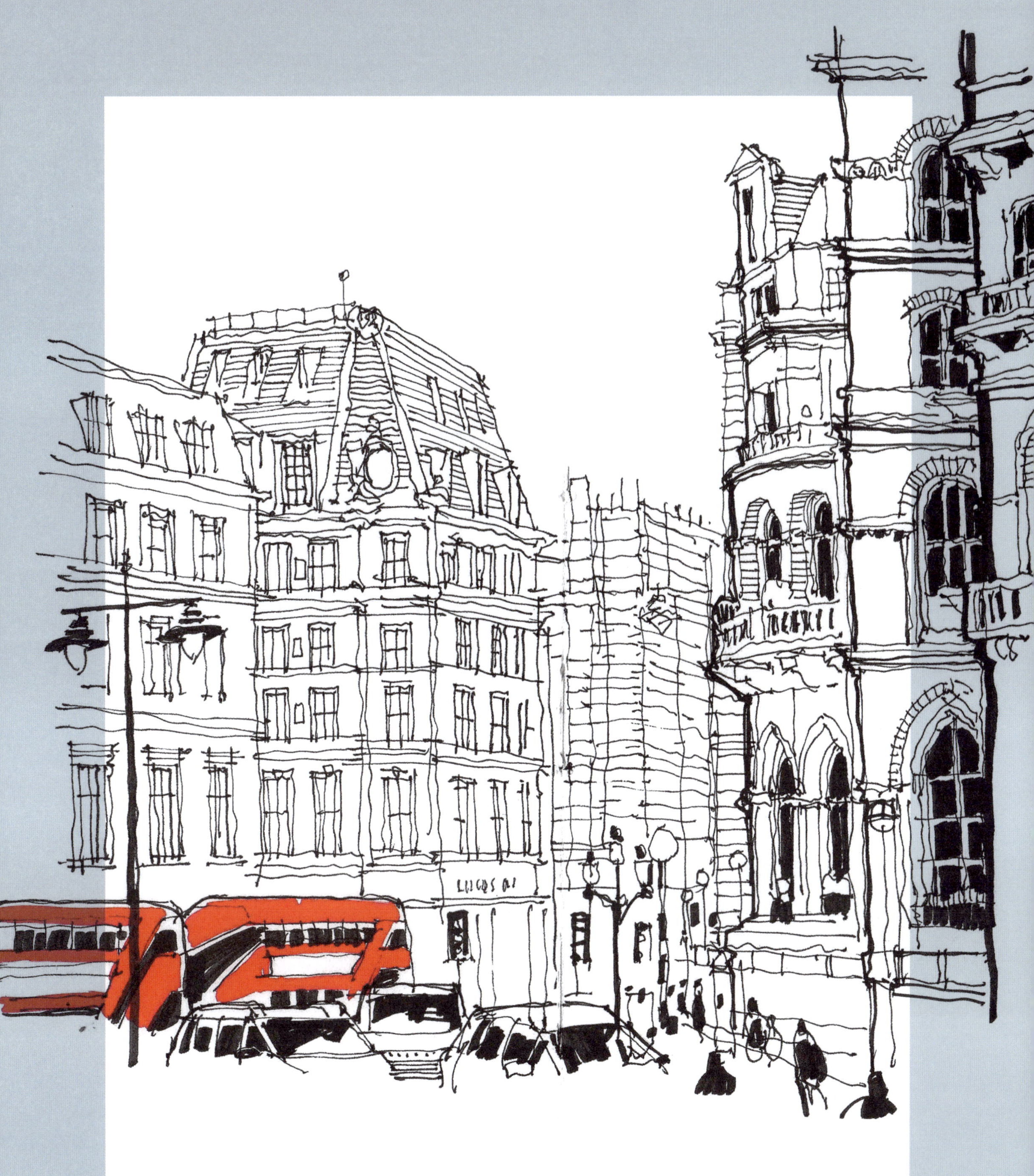

Monochrome Colour Exercise

This exercise explores the restrained use of minimal colour and the
power of a monochrome scheme to deliver impact and focus the eye.
In this exercise, I used Winsor & Newton brush markers because of the
control they give for both blending and adding detail. The original
sketch of this view was done quickly in Córdoba, Spain, in very hot
weather, so I decided to add to it later in the comfort of my studio
using a photographic reference.

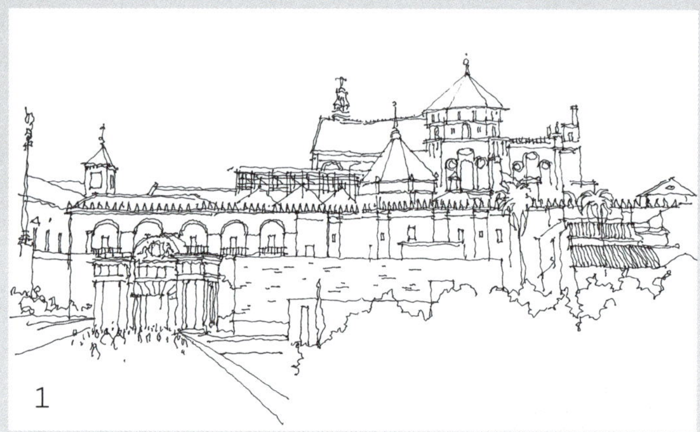

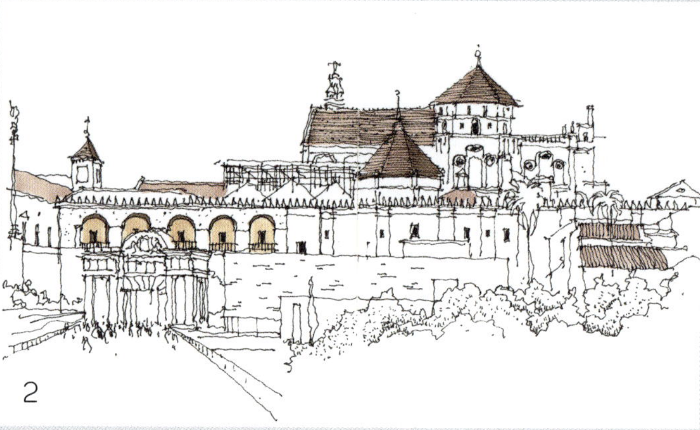

1. Pick one of your linework sketches where the original
view featured has some interesting pops of colour. This
exercise is all about using limited colour, so select no more
than four shades of one or two family of colours – warm,
cool or neutral – and also a black for contrast. Think about
the features you want to capture and their size and texture.
In this instance, I wanted to focus on the roof tiles as well as
parts of the main building. I chose warm oranges for the
brick and neutral colours for the stone. Try out your colours
on a scrap of paper (the same type that your sketch is on) to
see how the colours work together on the page.

2. From the outset, be clear what you want the finished
piece to look like. In this sketch, I was keen to retain
elements of bare line drawing around the edges but I
wanted to put the focus on the building in the centre by
adding colour there. Carefully begin to add colour to your
focal point. If you want to keep it fairly realistic, match the
colour as closely as possible to the original detail and take
care to observe where the sun hits and the shadows fall.

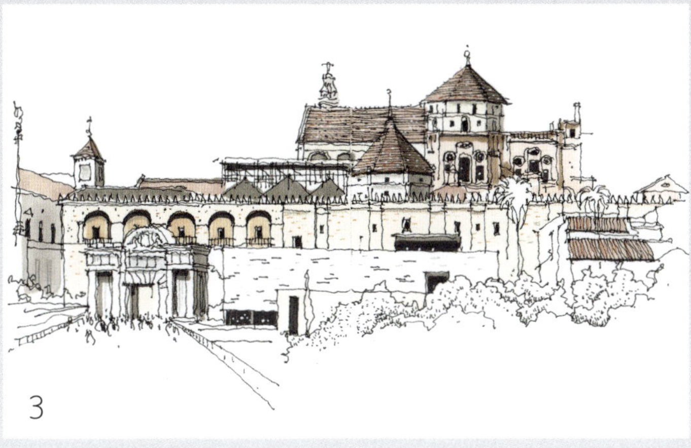

3

3. Lay the less dominant colours down first, then build depth by experimenting (cautiously) with overlaying colours that work well together. Solvent markers are particularly good for blending. A limited palette can be helpful in that you don't have to search endlessly for the perfect colour. Don't be afraid to leave white gaps in the drawing as it will help with the composition. Be fairly free with the colour application too; it is fine if colours overlap or don't quite fill the shapes.

4. Add a few more subtle details to the sketch with your colours, as I have done here on the brickwork and the roof tiles, but don't be tempted to fill every part of the sketch with colour. Go back over some of the earlier colours with the same pen and you will see how it gently builds depth. Beef up some of the black areas so that they don't get lost against the colours, and if the linework needs a little bit of adjusting, then work back into the lines as needed.

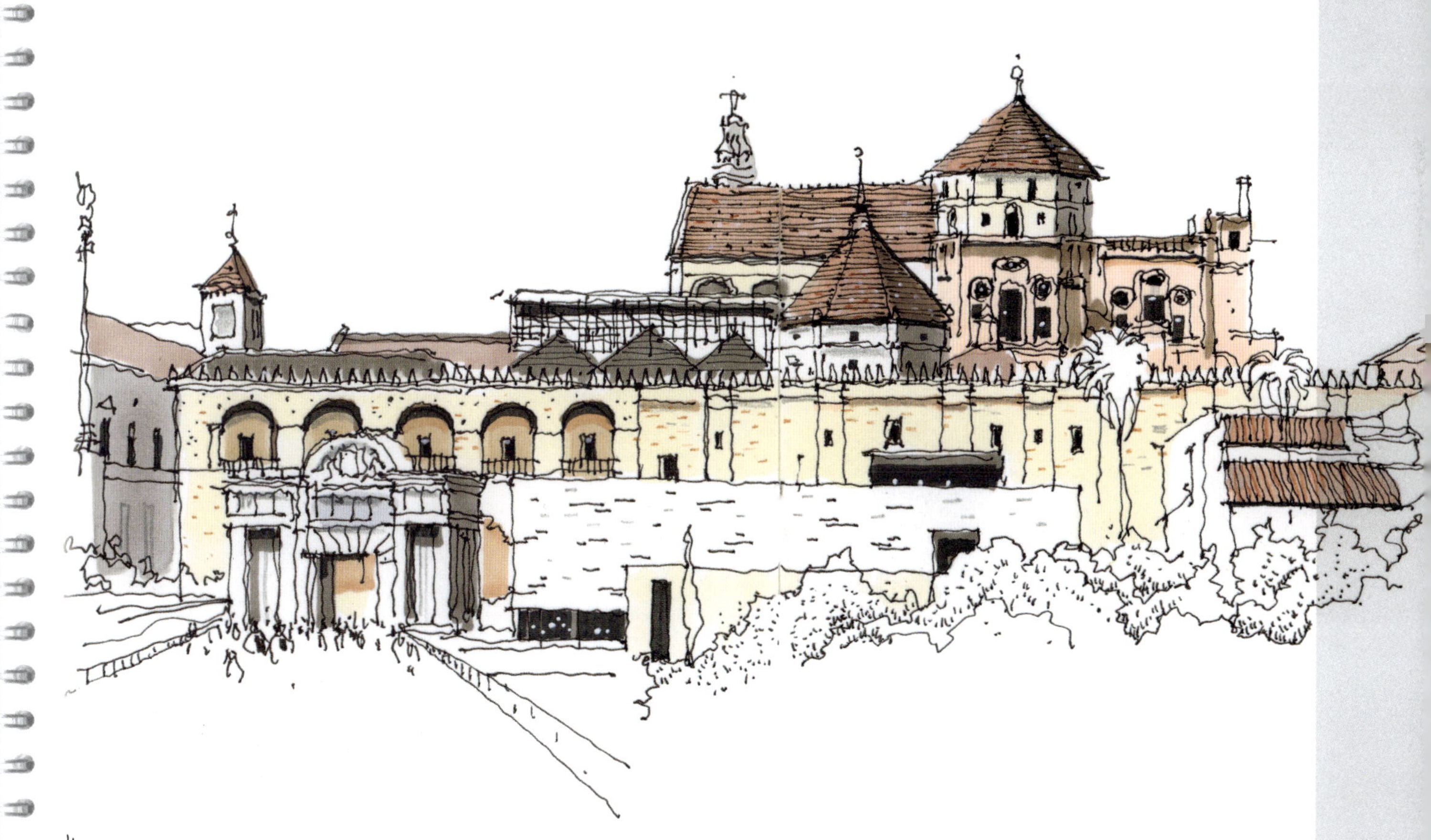

4

Complex Colour Exercise

This line drawing of the Hoxton Hotel in Amsterdam is a perfect example of a sketch that could be enhanced with the addition of colour. It has clean and precise lines, which will hold the colour nicely, and the original view had a bold colour scheme that I thought would work well on paper. I used Winsor & Newton Twin-Tip ProMarkers for this exercise.

1. First, choose the colour you would like to be most dominant – I accentuated the blue slate to make it a focal feature. Don't be afraid to boost the real colours slightly to add to the drawing. If there are any shadows present in your scene, use a darker shade of the colour you are using, rather than black, to avoid muddying the effect.

2. Add the next most dominant colour, which in this example is the reddy brown of the brickwork. The architectural features are distinctive on this building, so I took care to follow them fairly accurately to make sure the sketch remained tight. As you add each colour, assess whether more linework needs to be added; for instance, if more detail is needed in the brickwork, adjacent buildings or greenery. Think of the colour you are adding at this stage as a base layer that can be worked into, meaning you still have time to adjust the drawing and the final colours.

3. Accent colours are subtle tones that enhance the main colours and harmonize the sketch. When adding supporting colours, build from pale to stronger colour, allowing more control. Group the different shades of colours together – blues, browns, greens, creams and so on – as this will help you work quickly with the tools to hand.

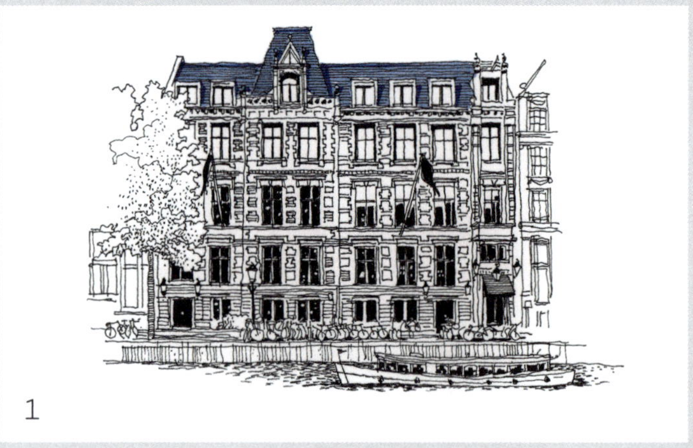

1

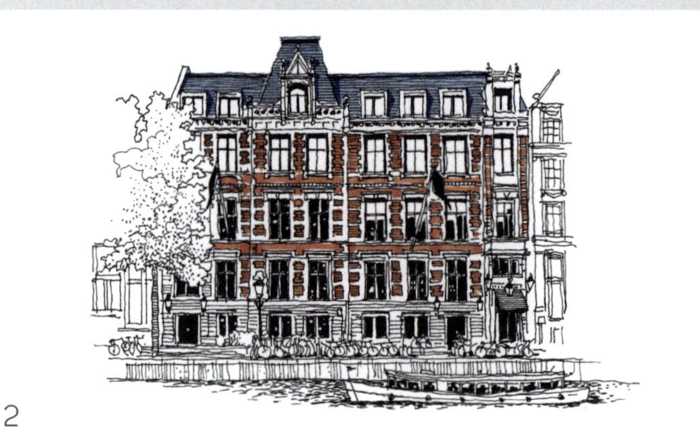

2

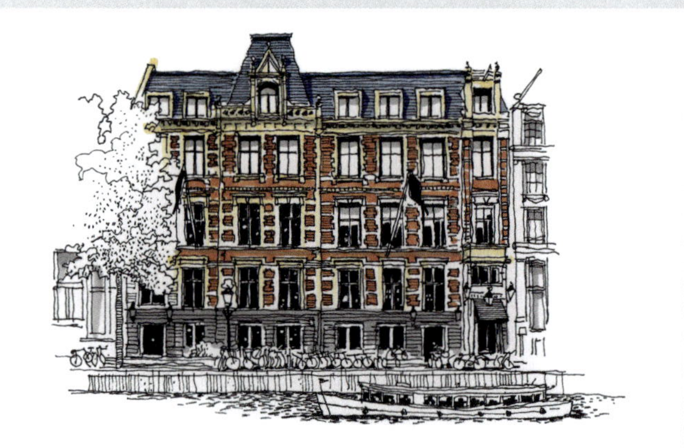

3

4. Finally, try adding some detail in coloured pencils, and use white gouache or gel pen to bring out highlights. Experiment with the opacity of the gouache or pen on a piece of scrap paper to ensure you have the density correct. Exercise restraint with the highlights, as the effect you are seeking is delicate and subtle.

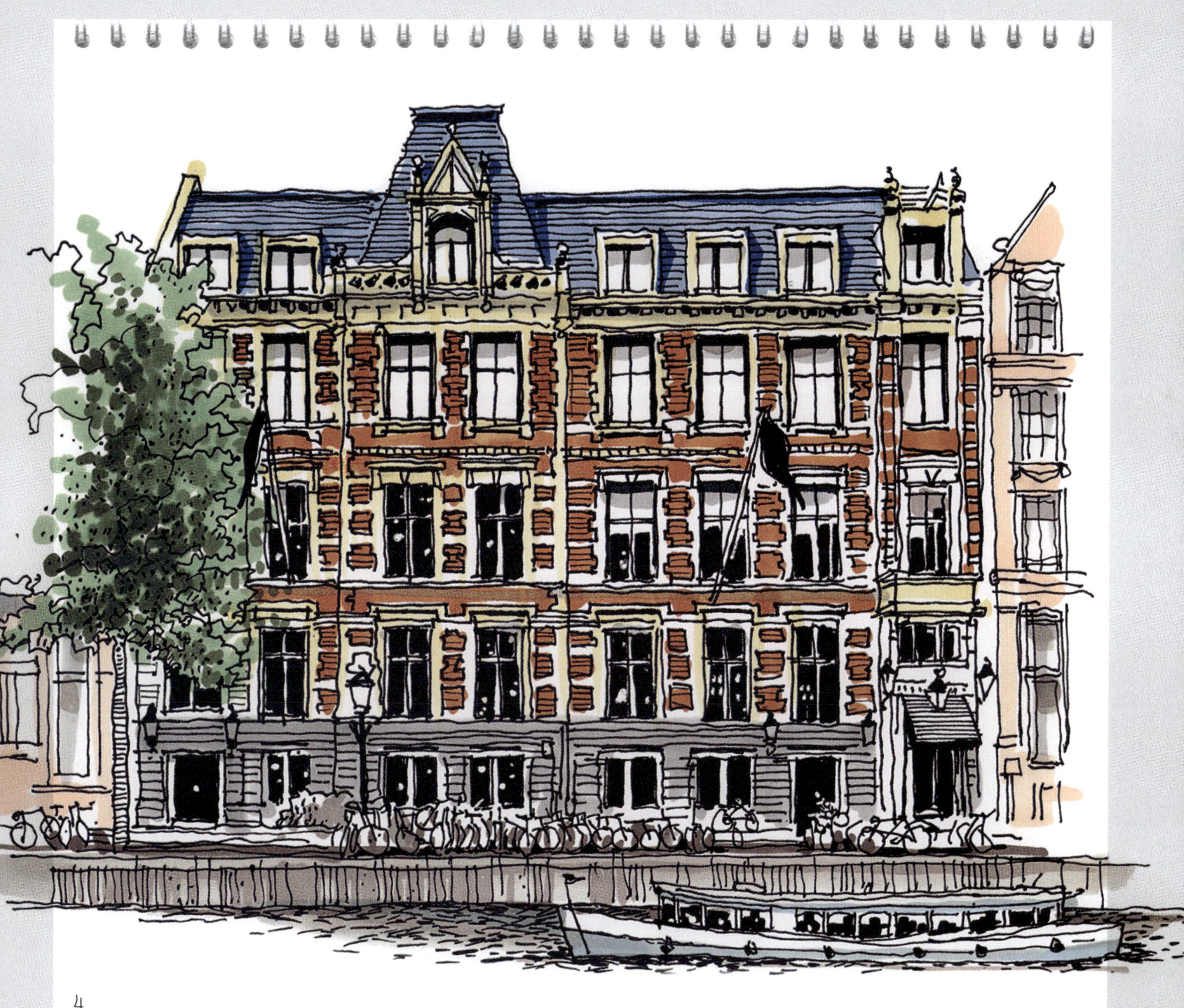

4

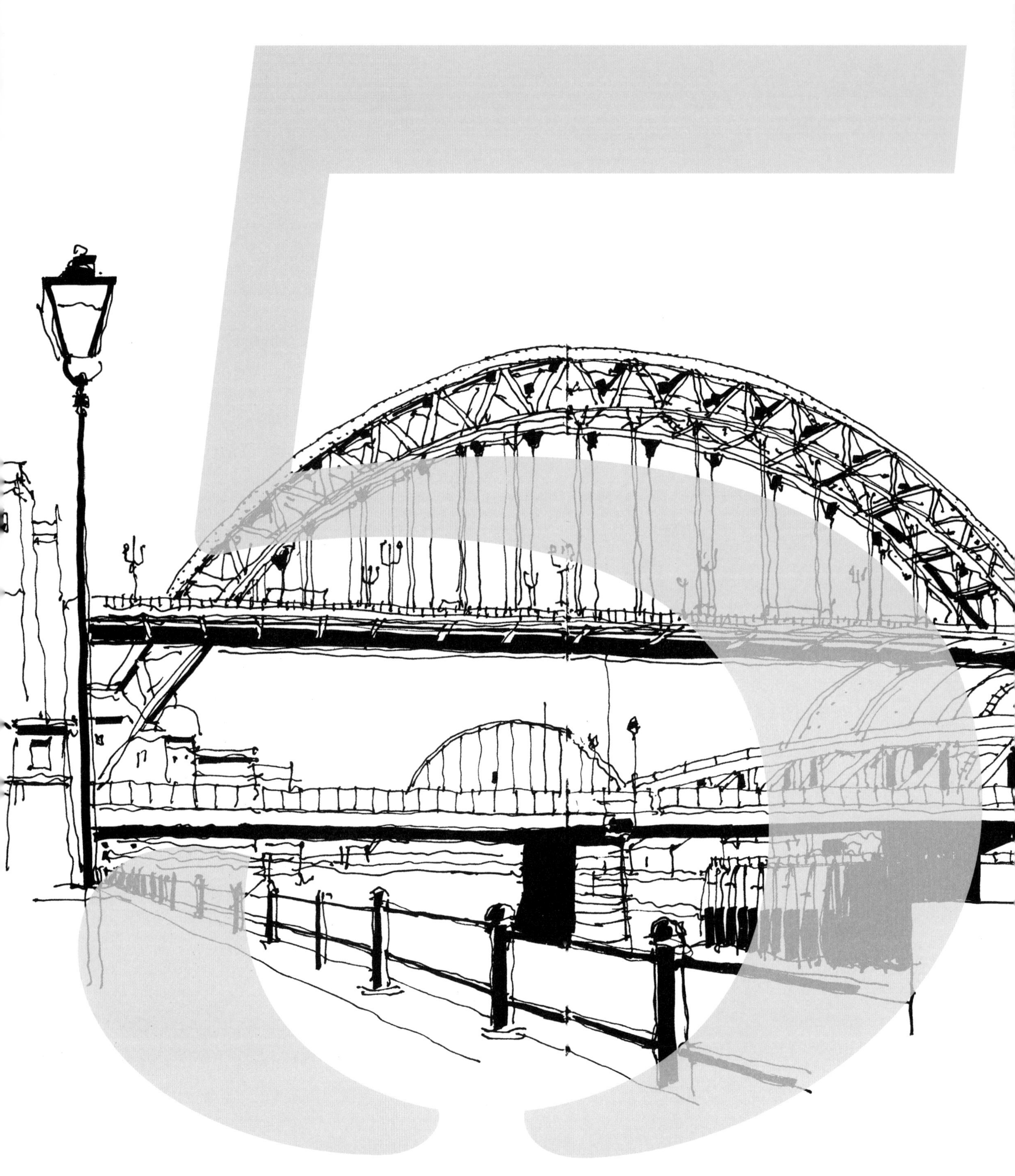

Finishing Touches

The point at which a sketch is finished is a decision that is solely in the hands of the artist. Following on from the last chapter, which looked at ways to develop your sketches further, this chapter gives tips on how to add that final polish. These small touches at the end of a sketch can be the difference between creating something good and something great. Add finishing flourishes to your sketches and you will be rewarded with artwork that really jumps off the page. At this point, it is the small details, the nuances and marginal gains that will elevate your work. We will explore techniques that will help embellish basic sketches and will inspire you to create better work going forward.

Once the sketch is complete — and in this chapter we will also look in more detail at how to decide when it's ready — we explore the archiving and display of your artworks. Putting down your pens and pencils doesn't have to be the end of a sketch's journey: next comes the opportunity to share your sketches with a huge community of urban sketchers all over the world.

Tips and Tricks

I use the following tips and tricks on a daily basis when urban sketching. They help to bring realism to my sketches and add depth to the finished artwork.

Brickwork

When you look closely at bricks on a building, you will notice that they are not entirely uniform. While they are all largely the same size and laid in the same way, they vary slightly in colour and texture, and it is important to represent this variation in your sketching. A top tip for colouring brickwork is to start with a medium colour that represents the entire wall and then add a darker and a lighter shade for the variations. If the mortar that binds the bricks is lighter than the bricks themselves (often it is), use a lighter shade or even white to draw in the brick shapes over the top of the wall colour. It's worth noting that when sketching brickwork you should never aim for 100 percent accuracy, but instead simply give an impression of the texture.

1. This example shows light mortar drawn with a white gel pen. Don't worry too much about subtlety of colour on the mortar, as you are looking to accentuate the contrast.

2. This example shows light brickwork with dark mortar represented using a darker line. Use this style when the bricks themselves are pale, and keep your linework fine to ensure the effect is not too heavy.

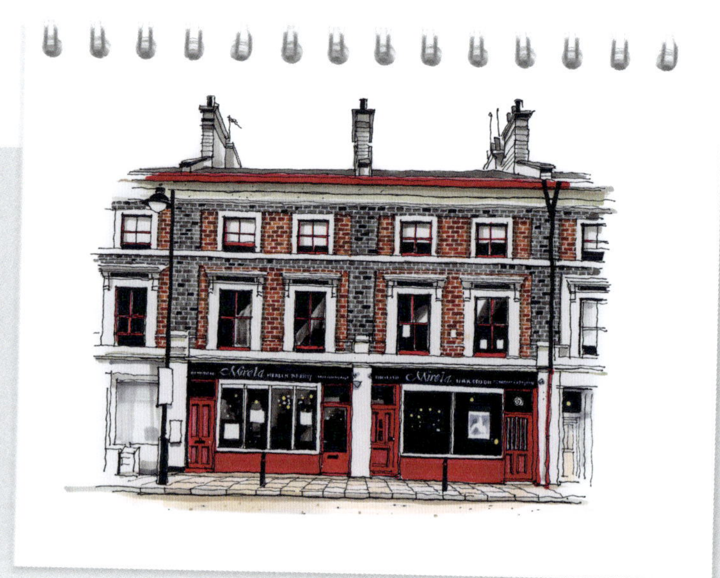

1

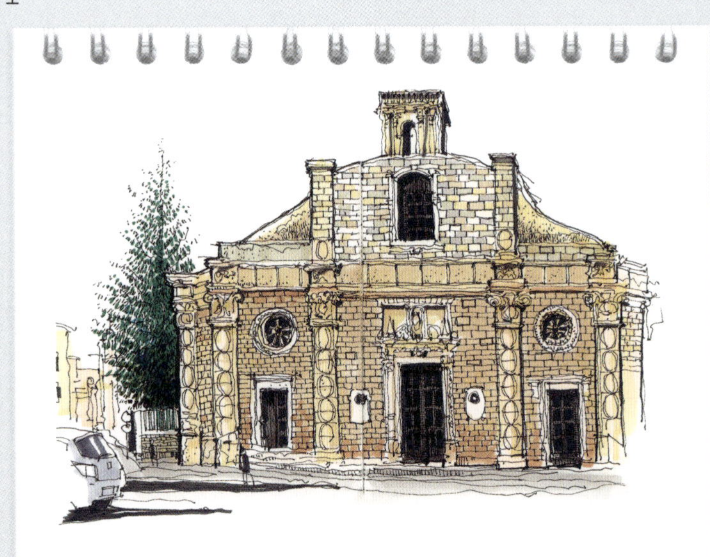

2

Trees and shrubbery

Including trees and shrubbery in a sketch can provide an effective contrast to hard architectural edges. Different approaches need to be used depending on the time of year. Deciduous trees in winter become spidery and intricate, but in the summer they are almost cloudlike. Good technique is required to make them look believable, but persevere as the addition of trees is worth the effort in the overall sketch.

1. Winter trees can be fun to sketch, just make sure that you try to show the tree itself and how the branches get more delicate towards the outer limbs. Use fine lines and small dashes to illustrate the sparseness of winter branches.

2. Adding solid black linework to represent the shadows under leaves creates contrast and weight. Allowing colour to fade upwards to white adds an airiness that complements the overall composition. Create a sense of depth by adding more line detail to the leaves that are nearer to you and make the trees that are farther away more abstract and pale.

3. Add texture and physical realism by adding rings to the tree to portray the structure of the trunk, which is essentially a tapering cylinder. Use a fineliner, pencil or gel pen to add detail. When adding this information, think of the trunk as having rippling musculature to represent the true shape of the tree – most trees do not grow in straight lines.

4. This sketch shows the outline of trees in full leaf with the colour added afterwards. The trees look like green pillows, but with the addition of a dark and light green and a white highlight, they look perfectly at home nestled in among the buildings. I also used flecks of black to add to the leaf texture.

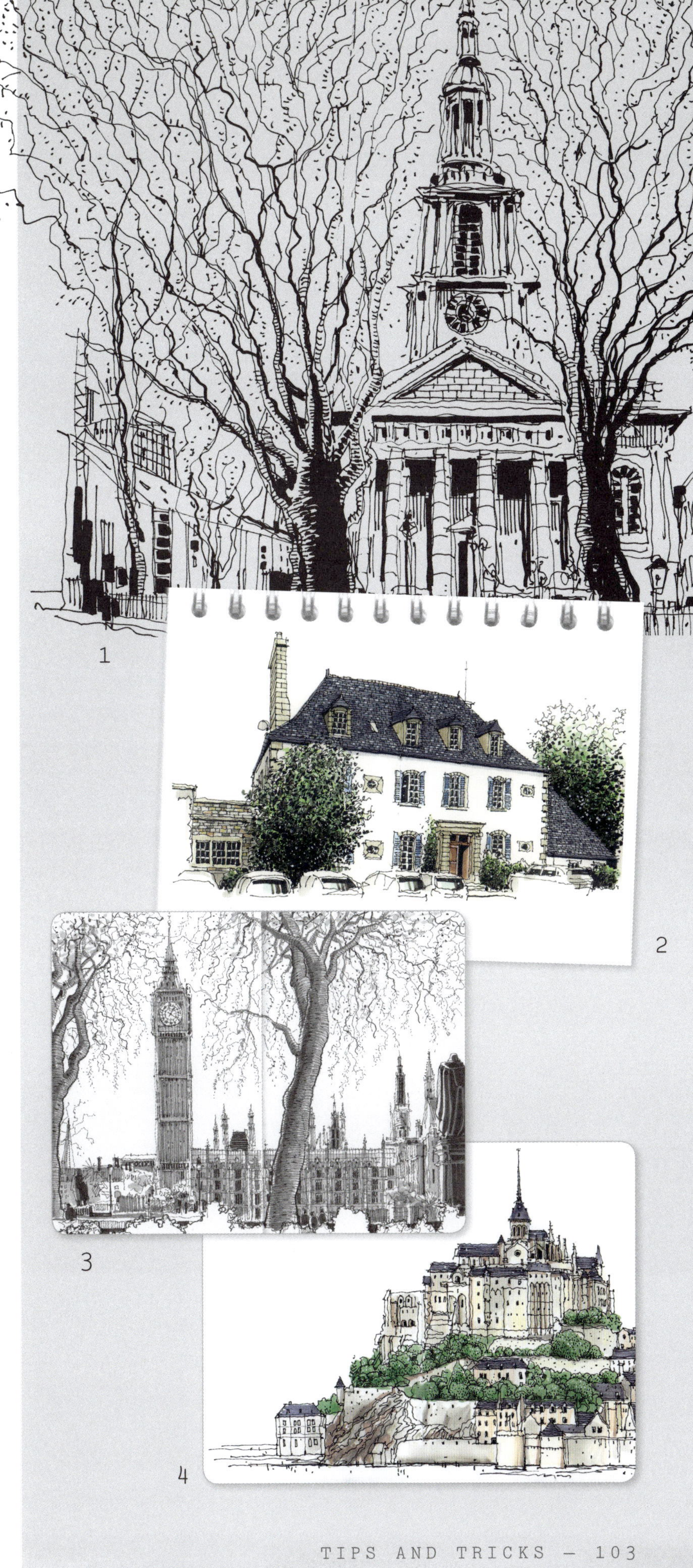

Texture

Adding further texture gives additional depth and realism to a sketch. Look carefully at your subject and see if there are details that should be added, then think about how this detail could be shown with the materials available to you. If the texture is fundamental to a scene, then make a feature of it, but if it's supplementary detail that is not essential to the story, then make it a background feature.

1. This sketch of a Georgian doorway is packed with characterful details that are essential to its charm. The masonry work is chipped and dented by years of wear and tear, the woodwork of the door is intricate and the delicate shrubbery frames the scene. This detail all requires a textural approach to bring the sketch to life – added here using pencil, marker and fineliner pen.

2. This doorway in Puglia, Italy, tells its story through the texture of the masonry, ironwork and its heavy wooden door. Textural details were added to the stonework and paving on location with a fineliner pen, and the colour was added afterwards from a photographic reference. Highlights on the door and ironmongery were added with a gel pen.

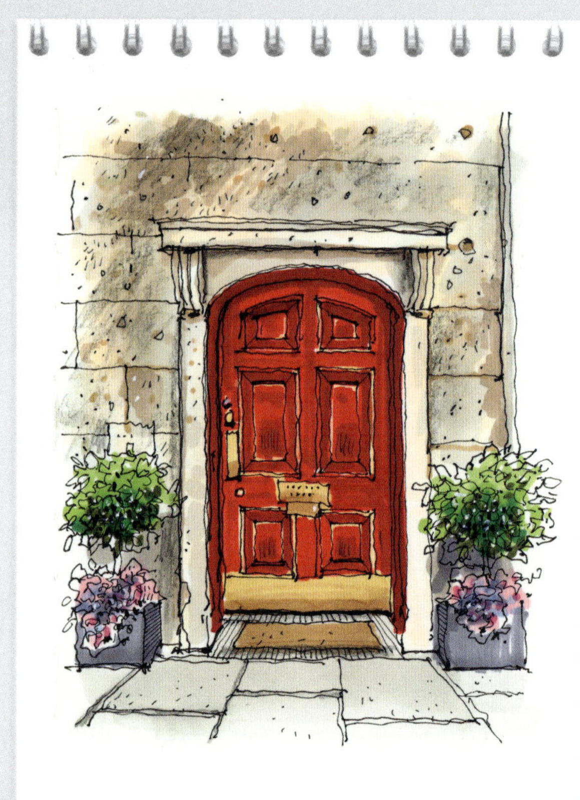

1

2

Wobbly lines

A top tip when drawing the hard, clean lines of architecture is to try not to make your lines too straight. This may sound counterintuitive, but it helps you to be more relaxed when sketching imposing scenes and gives you some artistic licence to interpret what you are seeing.

1. This sketch is a great example of where wobbly lines help with the challenging sweep of the curved bridge. They give permission for the entire drawing to have a loose style; there's not an entirely straight line in sight, which adds to the rough feel of the piece. It was sketched using a fineliner pen with heavy line weights to convey shadow and depth.

2. This linework drawing would be quite uninteresting if all the lines of the buildings were straight and precise. It is a great example of box-like buildings getting the wobbly line treatment. The lines create character and will give you the freedom to build the scene without being overly concerned with accuracy. This technique encourages a lateral-thinking approach to sketching.

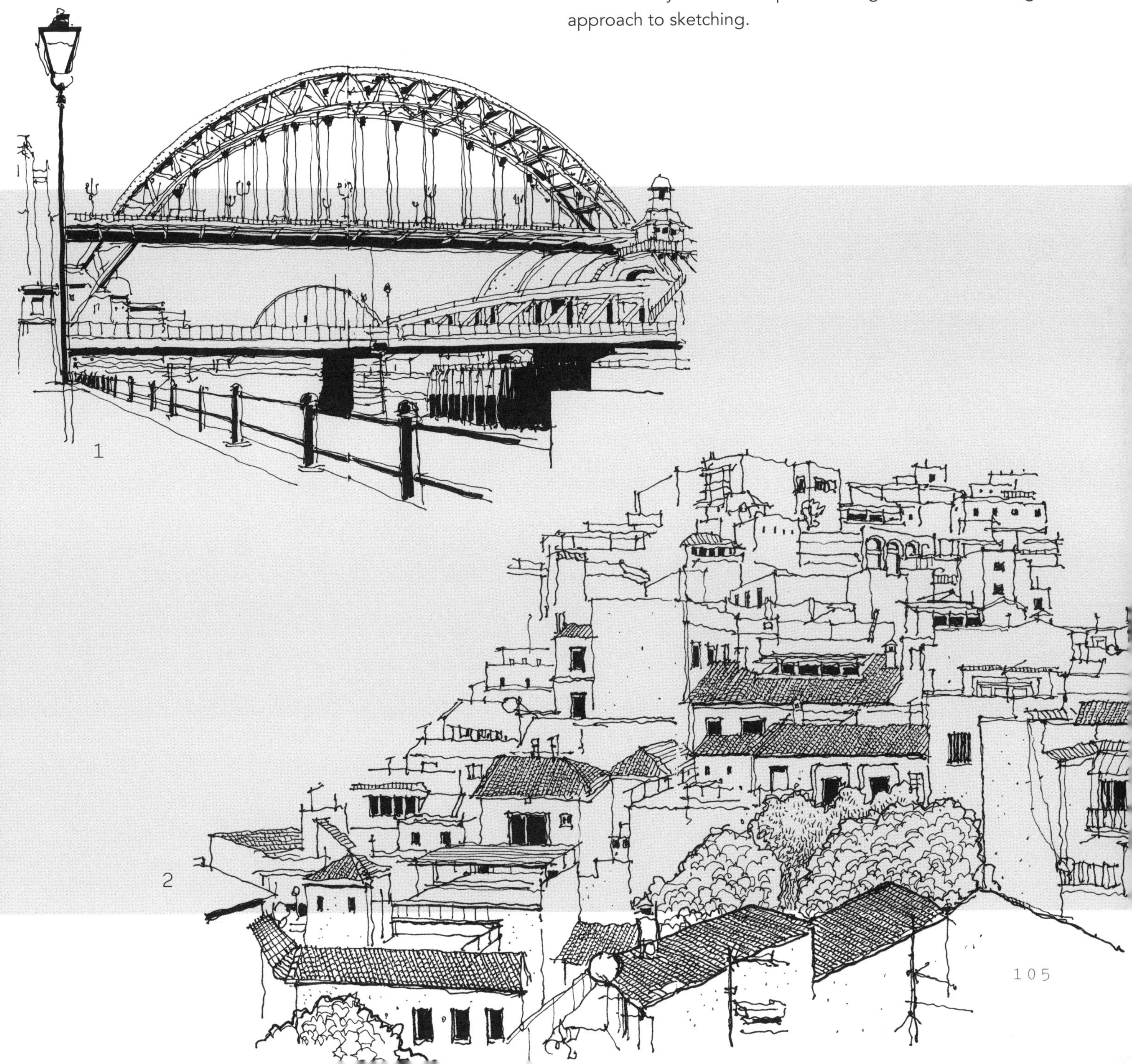

Shadow

The addition of shadow will always add dynamism and a touch of realism to a sketch. Shadows don't always have to be completely realistic in terms of their depth and strength, but they are mostly essential to any drawing.

1. Hard sunlight delivers drama and impact when it hits detailed stonework. In this sketch, the shadow is built out from the features of the stonework, combining the use of a solid black marker and a white highlight pen to create dramatic contrast.

2. Winter shadows will often create bold shapes, and in this sketch, the dark shadows of the trees were dramatically framing the scene. I added the shadows on location using black ink. Don't be afraid to add dramatic shadows if they are present, as they will add atmosphere to your drawing.

3. In a busy market scene like this, shadow is a useful signpost for sections of the drawing that you want the viewer to focus on. To define areas of the sketch, use solid black ink, creating bold shadows where appropriate. Remember to always consider where the light is coming from when drawing in shadow.

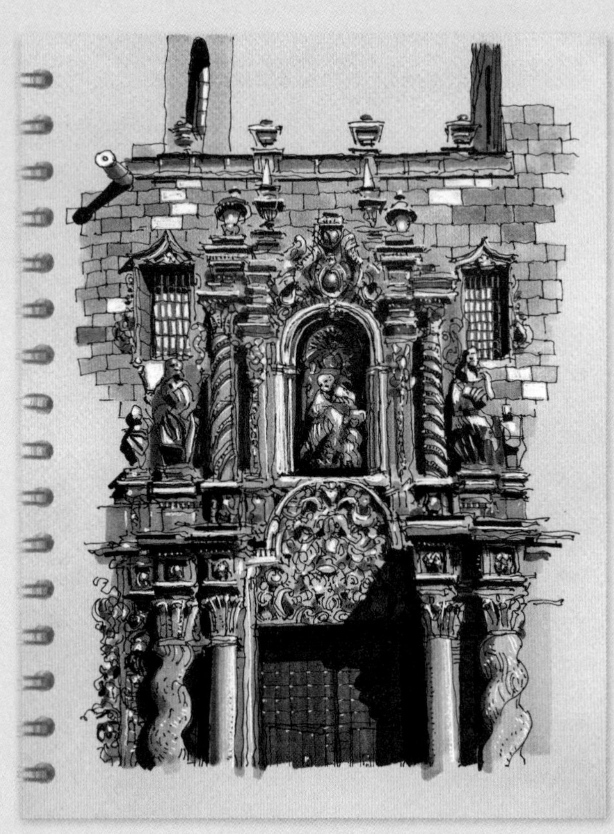

1

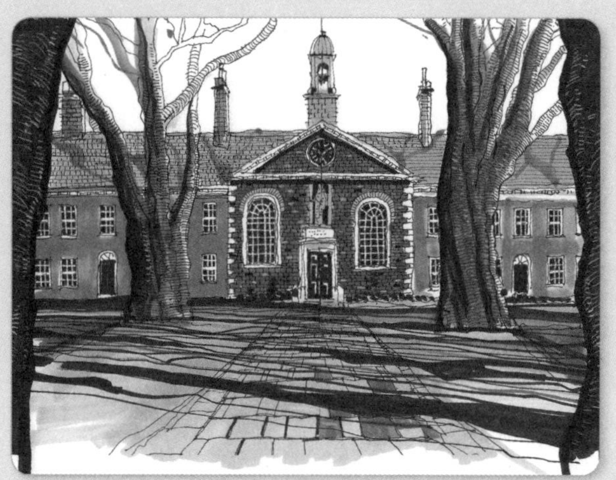

2

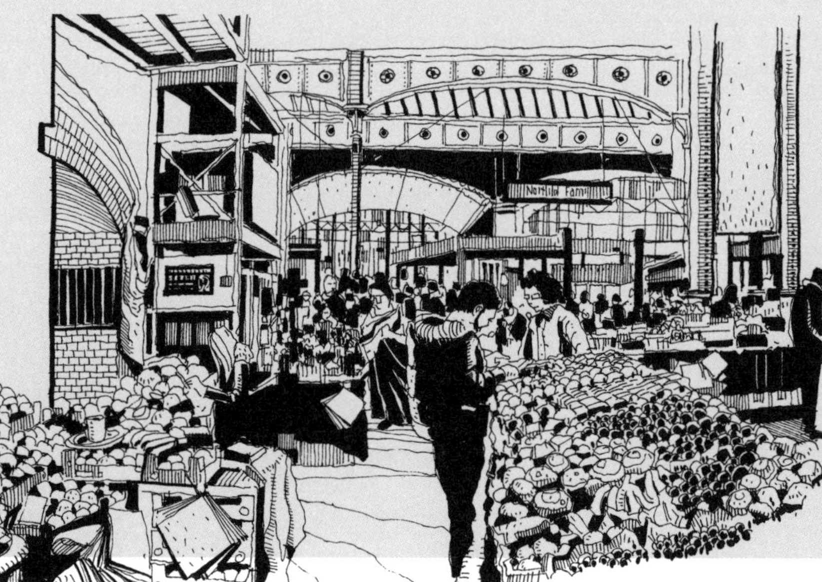

3

Highlights

In urban sketching, white highlights can be deployed in a number of very effective ways. The trick is to add white at the very end of the process to add that final hint of detail that will bring everything together.

1. White highlights need be only gestural, but their impact on a sketch can be significant. In this sketch they pick out the architectural detail, describe the lighting and create movement and contrast. Here, I used a white gel pen for the strong highlights and a white pencil to add softer lighting to areas such as the column.

2. In this sketch, white was used to pick out the window frames of the surrounding buildings, which contrasts nicely with the darker tones of the brickwork. White gouache has a very opaque pigment and sits well on top of the foliage to provide crisp highlights. For this reason, gouache is better than gel pen for chunkier highlights.

3. This sketch of a London pub is on tinted paper, which makes the highlights jump off the page even more. Use white gouache and pencil to convey depth with restraint. When adding the sky detail to a line sketch using white pencil, be loose and creative with the application.

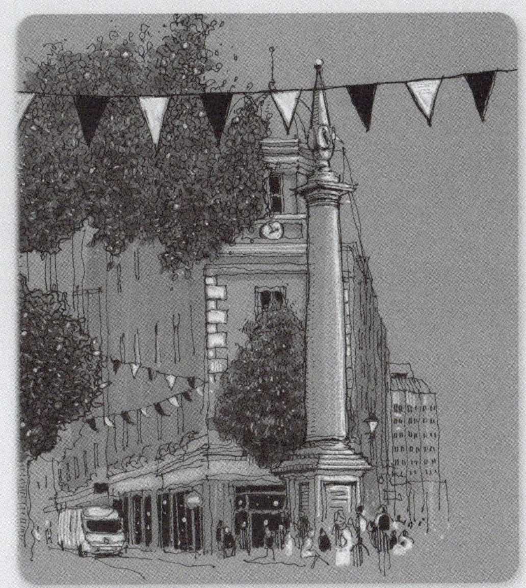

1

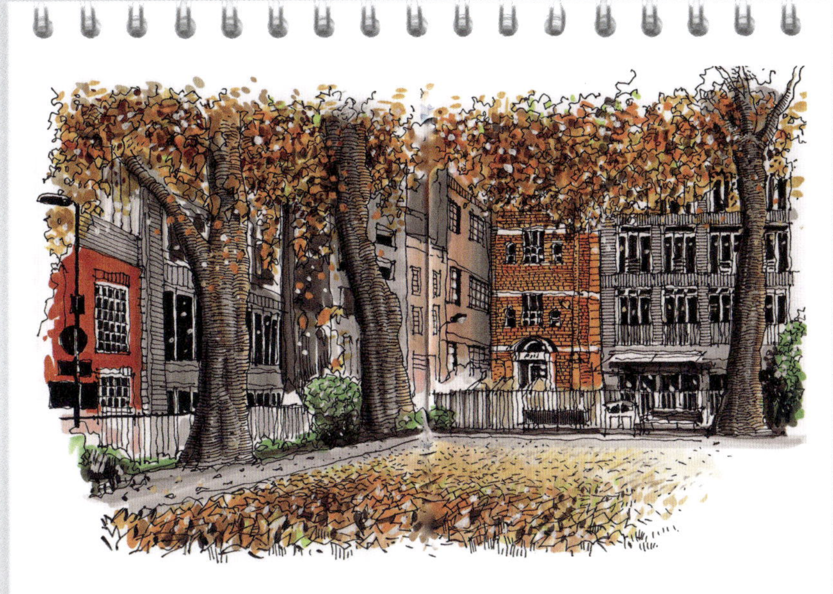

2

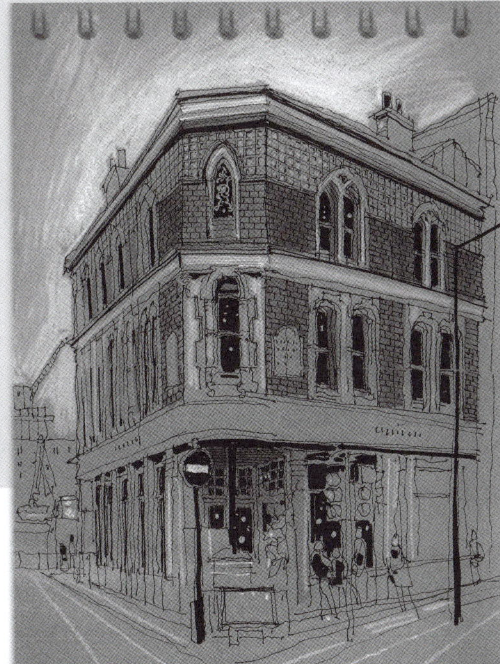

3

REMEMBER
It is important not to overdo white highlights — remember that they are only highlights and not the main narrative of the sketch.

When to Stop

One of the biggest challenges that artists often face is knowing when to finish a piece. We looked earlier at how to plan a scene, but sketching is an organic process and as the drawing develops, how you feel about it can change. Only one person can tell you when to close your book and stop the sketching, and it's you.

Many sketchers struggle with this stage of the process, as this is where careful judgement is needed. Key things to consider when making the decision to stop are:

Composition
- How is the drawing looking on the page?
- Is there enough or too much negative space?
- Do you need to add more detail to make it believable or recognizable?
- Will adding superfluous elements overcomplicate the aesthetic?

Detail
- Is there enough detail to bring the scene to life?
- Could adding any more details to the scene take away from its spontaneity?
- Would any parts benefit from the addition of textural detail to add richness?

Tone
- Is the linework enough to hold the viewer's attention?
- Would the scene benefit from more depth?
- Is colour important to the subject matter and would it help convey the sense of place?

You may have a gut feeling about when to stop, but my advice would always be less is more – unfinished areas of a sketch can be just as powerful as the areas filled with drawing. The mind fills the gaps that the eye sees, and the space becomes intrinsically part of the sketch.

This isn't to say that a page should never be completely filled. Making the most of the live sketch time has just as much merit. Sometimes I fill a whole page and there is a joy in that, as long as the subject matter benefits from it.

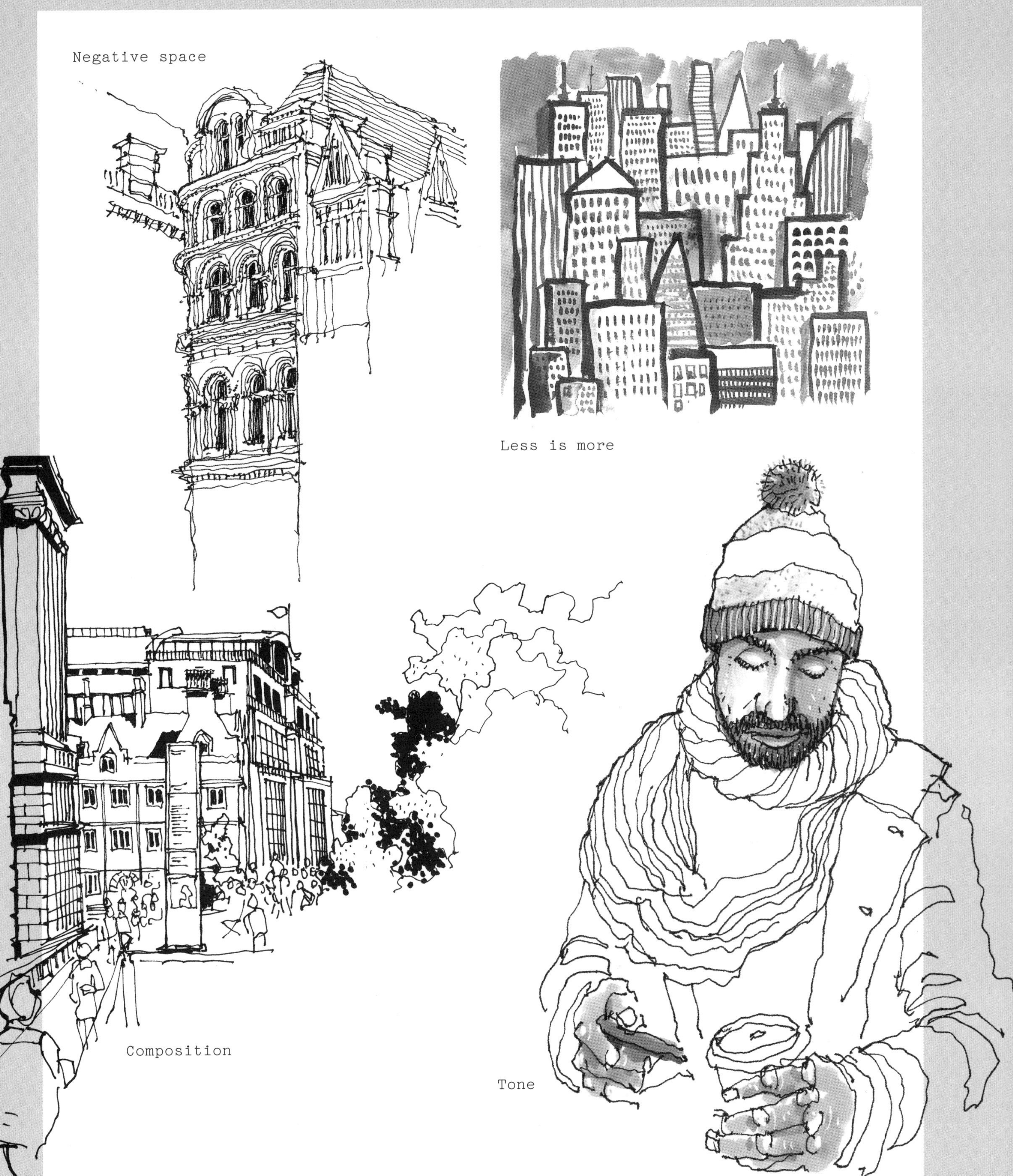

Negative space
Less is more
Composition
Tone

Sharing Your Work

How to become part of the online sketching community

It is very easy to tap into the vast online community of sketchers on social media. Sketching is incredibly popular in the online world and I can see why: where photography has become ubiquitous and everyday, hand-drawn, analogue content is unique and has the potential to really stand out.

Instagram is the most effective social media platform for urban sketchers to share their work and see what else is out there. Twitter and Facebook can also be used but Instagram is the best place to start for first-time posters. Begin by following people and hashtags and you will get a feel for the kind of content you enjoy and what inspires you. I recommend following these hashtags in the first instance:
#urbansketchers
#sketching
#sketch
#sketchbook
#drawing
#artistsofinstagram

The list of hashtags is endless, but when you start looking, you will quickly discover a world of inspiration that will drive you on to continue to create. Social channels can then become a conduit for you to be seen by other creative people. Understandably, sketchers may be nervous about this kind of exposure; not sure about how to embark on the digital journey or uncomfortable about letting other people see their work. These are valid viewpoints, but my personal experience is that the more people who see your work and the more work you see by other people, the better and more confident you will become as an artist.

I suggest you start small and set up a dedicated sketcher Instagram account that is separate to any personal accounts you may have. Search for artists doing things you like – watercolour, marker, ink, pencil drawing, etc. – and follow them. Interact, comment and like, and you will soon find that people will react in kind. It can be very rewarding and you will discover that having an active online presence with your art can lead to amazing opportunities to take your sketching journey forward.

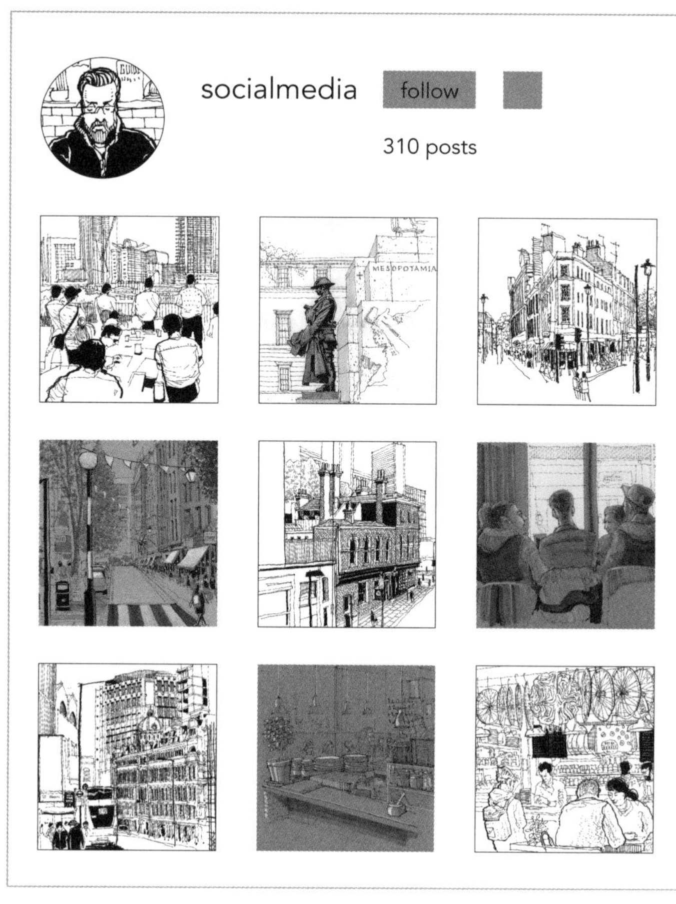

The effective platform of Instagram

Top tips for sharing your content on Instagram

- Make your content unique so it stands out on the channel and doesn't become wallpaper (repetitive)
- Crop your images effectively – remember, Instagram is a square format
- Videos tend to perform incredibly well so shoot some videos of you sketching to receive more attention
- Tag artists that you like and they might like and share your work
- Always use hashtags
- Reply to any comments on your posts – it will boost your ranking on Instagram
- Note that colour sketches tend to outperform black and white by 200 percent

Urban sketching groups

Many cities across the world have urban sketching groups that meet regularly to sketch on location. Sketching can be a solitary exercise if you so wish, but it can also be a very social experience, especially when in a diverse group of people with different abilities. Group sketching is great for sharing experiences, new ideas and techniques, and I highly recommend it for people starting out. Search for groups in your area to see how you can get involved. There is also a global urban sketchers organization – urbansketchers.org – that meets annually for a symposium where sketchers from all over the world meet up to sketch.

Print fairs

Most cities and major towns have print fairs where local artists sell their work as prints or original artworks. It is worth attending these fairs to see what kind of work is selling. Talk to the artists, see what their experience is and keep in touch with them and their work. It may inspire you to try to sell your own work at some point, and you may be surprised by what sells best and is the most commercial.

Local galleries

Check out the galleries in your town or city, chat to the gallery owners and see what other artists are doing. Find out when their next show is and what kind of art will be on display. Whether you have ambitions to show your work or not, you will learn about how art is presented well and what makes an impact.

Local businesses

If you sketch regularly in a city, town or neighbourhood, a great tip is to sketch the local businesses – bars, shops, restaurants and so on – and then talk to them about showing your work on their premises. Most owners of local businesses love their business being the focus of attention, so make the most of it and offer the sketch to them free of charge if they let you display your work. Customers will get a chance to see your work and word of mouth is a powerful thing in communities, creating a halo effect back on the business making them feel great as well.

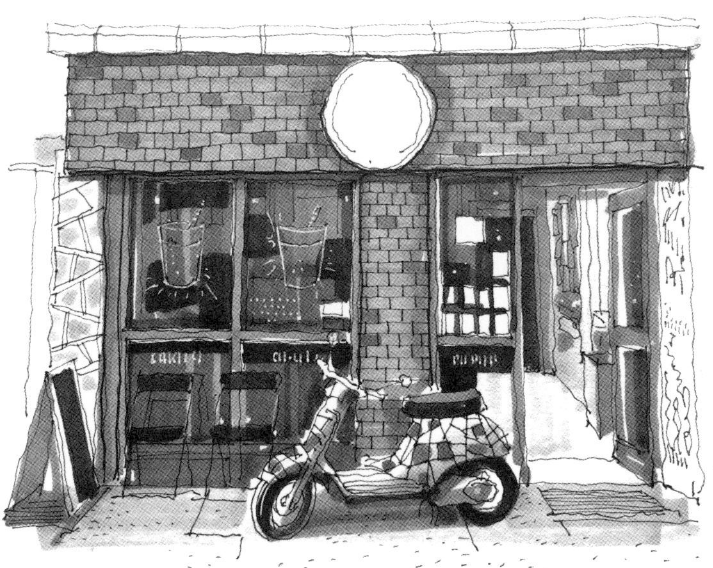

Displaying in local businesses

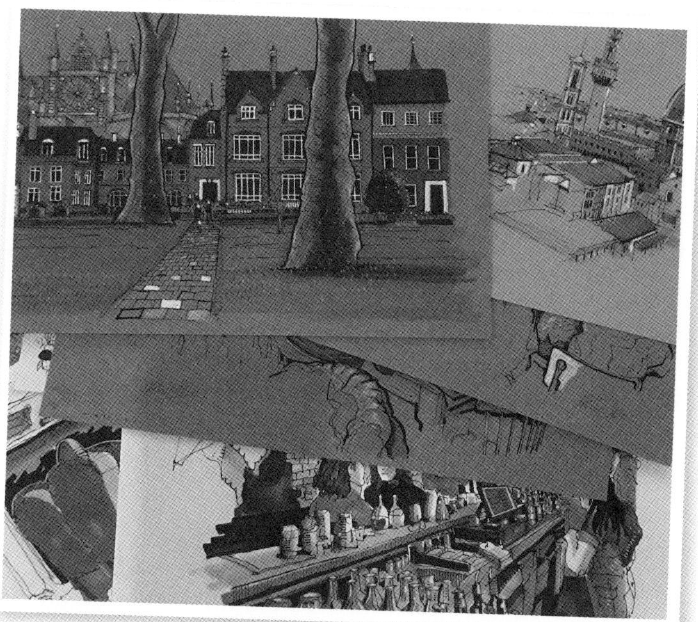

Exhibiting in galleries

Acknowledgements

This book would not have been possible without the endless patience and support from my wonderful wife, Julie. Thanks for being by my side on our adventures, your priceless words of wisdom and all round chivvying along. It's hard at times being the wife of a sketcher and every single drawing in this book would not have been possible without her unfailing encouragement and positivity. She knows how much this book means to me, and I love her for that. An enormous thank you to our children, Josh and Georgia, for their endless enthusiasm, passion and for making me proud. They have helped lift my spirits when the going was tough, stepped in when I was technically inept and generally put the wind back in my sails. Thank you to my parents, Pauline and Brian, for seeing the artistic potential in a young council house kid and supporting me through art college back when it wasn't fashionable or economically sensible to do so. I owe them everything.

To the amazing publishing team at Octopus Books – a huge thank you for your judicious editing and highly capable advice, and for helping to make sense of my words and pictures. Special thanks to Ellie Corbett for seeing my work and believing in me from the outset. I'm grateful to Ellen, Ben, Steph, Rachel and Lucy for bringing it all together and making the content sing.

Thank you to the people who have inspired me along my sketch journey: Glenn Hall, Ian Jackson, Richard Hind, Lyndon Hayes, Simone Ridyard, Martin Hayes, Lydia Thornley, Jordan Spilman, Richard Johnson, Brian Ramsey, the team at Certain, David Gentleman, Jason Brooks, The Gentle Author, Gérard Michel, Paul Heaston and Jared Muralt.

I am thankful to every one of my long-suffering friends (you know who you are) for putting up with my incessant drawing, regardless of the situation – I appreciate the kindness and support afforded to the sketcher in your midst. Thank you Karen Lynch for proofreading the final draft while sitting around a pool in the sun. To my first boss, guru and friend, Dean Brewer, always an influence. I'll never forget the blank sketchbook, which didn't stay blank for long.

Finally, this book is dedicated to the artistic tour de force that was Laimonis Mierins, my drawing tutor at Jacob Kramer College of Art in Leeds. Lem (as he was known) inspired me to draw everything that I saw and taught me to be brave in making a mark and to not be afraid of drawing anything. These are skills I still use to this very day. Lem, I salute you.

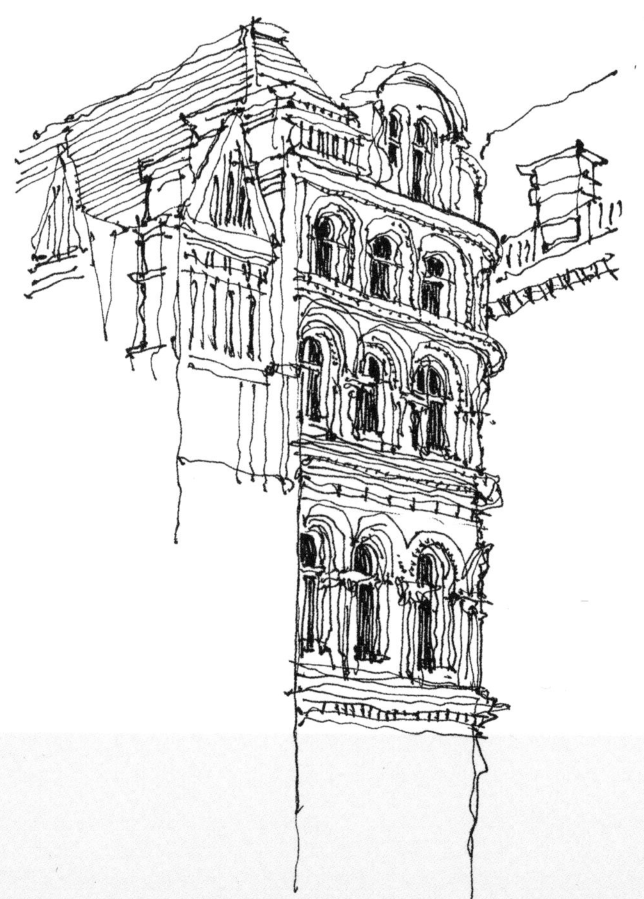